Political marketing

MANCHESTER
1824

Manchester University Press

Political marketing

A comparative perspective

edited by
Darren G. Lilleker and Jennifer Lees-Marshment

Manchester University Press
Manchester and New York

distributed exclusively in the USA by Palgrave

Published by Manchester University Press
Oxford Road, Manchester M13 9NR, UK
and Room 400, 175 Fifth Avenue, New York, NY 10010, USA
www.manchesteruniversitypress.co.uk

Distributed exclusively in the USA by
Palgrave, 175 Fifth Avenue, New York,
NY 10010, USA

Distributed exclusively in Canada by
UBC Press, University of British Columbia, 2029 West Mall,
Vancouver, BC, Canada V6T 1Z2

British Library Cataloguing-in-Publication Data
A catalogue record for this book is available from the British Library

Library of Congress Cataloging-in-Publication Data applied for

ISBN   0 7190 6870 3 *hardback*
EAN   978 0 7190 6870 6
ISBN   0 7190 6871 1 *paperback*
EAN   978 0 7190 6871 3

First published 2005

14 13 12 11 10 09 08 07 06 05   10 9 8 7 6 5 4 3 2 1

Typeset in Minion
by Servis Filmsetting Ltd, Manchester
Printed in Great Britain
by Biddles, King's Lynn

To Jennifer's sister Samantha and nephew Jack in Australia
who helped her to keep a world-wide comparative perspective;
and to Darren's partner Teresa

Contents

Figures, tables and boxes

Figures

Tables

Boxes

Contributors

Declan P. Bannon is lecturer in strategy and marketing at the University of Paisley, Scotland. His research interests include voter behaviour, electoral non-participation, segmentation and the application of marketing theory to non-commercial organisations.

Josiane Cotrim-Macieira is a Brazilian journalist who has an MA in political communication from Dublin City University. Her research interests include political communication, political marketing, discourse analysis, comparative politics, political posters, Irish politics and party organisation.

Jonathan Knuckey is assistant professor of political science at the University of Central Florida. His research interests are voting behaviour, elections and political parties, with particular emphasis on southern politics. His research has been published in *Polity*, the *American Review of Politics*, *Social Science Quarterly*, *Political Research Quarterly*, *Politics and Policy* and *Party Politics*. Currently he is working on a National Science Foundation-sponsored survey of grassroots party activists in the southern US.

Andreas Lederer lives in Austria where he works as a political consultant. He is currently researching political marketing and branding in politics at the Institute of Political Science, University of Vienna.

Charles Lees is lecturer in politics and director of the Institute for the Study of Political Parties at the University of Sheffield. He is editor of the PSA journal *Politics* and of the Manchester University Press series 'Issues in German Politics', managing editor of the *Journal of Common Market Studies* and secretary of the Association for the Study of German Politics. His research interests fall within the broad remit of comparative politics, including European party politics, the politics and policy of the Federal Republic of Germany, environmental politics and policy, and the use of institutionalist approaches to empirical research. His publications include *Party Politics in Germany: A Comparative Politics Perspective* (Manchester University Press, 2004), *The Red–Green Coalition in Germany: Politics, Personalities and Power*

(Manchester University Press, 2000), two edited volumes, as well as numerous articles in leading refereed journals and book chapters in edited volumes. He has also provided advice and consultancy to the New Zealand Green Party, the Australian Embassy in Berlin and the Scottish Executive.

Jennifer Lees-Marshment is founding director of the Centre for Political Marketing within the Department of Management at Keele University (www.keele.ac.uk/depts/mn/cpm) and is a leading theorist in political marketing, taking a comprehensive and cross-disciplinary approach in her research and related activities. Jennifer published *Political Marketing and British Political Parties* (Manchester University Press, 2001), which broadened the focus of political marketing from campaigns to party behaviour, and *The Political Marketing Revolution: Transforming the Government of the UK* (Manchester University Press, 2004), which argued that marketing is being used by all political organisations, including the BBC, the monarchy, universities, as well as charities, local government and the National Health Service. In response to the emergence of the 'political consumer', Jennifer has published numerous journal articles in both political science and marketing, covering the marketing, strategies employed by both the Labour and the Conservative Party over the period 1997–2004. She was academic convenor for the 2002 political marketing conference in Aberdeen and the editor of several journal special issues in political marketing (2003 and 2005), as well as the founding chair of the Political Marketing Group within the Political Studies Association.

Darren G. Lilleker is senior lecturer in the Bournemouth Media School and course leader of the MA in political communications. His current research focus is the ways in which politicians interact with society and citizens, and his recent publications include a study of class de-alignment and a number of articles covering the professionalisation of political communication, the use of political marketing and the impact of such trends. He is developing research on the importance of a local profile in parliamentary elections in the UK. In addition Dr Lilleker has researched the ideological debates surrounding British and European defence policy, out of which emerged *Against the Cold War* (IB Tauris, 2004). He has reviewed papers in political marketing and is vice-chair of the PSA Political Marketing Group.

Alex Marland is a director of communications with the Government of Newfoundland and Labrador. He has taught political science at the Memorial University of Newfoundland, authored the article 'Marketing political soap' (*Journal of Public Affairs*, May 2003) and is currently preparing a PhD thesis (Lancaster University) examining marketing in Canadian constituency campaigns. Alex has held marketing, communications and opinion research positions in Ottawa and St John's, where he worked on projects such as airline branding and government tobacco policy, and has been involved with the Liberal Party, the New Democratic Party, the Progressive Conservative and Reform Parties.

Sean McGough has a PhD from the University of Birmingham on British policy in Northern Ireland and conflict resolution. His research interests include terrorism, conflict resolution, political risk, European politics and international relations. Since January 2003 he has been an associate professor of international politics at the University of Huron, London. He is currently a researcher on the Leverhulme project 'Politics of food and farming', at the University of Birmingham, and a lecturer in international, European and British politics at Coventry University.

Robert Mochrie is lecturer in economics in the School of Management and Languages, Heriot-Watt University, Edinburgh.

Pedro Patron Galindo has a BA in Communication, with emphasis in organisational communication, from the University of Lima (Peru) and an MA in political communication from Emerson College, Boston (USA). He has worked as a journalist in Peru, as a consultant in Lima, Boston and Barcelona, and as a professor of the School of Communication of the Catholic University in Lima, Peru. He presented a paper on Peruvian politics at the 2002 political marketing conference at the University of Aberdeen. Presently he works as communication director at the National Centre for Agricultural Research, Peru, dealing with press, marketing and information issues regarding the social and economic impact of the innovation projects held by the Centre.

Fritz Plasser is professor of political science at the University of Innsbruck and director of the Centre for Applied Political Research in Vienna. He is the author, co-author and editor of twenty-six books and has published widely on campaigns and elections from a comparative perspective. His recent publications include *Global Political Campaigning: A Worldwide Analysis of Campaign Professionals and Their Practices* (2002) and (as co-editor) *Political Parties and Electoral Change: Party Responses to Electoral Markets* (2004).

Chris Rudd is senior lecturer in the Department of Political Studies at the University of Otago, Dunedin, New Zealand. He is co-editor of *The Political Economy of New Zealand* and has published articles on New Zealand politics and the media. Currently he is working on an edited volume on political communication in New Zealand.

Christian Scheucher, a graduate of Harvard University and the University of Vienna, is an international political and public affairs consultant. He works for parties and candidates throughout Europe, and consults for corporations in the biotechnology, medical systems, telecommunications and chemical industries. He is a speaker at international conferences such as the British Academy of Marketing, the John F. Kennedy School of Government and political marketing conferences throughout the UK and is a frequent commentator in print media and on radio and television. A lecturer at the universities of Vienna and Krems, he has published in the *Handbook of Political Marketing* (Sage), for which he was an advisory editor, in the *European Journal of Marketing*; he is European editor of the *Journal of Public Affairs* (Henry Stewart, London), and board member of the *Journal of Political Marketing* (Haworth, New York), for which he frequently reviews papers.

Preface

In the wake of both the tumultuous world events that rocked political and social structures and of the more gradual erosion of public trust and attachment to traditional political systems and organisations, researchers from around the world converged to discuss the global phenomenon of political parties and organisations employing marketing at the 2002 political marketing conference at the University of Aberdeen, Scotland. Many of these researchers used the Lees-Marshment model of comparative political marketing as a benchmark in an attempt to understand political party behaviour, which, despite its origination and development in the single context of the UK, was found to have significant explanatory power. Nevertheless, presentations generated heated and critical debate about the utility of a UK Thatcher–Blair-generated model to explain politics worldwide. Academics are always, perhaps justifiably, nervous and critical of claims that one model can explain all, even if this was never argued by the model's author. However, we felt that the interest generated by Lees-Marshment's first book *Political Marketing and British Political Parties* (2001) justified further investigation, particularly in view of the apparent similarities between Clinton in the US, Blair in the UK and Clark in New Zealand in terms of conducting focus groups, creating pledges and utilising (some of the same) staff in the area of marketing.

At the end of the conference, Lilleker attempted to persuade Lees-Marshment to put together in an edited collection existing and new studies of party marketing, to investigate the explanatory power of the model. Despite the inevitable post-conference fatigue, she agreed, provided that he acted as co-editor, to share the workload but also to offer a critical perspective on the work, one distinct from that of the author of the model. The privilege of putting together a collection of individual writings each of which utilises one's own framework, particularly at such an early stage in a career, is granted to few academics. While it was undoubtedly intellectually exciting to embark on such a project, one can be guilty of being over-protective or, equally, overly critical of one's own theory. Having another editor on board has worked well to ensure a constructive dialogue that has stimulated refinement as well as re-articulation of the original tenets of the product–sales–market-oriented party model.

From the conference we already had around five potential chapters that had been taken through double-blind review and could be updated and unified in structure; we recruited additional researchers who would apply the model to a range of political parties and candidates across diverse political systems, including Brazil and Peru. The aim was not to prove beyond doubt its applicability, but to test the model, as well as the extent to which political marketing is being used by politicians outside of the UK and the USA, to what end and with what measure of success. This, we believed, would allow us to redevelop the model for global application.

The chapter authors fulfilled all our hopes, and more, and while, as with all research, there remain questions and gaps outstanding, this volume highlights the facts that political marketing is now a global phenomenon; that political actors employ marketing in the hope of gaining votes; and that, in some cases, voters are responding positively. The book asks whether this phenomenon is a good thing – for pluralist democracy, the future of political party organisations or for political competition: political marketing may be a different or new way of operating but the issues to which it gives rise are time-honoured, classical questions for all of us interested in the functioning of democracy via parties and elections.

The countries included present a range of differing systems with contrasting histories and traditions. This is partly by design and partly by accident. Political marketing has developed significantly in recent years, but we are not yet at the stage of having a band of researchers in every country, or at least not in time to complete the draft of this book. Like all overworked but committed editors we could already envisage a second edition, with countries like Sweden, Finland, Ireland, Denmark, France, Spain, Greece and Australia added to the crosssection. Our first comparative project nevertheless possesses an exciting mixture, both interesting and illuminating, and the range of contexts offer a rich picture of the ways in which political marketing is evolving, and being adapted and employed. Our authors take different lines on assessing the phenomenon, based on their analysis of their respective countries and/or parties. In developing democracies it is seen as a force for the stabilisation and deeper rooting of democracy; in more developed countries we hear more criticism, of marketing practices breaking the link between party and members, voter groups or parliaments. These differing perspectives afford us an understanding of the effects of political marketing and some insight into the future as the phenomenon becomes even more widespread and engrained in political party behaviour. We hope that this book begins a global debate focusing on the uses and effects of political marketing that will stimulate academics and practitioners to consider what shape future political behaviour will take and what role marketing practices will play.

This volume would not have been possible without the co-operation and hard work of all the chapter authors. We thank them all for meeting the deadlines, some at extremely short notice, and producing excellent, original pieces of work; for dedicating their time to this volume, especially those who are not employed as full-time academics and who have done so out of sheer passion for the topic; and for responding constructively to our suggestions for revision.

On a more personal note we would like to thank the Political Marketing Specialist Group of the Political Studies Association for its support and friendship; everyone at Manchester University Press, particularly Tony Mason for his belief in the importance of this topic; and those people in our lives who have put up with us as we completed all the duties of an editor, often on Sunday afternoons when they wished to do something else. Darren wishes to thank Teresa Thorn for her continuing love and support, and Mark and Kayleigh for their understanding. Jennifer would like to thank the Management Department at Aberdeen for the support necessary to run the 2002 conference that began it all, and those in the Centre for Political Marketing and Management at Keele who share our passion for this growing field. She thanks also her family, both in England and Australia, especially her nephew Jack, who could not fathom why she did not play with him constantly on her last trip to Brisbane – her time was spent on the computer reading draft chapters for this book – and hopes that he, and others, will in time at least grow to consider that the output of that work made it worthwhile.

Darren G. Lilleker, Bournemouth University
Jennifer Lees-Marshment, Centre for Political Marketing and Management,
Keele University

Introduction:
rethinking political party behaviour

Darren G. Lilleker and Jennifer Lees-Marshment

Political marketing is a global phenomenon with parties from all corners of the world developing political manifestos based around the results of qualitative and quantitative marketing research. Commercial techniques and strategy have permeated the political arena, in response to the rise of more critical, better educated and informed electorates that are independent of particular parties (see Lees-Marshment 2001a: chapter 1). Voters choose parties as consumers choose products. This has led academics to examine the extent to which marketing techniques and approaches are employed; they also recognise the emergence of the market-oriented party – a party no longer tied to historical ideology and futuristic rhetoric but one more focused on developing a credible product with which to satisfy its core electoral market.

Jennifer Lees-Marshment's analysis of UK party behaviour (2001a) identified three approaches parties could take by becoming a *product*-oriented party, a *sales*-oriented party or a *market*-oriented party, with the latter being perceived as the paradigm for a party seeking to win election. Lees-Marshment's model was constructed to explain major party response to developments within the UK duopolistic political system, although it has been applied increasingly to smaller parties and countries around the world with different goals, markets and political systems. The extent to which this UK-generated model can be employed for comparative analysis requires questioning, however, because of differences in the structure of government, constitutional arrangements, separation of powers, type of legislature, electoral system and political culture (Lees-Marshment 2001a: 220). Such factors would condition the potential scope, use, influence and effectiveness of a party-based political marketing framework (Ingram and Lees-Marshment 2002). This book seeks to explore this and related questions by analysing political marketing around the world from a comparative perspective alongside a consideration of the efficacy of the Lees-Marshment model in enhancing our understanding of this global phenomenon.

In developing a comparative framework for analysing current trends, and for testing the applicability of the model, we use a cross-section of nations, as

---

Box 1.1 *Chosen democracies*

Established democracies: Canada, New Zealand, the UK and the USA, as well as a devolved democracy within an established system: Scotland.

Countries with current or historic anti-democratic movements that have become strong democracies: Austria and Germany.

Second wave democracies: Brazil.

Emergent democracies: Northern Ireland and Peru.

---

categorised by Derbyshire and Derbyshire (2002; see box 1.1). While not a perfect sample of political systems, this initial analysis allows us to examine a range of political systems with contrasting histories, traditions and structures.[1] Each case study enables us to understand responses to global trends, such as the rise of consumerism, as well as to test the model under a variety of different political environments. Each chapter looks at either a single party or a collection of parties[2] and is conducted by one or more researchers specialising in a given nation's politics. Each attempts to access what is currently happening in a country, as well as contemplating the implications of the political-party behavioural changes for its political system as a whole.

To date, no such comparative analysis of political-party marketing has been conducted; studies that come closest are those dealing with the globalisation or Americanisation of political communication and election campaigning (see e.g. Norris 2000). Few go beyond considering campaign communication to elicit the reasons for changes in party behaviour (an exception is Mair 1998). Comparative analysis of political behaviour is important for several reasons. Political parties emerge out of specific national contexts and have to develop within the constraints of their political environments. In each nation one finds that the political organisations are shaped and moulded by the histories, political traditions, societal forces and political structures in which they have developed and now seek election. Nevertheless, recognising certain commonalities and areas of convergence is important to comprehend the growing use of political marketing across the world.

Global convergence and the rise of consumerism

Certain patterns of convergence have been noted by political observers such as Lane and Ersson (1996), who observed convergence in Europe, for example the harmonisation of political structures, with moves towards democratisation across the Continent, as well as increasing similarity between the organisation of democracy in countries. Such convergence is driven by economic forces which affect any nation that embraces international trade, and harmonisation moves through the financial sectors to the business sector and, finally, to the political sector (Beck 2000). Political culture – the ways in which the public acts and responds towards the political system – is also converging. These forces are argued to be global phe-nomena (Baylis and Smith 1999), and one can conclude therefore that they are shaping not just the political economies of Europe but the political structures of the entire world. Such developments have implications for the utilisation of polit-ical marketing.

Another relevant trend is the internationalisation of consumerism: the global public is increasingly thinking and behaving like a consumer in all areas of life. Some call this 'Americanisation', others refer to it as 'coca-cola-isation' or 'McDonaldisation' (see Barber 1996; Berger 1997), though it could also be claimed to be a liberation. Many argue that consumerism, or what Marx referred to as commodity fetishism, has supplanted higher culture and religion, turning us all into mindless clones desiring to dress like and to drink the same things as the movie stars (Brownlie *et al.* 1999; Du Gay and Salaman 1992; Elliott 1997; Miller 1997; Morgan 1992). It could, however, be said that within this consumerism the individual has more power than ever before (Belk 1996; Brownlie *et al.* 1999; Dermody, Moloney and Scullion 1999). While advertising tries to bamboozle and control, the increasing cynicism of viewers enables them to discriminate about what they believe, what they want, what they think about and what they think about it. The consumer is a beast difficult to influence, one it is argued, that is becoming far more sophisticated in forming its perceptions about all aspects of life (Dermody *et al.* 1999; Dermody and Scullion 2001; Spogard and James 2000) – politics included.

Politics sets the parameters for society and its economic relations (Giddens 1991), dominating individual lives from the macro level where the rules of society are made, but also – more directly visible perhaps – at the micro level where services and benefits are delivered and received. Here, too, consumerism is developing as citizens exhibit increasingly critical and challenging attitudes towards the local council, MP or doctor. It is no longer accepted that public figures and organisations know best: the public expects individuals' opinions to be considered. Academics have attended to the recent development of the political consumer (Lees-Marshment 2004) and have observed that politicians appear increasingly to respond to and follow their markets rather than try to lead them (Butler and Collins 2001; Lees-Marshment 2001a; Lees-Marshment and Lilleker 2001; Lock and Harris 1996; Scammell 1999). The spread of consumerism and political marketing through many nations necessi-tates comparative analysis if we are to understand the transformations taking place and their consequences for global democratic governance.

Using the Lees-Marshment model

Political marketing is the study of how politicians interface with their electorates. If, as we hypothesise, the use of political marketing is related to the growth in political consumerism, which in turn is due to the global reach of consumerism, then we would expect to find that marketing is being used by political parties worldwide. However, testing for the extent of the effects of marketing in politics is a difficult process, one that needs, at the very least, benchmarks against which to measure political parties' behaviour for a market orientation. This is one reason for employing the Lees-Marshment model (Lees-Marshment 2001a). The model provides a series of stages through which a party desiring to adopt a market orientation, it is argued, proceeds, enabling the contributors to this book to rigorously test the ways in which parties from a cross-section of nations are or are not altering their behaviour in response to market forces. This allows us to understand the extent of marketisation, as well as the fit of the model.

The Lees-Marshment model takes a highly systematic approach to the study of political parties, avoiding the tendency to simplify or to ignore key aspects of party behaviour such as party policy, leadership, organisational structure, membership, and both external and internal communication. The model distinguishes political marketing from other, less subtle, analyses which reduce it to salesmanship, populism or following majoritarian opinion with no provision of leadership.

The model was developed through a study of UK political parties. We suspect, therefore, that the model is insufficiently developed to be applicable across other national contexts. While we consider the model to be an adequate starting point, a study of this nature may suggest necessary modifications and development, taking account of its comparative use and application, its utility for party leaders and its generation of more prescriptive and/or predictable outcomes for academics. The model could be developed for use by parties in any country wishing to truly understand their markets and so regain the support of swathes of the electorate and by academics seeking to predict voting behaviour. The adoption of a global comparative focus so as to learn from other national experiences and contexts is one means by which the model can be enhanced. Such improvement is essential if the model – and the study of political marketing in general – are to become tools of the practitioner as well as the academic. While we do not expect to find all the answers in this first comparative study, we will make significant progress in broadening our understanding of political marketing practice and theory.

Before we move to such comparative analysis, we provide a brief overview of the basic nature of a political party, of political marketing and of the Lees-Marshment model to form a basic framework for discussion in the rest of the book.

Political parties

Political parties are the life-blood of democracy: they are the main channel of representation and determine the nature of a nation's government. They have different goals, markets and products, all of which affect how they might use marketing but they are likely to vary from one nation to another.

Goals

Political parties can have many goals, but usually one is more important than the others. Historically parties were viewed as pursuing a particular ideology, from which standpoint they determine their policies and try to put them into practice to suit those whom they represent. The development of rational-choice literature in the 1960s and after led to the assertion that the dominant goal of the major parties is to obtain control of government through long-term electoral success (see Downs 1957: 28; Harmel and Janda 1994; Laver 1997: 111; Lock and Harris 1996: 25; Schlesinger 1984 and 1994 for discussion). Smaller parties which do not aim to win control of the national government can be inclined to exert influence over the political agenda on behalf of one section of society. When analysing the use of political marketing it is important to understand a party's goal because this is the starting point from which all its behaviour is observed and its marketing effectiveness measured.

Market

In the twentieth century, parties were thought to have a 'natural' – class-based – constituency or market, but this idea appears to have been revised drastically over the last two decades (Katz and Mair 1995; Lilleker 2003) due to a number of changes in society or in the overall market environment. The availability of information, its independent or biased nature, the space for debate, the stage of information and communication technology development, levels of education, geographical and occupational mobility, distinctness of socio-economic groupings – all these affect the overall degree of consumerisation and the attitude of the citizenry to its politicians and, in turn, its demand for more market-oriented/ consumer driven politics (Lees-Marshment 2001a: 14–25). These non-political factors are, after all, those portended to determine the strength of party identification by the political science (or the sociological) model of voting behaviour (Campbell *et al.* 1960). Thus, the market is much more open and fluid.

A party's market also varies according to its goals and size. While smaller parties are still able to focus on representing a small section, or niche, within society, major parties seek to serve various larger sections and sub-groups in society. The prime market for a major party will include the voters whose support it requires to achieve electoral success, according to the electoral rules of individual nations, but also the party's membership which may make demands that conflict with those of the wider electorate.

Product

'Product' is not a word generally used within political discussion, but from a market-oriented perspective politicians need to hear what the political consumer demands in order to analyse how that may be designed, communicated and sold. In political terms, the product is quite simply how a party behaves – in terms of both the past and the present, and in terms of future promises. It can include the aspects listed in box 1.2.

The product is ongoing and is offered at all times (not just at election times) and at all levels of the party. The goals, market and product, however, will vary according to the party and the political system in which it operates, as will be explored in the following chapters.

Box 1.2   *A party's product*

- **Leadership:** powers, image, character, support/appeal, relationship with the rest of the party organisation (advisers, cabinet, members, MPs), media relationship.
- **Members of Parliament** (existing or proposed): candidate nature, relationship with constituents, etc.
- **Membership:** powers, recruitment, nature (ideological character, activity, loyalty, behaviour, relationship to leader).
- **Staff:** researchers, professionals, advisers, etc. – their role, influence, office powers, relationship with other elements of the party organisation.
- **Symbols:** name, logo, anthem.
- **Constitution:** formal, official rules.
- **Activities:** party conferences, rallies, meetings.
- **Policies:** those proposed in manifestoes and those enacted in office.

Source: Lees-Marshment 2001a: 27

Political marketing

Political marketing is the use of marketing concepts and techniques in politics. Marketing is concerned with how organisations behave in relation to their 'customers'; politics, with how political actors and institutions behave with regard to citizens. Marketing is used, in varying forms with different consequences, by all political organisations including parties, but also parliaments, local councils, hospitals, universities, charities or interest groups, government departments and, in the UK, the BBC and even the monarchy (Lees-Marshment 2004). While such organisations differ from businesses in many ways, they are able to adapt and use the basic concepts of business marketing. They increasingly conduct market intelligence to identify citizen concerns, change their behaviour to meet those demands and communicate their 'product offering' more effectively.

Political marketing has moved beyond the narrow focus on communication that characterises much of its literature prior to the twenty-first century – a focus that perhaps stemmed from the common mistake that marketing itself is the same as advertising or selling. Political marketing is concerned with the demands of the market and political behaviour in a much broader sense, so that we can say political marketing studies the relationship between a political organisation's *product* and the demands of its market. Because such political organisations include parliaments, political parties, interest-groups and bureaucracies, their products include legislation, policies and meetings; their market, the public, electorate, members, financial donors, tax-payers or benefit receivers.

As an activity, political marketing is about political organisations (such as political parties, parliaments and government departments) adapting techniques (such as market research and product design) and concepts (such as the desire to satisfy voter demands) originally used in the business world to help them achieve their goals (such as win elections or pass legislation). While politics generally does not hold profit-making as its dominant goal, business too is increasingly acknowledged to have wider objectives than mere profit, and both politics and business offer much the same basic tenets of responding to your market, thinking carefully about what you do or about your product, and engaging in effective communication.

Political marketing, like marketing generally, has several approaches or orientations – its orientation being the basic drive of an organisation. To put it simply, in a *product*-oriented political organisation the leadership and/or the members will set policy and expect others to support the organisation on the basis that the policy is right. A *sales*-oriented political organisation will follow the above course, but uses market intelligence to design its communications strategy in order to persuade voters to support the party. A *market*-oriented organisation, however, gathers intelligence on voter requirements and considers them, together with the views of internal staff members and any target or core segment of the market, prior to designing the product. Communication is then a process of informing voters that the organisation is offering the product that they want (for further detail see Lees-Marshment 2004: chapter 1).

To follow these orientations through, an organisation can engage in a wide range of activities and processes. These can be adapted for politics, although not all will be relevant because, as political marketing scholars widely acknowledge (see Scammell 1999), there are differences between business and politics. There are core activities that all political organisations can choose to engage in, such as market intelligence, product design and communication, but the ways in which these are used vary from one organisation to another.

The Lees-Marshment (2001a) model was developed to incorporate these, along with an understanding of party behaviour from the political science literature, and provides the framework for comparative empirical analysis. We now explore that model in more detail.

Marketing political parties: the Lees-Marshment model

Lees-Marshment (2001a: 21–43) identifies three approaches in the political marketing of a party: the POP (product-oriented party); the SOP (sales-oriented party); and the MOP (market-oriented party). Each party considers its relations with its market and so behaves in ways deemed appropriate to that market. The stages of behaviour for each approach are depicted in figure 1.1. It is necessary to explain both the philosophy behind each orientation and the stages they go through. In particular we will detail the eight-stage process for the model of a *market*-oriented party, as it is that approach which, we argue, is becoming a global phenomenon.

Figure 1.1   *The marketing process for POPs, SOPs and MOPs: the Lees-Marshment model*

PRODUCT-ORIENTED PARTY	SALES-ORIENTED PARTY	MARKET-ORIENTED PARTY
STAGE 1 PRODUCT DESIGN	STAGE 1 PRODUCT DESIGN	STAGE 1 MARKET INTELLIGENCE
	STAGE 2 MARKET INTELLIGENCE	STAGE 2 PRODUCT DESIGN
		STAGE 3 PRODUCT ADJUSTMENT
		STAGE 4 IMPLEMENTATION
STAGE 2 COMMUNICATION	STAGE 3 COMMUNICATION	STAGE 5 COMMUNICATION
STAGE 3 CAMPAIGN	STAGE 4 CAMPAIGN	STAGE 6 CAMPAIGN
STAGE 4 ELECTION	STAGE 5 ELECTION	STAGE 7 ELECTION
STAGE 5 DELIVERY	STAGE 6 DELIVERY	STAGE 8 DELIVERY

The product-oriented-party

The POP exemplifies the classical conviction-based form of party behaviour of arguing for what it stands for and believes in. It assumes that voters will realise the worth of its ideas and will therefore vote for it. This type of party refuses to change its ideas, or product, even if it fails to gain electoral or membership support. A POP goes through a five-stage marketing process.

- In stage 1, *product design*, the party designs its behaviour according to the beliefs of members and leaders.
- Stage 2, *communication*, addresses the party's campaign, whether conducted over the short term or the long term but also ongoing behaviour. Not just the leader, but all MPs and party members send a message to the electorate. The organisation is clear and effective; designed to advance the party's arguments to voters.

- Stage 3 is the official campaign period leading up to the election when the party makes its case to the electorate.
- Stage 4 is the general election itself.
- In stage 5, *delivery*, the party indicates how it aims to deliver its promised product in government.

Lees-Marshment argued initially that electoral conditions in Western liberal democracies are such that voters do not support a party that appeals for support simply on the basis that it is right or because the ideology it argues for is normatively valuable. This book explores the possibility of parties in countries outside of the UK adopting the POP approach and being successful in influencing political debate and achieving their goals.

The sales-oriented party

The pure POP argues the case, hoping to engage the support of people, whereas the SOP seeks to persuade voters through extensive marketing communications founded in an understanding of ways in which a market can be manipulated. This would involve conducting research for advertisement and message construction, but not for product design. An SOP does not change its behaviour to suit what people want, but tries to make people want what it offers.

An SOP is therefore much more focused than the POP and the MOP on selling its product. After designing its product according to the party's beliefs, the SOP in stage 2 conducts market research to ascertain voters' response to its behaviour: which voter segments like it, which do not and which might be persuaded if certain aspects are communicated in a targeted manner? Communication is then devised to suit each segment.

Market intelligence will then inform both ongoing communication (stage 3) and the official election campaign (stage 4). Communication is well-organised, coherent, centralised and unified. It is designed not just to advance arguments but to persuade voters that the party is right and that they want to vote for the party. It uses all available selling techniques and marketing communication techniques, including mail, leaflets, posters and direct-mail videos, party-election broadcasts, mobile phone texts (Fill 2002). At the general election (stage 5), the successful SOP would win. The final stage is delivery: major parties that win power need to deliver their policies and objectives in government.

Lees-Marshment (2001a) argued that an SOP approach is likely to fail at an election because it does not respond to the emergent political consumer and continues to seek to change voter demands rather than to follow them. This book will, however, take a more open perspective and consider the potential advantages of an SOP approach for parties in other countries or with different goals.

The market-oriented party

The MOP model turns around traditional ideas about politics and argues that to win an election a party needs to identify and understand public priorities, concerns and demands before then designing a product that reflects them. It does not attempt to change what people think, but to deliver what they need and want. An MOP is driven not by ideology or leader opinion, but by the desire to develop and deliver a set of realistic policies and structures that will meet the needs of its market. Party tradition, the views of members and expertise, whether of professionals or of the leadership, are utilised to develop responses to demands rather than to dictate them.

An MOP therefore goes through a more complex eight-stage process to develop a product that will satisfy voters' demands, is supported and implemented by the internal organisation and is deliverable in government.

Market intelligence (stage 1) aims to discover voters' behaviour, needs, wants and priorities. Data deriving from many sources are collected using various methods (including polls, focus groups, public consultations and meetings, and internal discussions at all levels) to provide information about all aspects of the product. The focus can be on intelligence for short-term goals and election manifestos and on specific areas, or it can be on long-term goals, for example the future of health-care provision. The gathering of intelligence should not always look at the electorate uniformly, but should involve strategic segmentation that will allow the product and its communication to be designed for specific groups. Data will normally be professionally collected, to avoid political bias, but must then be disseminated throughout the membership to increase the chances that the party, as a whole, will accept market-oriented changes in behaviour.

The party will then design a model 'product' (stage 2) on the basis of market intelligence data. This can mean making changes, where necessary, to any aspect of the party; such changes may well be trivial or to one particular area (e.g. to the leader), or they may be dramatic and indicative of a wholesale transformation in image and behaviour. The latter can generate internal opposition and is unlikely to be effectively implemented without some adjustment and careful management.

The product design is adjusted (stage 3) according to four factors: achievability, internal reaction, competition analysis and support analysis.

- *Achievability*: the party should not promise what it cannot deliver in government. Promises to reduce tax and then a failure to do so, for example, would result only in voter dissatisfaction.
- *Internal reaction*: analysis concerns linking the demands and priorities of the market with those of the party members, elected as well as grassroots. Political parties commonly depend on members for funding, support and campaigning. Because these people are often ideologically motivated (Lilleker 2005; Seyd and Whiteley 2002), changes have to be congruent with the party's ideology and history, as well as with the ideas of the market, suggesting that an MOP must perform a delicate, yet essential, balancing act between the demands of external (voters) and internal (members) supporters. This activity can be facilitated by extensive consultation, within which members must, however, be allowed to have their say.

- *Competition analysis*: the strengths and weaknesses of the opposition parties are taken account of and response to them made in the product design. This allows for the product to be distinctive and so fill gaps in the market. Differences will inevitably occur as the party adjusts its behaviour to suit its internal support, because each major party has its own historical and ideological background. Additionally, the party may either highlight or downplay a particular ideological difference with regard to the competition, depending on whether a strength or a weakness is involved. A party which simply copies another electorally success-ful party would not be using political marketing correctly.
- *Support analysis*: the final phase of adjustment consists of identifying the key groups within the electorate whose support is required in order to secure elec-tion. These groups, or segments, are then targeted by further product adjust-ments as well as by communication.

Implementation (stage 4) involves unifying the party around the proposed product. Only when an overall majority of party members, candidates and MPs broadly accept the logic of the market-oriented product will voters be convinced of the credibility of what is on offer. This must be carefully managed internally to minimise any conflict that can 'contaminate the brand'. This stage is perhaps the most difficult, though the most important; ineffective implementation may gain short-term goals but will hinder delivery and long-term electoral success.

Once the product is implemented throughout the party, it must be conveyed to the electorate using the most appropriate and effective communication techniques. Communication (stage 5) is a continual process that allows interaction with both internal and external supporters, and is carried out in a coherent way nationwide by members of the party from all levels. The official election campaign (stage 6) will simply re-emphasise the more important aspects of the product to remind the electorate what is on offer and will employ the more innovative practices of mar-keting communication. If the product is effectively communicated and the party is accepted as a viable potential government, the party will be elected (stage 7) and will gain support in terms of favourable voter and member assessment of the party's product. The eighth and final stage is to deliver the promised product in government. This difficult task is crucial if voters are to be satisfied and also con-tinue to support the party. If the party is to remain market oriented once in gov-ernment, it must engage in continual market intelligence and adjust its behaviour as demands change.

Testing the model

The model was constructed in 1999 with reference to the UK, without the benefit of primary empirical testing. The chapters of the book gather together a range of international scholars to apply the theory to a variety of cases around the world from a comparative perspective. In doing so, they explore the extent to which polit-ical marketing is a global phenomenon, the academic utility of the MOP–SOP–POP

Lees-Marshment 2001a framework, the difficulties parties encounter when practising political marketing, discussing the democratic and philosophical implications of the use of political marketing around the world.

Each of the book's chapters directs attention to a particular nation and tells a strong story in its own right. The contributors write within a clearly defined structure that includes the following:

- an overview of the political context;
- a history of the application of political marketing;
- the introduction of the case study or studies;
- an analysis of the case study using the Lees-Marshment (2001a) model;
- a discussion of the implications for the democratic function;
- a critique of the model in the light of findings.

However, read as a whole, the book contributes to an overall understanding and analysis of party political marketing. It will be an interesting journey round the world.

Notes

1 A future project may revisit these cases and expand the number to include other European countries such as France, Spain and Finland. We initially planned and contracted a chapter on Denmark, but unfortunately the author, Robert Ormrod, had to pull out. The editors wish to acknowledge his support for the initial project design.
2 Such variance is dictated both by the research of our international authors and by a desire to ensure expert analysis conducted by those who understand the politics of their nation. The other advantage in allowing variety is that, overall, we provide both depth with wide overviews of political marketing by all parties in a nation such as Canada, as well as more in-depth studies focused on one party such as the APRA in Peru and Bush's Republican organisation in the USA.

Bibliography

Barber, B. R. (1996), *Jihad vs. McWorld*, New York: Ballantine.

Baylis, J. and Smith, S. (1999), *The Globalisation of World Politics*, Oxford: Oxford University Press.

Belk, R. W. (1996), 'On aura, illusion, escape and hope in apocalyptic consumption: the apotheosis of Las Vegas', in Brown S., Bell, J. and Carson, D. (eds), *Marketing Apocalypse: Eschatology, Escapology and the Illusion of the End*, London: Routledge.

Beck, U. (2000), *What is Globalisation?*, Cambridge: Polity.

Berger, P. L. (1997), 'Four faces of global culture', *The National Interest*, Fall.

Bowler, S. and Farrell, D. (1992), *Election Strategies and Political Marketing*, Basingstoke: Macmillan.

Brownlie, D., Saren, M., Wensley, R. and Whittington, R. (eds) (1999), *Rethinking Marketing: Towards Critical Marketing Accountings*, London: Sage.

Butler, P. and Collins, N. (2001), 'Payment on delivery: recognising constituency service as political marketing', *European Journal of Marketing*, 35(9–10): 1026–37.

Campbell, A., Converse, P. E., Miller, W. E. and Stokes, D. E. (eds) (1960), *The American Voter*, New York: University of Chicago Press.

Derbyshire, J. D. and Derbyshire, I. (2002), *Political Systems of the World*, Oxford: Helicon.

Dermody, J., Moloney, K. and Scullion, R. (1999), 'Political marketing: past, present and potential future. New insights attempting to understand the meaning of political consumption', *Conference Proceedings of the Academy of Marketing Special Interest Group in Political Marketing*, Bournemouth University, 15–16 September.

Dermody, J. and Scullion, R. (2001), 'Delusions of grandeur? Marketing's contribution to "meaningful" Western political consumption', *European Journal of Marketing*, 35(9–10): 1085–98.

Downs, A. (1957), *An Economic Theory of Democracy*, New York: Harper & Row.

Du Gay, P. and Salaman, G. (1992), 'The cult(ure) of the customer', *Journal of Management Studies*, 29(5): 616–33.

Elliott, R. (1997), 'Existential consumption and irrational desire', *European Journal of Marketing*, 31(3): 285–96.

Fill, C. (2002), *Marketing Communication*, London: Prentice-Hall.

Giddens, A. (1991), *Identity and Modernity*, Cambridge: Polity.

Harmel, R. and Janda (1994), 'An integrated theory of party change', *Journal of Theoretical Politics*, 6(3): 259–87.

Ingram, P. and Lees-Marshment, J. (2002), 'The Anglicisation of political marketing: how Blair out-marketed Clinton', *Journal of Public Affairs*, 2(2): 44–56.

Katz, R. S. and Mair, P. (eds) (1994), *How Parties Organise: Change and Adaptation in Party Organisation in Western Democracies*, London: Sage.

Katz, R. S. and Mair, P. (1995), 'Changing models of party organisation and party democracy: the emergence of the cartel party', *Party Politics*, 1(1): 5–28.

Lane, J. and Ersson, S. O. (1996), *European Politics: An Introduction*, London: Sage.

Laver, M. (1997), *Private Desires, Political Action*, London: Sage.

Lees-Marshment, J. (2001a), *Political Marketing and British Political Parties*, Manchester: Manchester University Press.

Lees-Marshment, J. (2001b), 'Comprehensive political marketing: what, how and why?', Proceedings of the Academy of Marketing Conference, Cardiff University 2–4 July.

Lees-Marshment, J. (2001c), 'The marriage of politics and marketing', *Political Studies* 49(4): 692–713.

Lees-Marshment, J. (2001d), 'The product-, sales- and market-oriented party and how Labour learnt to market the product, not just the presentation', *European Journal of Marketing*, special issue, 'Political marketing', 35(9–10): 1074–84.

Lees-Marshment, J. (2001e), 'Marketing the British Conservatives 1997–2001', *Journal of Marketing Management*, special issue, 'The Marketing campaign: the British general election of 2001', 17: 929–41.

Lees-Marshment, J. (2001f), 'The world's most unpopular populist, a poorly sold product, or just mission impossible? A Political marketing analysis of Hague's Conservatives 1997–2001', paper presented at the EPOP conference, 2001, University of Sussex.

Lees-Marshment, J. (2003a), 'Marketing political institutions: good in theory but problematic in practice?', Academy of Marketing peer-reviewed conference proceedings, University of Aston.

Lees-Marshment, J. (2003b), 'Political marketing: how to reach that pot of gold', *Journal of Political Marketing*, 2(1): 1–32.

Lees-Marshment, J. (2003c), 'Marketing good works: new trends in how interest groups recruit supporters', *Journal of Public Affairs*, 3(4): 358–70.

Lees-Marshment, J. (2003d), 'Marketing UK political parties: the potential and limitations of political marketing', staff–student seminar, Politics Department, University of Otago, New Zealand, 13 August 2003.

Lees-Marshment, J. (2003e), 'Marketing British political parties from Thatcher to Blair: the potential and pitfalls of political marketing', talk given at the National Europe Centre, Australian National University, Canberra, Australia.

Lees-Marshment, J. (2003f), 'New Labour, new danger: the pitfalls of political marketing in the UK', talk given at the Public Relations Institute of Australia, the Press Club, Canberra.

Lees-Marshment, J. (2004), *The Political Marketing Revolution*, Manchester: Manchester University Press.

Lees-Marshment, J. and Lilleker, D. G. (2001), 'Political marketing and traditional values: "Old Labour" for "new times" '?, *Contemporary Politics*, 7(3): 205–16.

Lilleker, D. G. (2005), 'Whose Left? Working class political allegiances in post-industrial Britain', *International Review of Social History*, 47(10): 65–86.

Lilleker, D. G. (2005), 'Political marketing: the cause of a democratic deficit?', *Journal of Non-Profit and Public Sector Marketing*.

Lock, A. and Harris, P. (1996), 'Political marketing: vive la différence', *European Journal of Marketing*, 30(10–11): 14–24.

Mair, P. (1998), *Party System Change: Approaches and Interpretations*, New York: Clarendon.

Miller, D. (1997), 'Consumption and its consequences', in H. Mackay (ed.), *Consumption and Everyday Life*, London: Sage: 14–50.

Morgan, G. (1992), 'Marketing discourse and practice: towards a critical analysis', in M. Alvesson and H. Willmott (eds), *Critical Management Studies*, London: Sage: 136–85.

Neubaur, C. and Wilkens, L. (1997), 'Propaganda as religion in National Socialism', *Psyche-Zeitschrift für Psychoanalyse*, 50(3): 85–99.

Norris, P. (2000), *A Virtuous Circle*, New York: Cambridge.

O'Cass, A. (1996), 'Political marketing and the marketing concept', *European Journal of Marketing*, 30(10–11): 45–61.

Opello, W. C. and Rosow, S. J. (1999), *The Nation-State and Global Order*, Boulder, CO: Lynne Reinner.

O'Shaughnessy, N. (1990), *The Phenomenon of Political Marketing*, London: Macmillan.

O'Shaughnessy, N. (1999), 'The marketing of political marketing', *European Journal of Marketing*, 35(9–10): 1047–57.

Scammell, M. (1999), 'Political marketing: lessons for political science', *Political Studies*, 47(4): 718–39.

Seyd, P. and Whiteley, P. (2002), *New Labour's Grassroots*, Basingstoke: Palgrave.

Spogard, R. and James, M. (2000), 'Governance and democracy – the people's view: a global opinion poll', address to the United Nations, available online: www.gallup-international/survey18.htm (accessed 19 August 2003).

2

Political marketing in the UK:
a positive start but an uncertain future

Jennifer Lees-Marshment and Darren G. Lilleker

Politics in the UK since the 1970s can be described as having a strong market orientation. Margaret Thatcher, prime minister (1979–90), implemented a market-oriented approach, not just in presentation but in the design of the political product. Labour's leader since 1994 and prime minister from 1997, Tony Blair has directed UK politics towards a full market orientation whereby public demands influence the redesigning of the whole party 'product', including emblems and logos, policies, internal structure and even the party constitution.

Labour enjoyed a landslide electoral success in 1997, since when a consensus in favour of the MOP approach has emerged within the two major parties. Our analysis of their behaviour from 1997 to 2003 suggests, however, that although there is the will to become market-oriented both parties have experienced significant difficulties in implementing an MOP approach. Furthermore, philosophical concerns about the effect of market-oriented political behaviour on leadership, agenda-setting and the constraints of governance have become clear in Britain in the last few years. The UK may appear to lead the rest of the world in the use of comprehensive political marketing (Ingram and Lees-Marshment 2002), yet it is also one of the first users to show that significant problems exist for the political marketing approach.

This chapter focuses on the behaviour of the Conservative and Labour Parties following the 1997 election and their attempts to regain or maintain a market orientation. Rather than go through each stage of the MOP model, which is explored elsewhere (Lees-Marshment 2004a: chapter 2), we concentrate on the aspects of political marketing which require particular attention, providing a detailed critique of the following key areas of the MOP model:

- difficulties with delivery;
- maintaining a market-orientation in government;
- internal political marketing and problems in implementation;
- room for ideology and culture within an MOP framework;
- the local political market;

• the role of leadership within an MOP framework; and
• marketing and controversial issues such as war.

This critique raises interesting questions about political marketing in the UK and beyond. Firstly, though, we must consider the nature of the UK political market.

UK political marketing in context: market, system and environment

The UK has a traditional majority system, the party elected to government being the party which wins the most seats in a general election, decided by a first-past-the-post electoral system held every five years, if not sooner. The system is dominated by two main parties, Labour and Conservative, and has functioned as a duopoly for the greater part of its existence; third parties tend to be marginalised. The main chamber in the legislature is the House of Commons, to which all MPs are elected by their constituencies. A second chamber acts as a check on government legislation.

The electoral system does not provide an overall proportionality between votes for a party nationally and seats in the House of Commons. This proves a barrier to small parties, which may have significant support that is diffused across the nation.

The Conservative and Labour Parties are major organisations. They compete at all elections, employ professional staff and advisors but also utilise voluntary labour through their membership. Membership remains an important part of the party product in Britain, which is perhaps the broadest of any of the systems studied in this book. Because two parties dominate politics, they gain more media attention, though this also means that every aspect of their behaviour can be conveyed nationally and therefore has potential influence on voters. Leadership is very important and can exercise significant control over the party organisation. The legislative system and the comparatively high levels of party unity enable a prime minister elected with a good majority to pass policies relatively easily through Parliament. The scope for party leaders to utilise political marketing is therefore potentially high.

The Conservative Party is the oldest established UK party, with a tradition going back to the seventeenth century. The party developed out of a loose association of landowners and has predominated for much of the last three centuries, surviving by responding effectively to changes in society. Having evolved from a party of landowners, the rich and the aristocracy, the Conservatives courted the expanding middle classes and later the skilled working class as the franchise was expanded.

In contrast the Labour Party was formed in 1899 as the political arm of the trade unions. It adopted 'labourism' (Allender 2001) as the platform from which to represent the working class in the 1920s, and by the 1930s had established itself as the second main party. Despite electoral successes during the twentieth century, it experienced eighteen years out of government (1979–97), as its core market was eroded by industrial restructuring (Lilleker 2003). Significant internal divisions,

exemplified by the short-lived but significant formation by former Labour politicians in 1981 of the Social Democratic Party, hindered the party's adaptation to
social changes, and it was not until 1997 that Labour won the broad support base
(geographically, socially, occupationally), including middle class affluent professionals, as well as the socially deprived, needed to form a government.

Until the 1980s, there were no other significant parties. It was only in 1988 that
the Liberal Democrats were formed, out of the remnants of the Social Democratic
Party and the Liberal Party. They have solidified a support base at the local level
and offer some challenge to both main parties. Smaller parties, such as the Greens
and the British National Party, have competed in elections, increasing their overall
public support in the 1990s, but with no success in terms of seats because of the
electoral system.

Despite their continued dominance, it is clear that the main parties have perpet-
ually had to adapt. The force for change is the electorate. Most recent changes
mirror those experienced by the other Western liberal democracies: a decline in
class cohesion, partisanship, political party participation, deference to political and
public elites; alongside an increase and diversification in education, geographical
and occupational mobility, information provision, technological advancement,
wealth and the development of a critical–consumerist attitude to elites (Lilleker
2003). These changes have led political parties to update their core beliefs, or at least
the policies they lead on, and to look for innovative ways of interacting with the
electorate.

The constantly evolving environment provides the space, if not the necessity, for
marketing to be introduced within the political arena. Since Thatcher's demise and
their loss of power in 1997, the Conservative Party has struggled to find its own
natural market – a reflection perhaps of the fluidity of the market environment as
well as the party's failure to utilise political marketing effectively. Conservative
voters have been captured by Labour and support for the party in Wales and
Scotland is particularly low. Equally New Labour's support is dependent on a
public perception of delivery; while being aided by an ineffectual Conservative
opposition. Meanwhile the growth of support for the Liberal Democrats represents
a challenge to both parties.

The party system, although appearing stable, is perhaps also under challenge at
the beginning of the twenty-first century, and this may be exacerbated by the introduction of devolution in Scotland and Wales, taking some of the emphasis away
from Westminster and potentially producing contrasting legislative policies. The
Liberal Democrats have also challenged the current Labour Government's hegemony as power is shared between Labour and the Liberal Democrats in Scotland
and they have only a narrow majority over Plaid Cymru in Wales. Moreover, by
introducing new proportional electoral systems, they have seen the growth of
smaller parties and with it a wider variety of political marketing behaviour. While
the conditions for political marketing are ripe in the UK, it is not as straightforward as it may at first appear for all political parties to utilise its approaches and
techniques.

A brief history of political marketing in the UK up to 1997

Politics and political communication have become increasingly professional (Negrine and Lilleker 2002) and parties have adopted a range of techniques from the commercial area (Scammell 1995). Historically, professionalisation was discussed with regard to image projection, attempting to court the voter through salesmanship, though it was Margaret Thatcher, prime minister 1979–90, who pushed the boundaries forward. Her ability to tap into the public mood represented a 'quantum leap', to adopt Scammell's phrase (1995), although debate continues about how much she was a market-oriented leader or was simply skilled in salesmanship. Thatcher certainly utilised consultants to inform her presentation skills and to design media events (Thomas 1989), but Lees-Marshment (2001a: 49–94) contended that, at least in her first term of office, she utilised marketing to inform how she designed policies. Sir Bernard Ingram (2003), Thatcher's press secretary, commented at the 2003 Political Marketing Conference: 'She didn't worry about how to sell policies. She always said that if the policy was right, it would sell itself.' However, in later years Thatcher became more dogmatic, stopped listening to market intelligence and dismissed advice given by party colleagues, and ultimately resigned because her conviction-led, product-oriented attitude lost her both internal and external support (Lees-Marshment 2001a).

Labour had suffered a succession of electoral defeats in 1979, 1983 and 1987 – and even in 1992 when voter dissatisfaction with the Conservative Government was high. While in the 1980s Labour utilised elements of political marketing, redesigning the party's communication system, creating a new logo and smartening appearances, marketing was confined to *presentation* rather than the product itself – more of a sales-oriented approach (see Lees-Marshment 2001a: 134–80). But senior figures, such as Tony Blair and Gordon Brown, and advisors Phillip Gould and Peter Mandelson, argued that the party needed to redesign all aspects of behaviour, especially policy, and respond fully to the market intelligence it had long been gathering (Gould 1998).

Under the leadership from 1994 of Tony Blair, 'New Labour' redesigned every aspect of the party's product according to the results of market intelligence. In addition, careful support analysis identified the need to target the 'middle England' segment, including former Tory voters, who wanted better public services as well as cautious economic management and lowered income-tax rates. Policies were developed that focused on the issues these voters cared most about (Lees-Marshment and Lilleker 2001). Furthermore, Blair had been selected as leader because of his presentational appeal and strongly market-oriented approach. Membership rights were increased and new members from middle class and professional backgrounds were recruited while the symbiotic relationship with the trade unions was significantly weakened. Communication was long-term so that by the time of the campaign the product sold itself (see Lees-Marshment 2001a: 181–210).

New Labour, one of the clearest examples of an MOP, enjoyed a landslide victory in the 1997 election, taking seats that had previously been thought unwinnable. In contrast, the peformance of the Conservatives under John Major declined considerably, suffering from non-delivery of promises, internal disunity over Europe (an issue voters cared little about) and allegations of sleaze. The use of market intelligence to identify public demands was limited, the product was unclear and unpopular, party organisation was divided and membership was falling, and the response to Labour's new challenge was to be negative and historical. In terms of communication they produced a 'New Labour – New Danger' campaign, which depicted Tony Blair with demon eyes. This was rejected by a public who preferred Blair's carefully designed positive image and the re-branding of Labour as a modern party ready for government (Lilleker 2005).

Labour's success in 1997 and again in 2001 has led the Tories, and indeed other parties in the UK, to consider adopting an MOP model. Smaller parties may have different goals, but still use political marketing. It can be argued, for example, that the Liberal Democrats also have moved towards market-oriented politics. The party has focused on building up support at the local level and in certain geographical areas, in response to market intelligence and an understanding of the local context. Though traditionally eschewing political marketing, the party has made use of political marketing, though it is most visible in targeted constituency campaigning (Denver *et al.* 2002), rather than in product design. This has lead opponents to criticise the Liberal Democrats for trying to represent 'all things to all voters' (Lilleker interview with Conservative candidate, 2001). However, as the party's share of seats in the Parliament has grown, its communication and campaigning strategists have recognised the necessity to change its behaviour:

> Having more MPs mean . . . we have more staff . . . and because we're a larger party we are taken more seriously by the media, which in turn has forced us to raise our game . . . It's a much more cohesive and professional organisation than it was even five years ago . . . We don't want to be a party that muzzles individuality . . . but having said that I think there has to be more of a party line on a lot of things than there used to be. (Walter 2002)

The Liberal Democrats market-test policy (Lees-Marshment informal conversation with senior party official, September 1999), and there are indications that the party has begun to respond to public opinion when developing its behaviour and policies. A recent *Guardian* article (Ward 2002) noted how party strategists are discussing plans to segment the electorate and target specific types of voter. Using the complicated descriptors 'innovators', 'self-actualisers' and 'contented conformers' to designate voters seen as those most likely to switch support to the Liberal Democrats, the party plans to identify the concerns of these target voters, design policies to suit and then test them. The outcomes could then be used in the design of the next party manifesto.

Smaller UK parties have largely rejected market-oriented politics. The Scottish National Party, a sub-state nationalist party, has evolved through the product- sales- and market-oriented cycle. However this is limited due to the need to follow policies specific to Scotland. Similarly, the environmentalist Green Party and the Eurosceptic

UK Independence Party are receptive to the benefits of political marketing, both of them adopting a sales-oriented approach. In contrast, as Bannon and Mochrie show (chapter 11, this book) the Scottish Socialist Party (SSP) remains product oriented, driven by the desire to influence policy and to represent particular sections of the political market, rather than to win office. Like the British National Party, the SSP is much more ideological: the product is determined by party principles, rather than developed to suit the changing demands of the electorate.

Arguably there is a role for such product-oriented parties in the electoral market, even while market-oriented parties dominate, not just in the UK but elsewhere. They enjoy limited electoral success, however, and this chapter therefore concentrates on the use of political marketing by the Labour and Conservative Parties between 1997 and 2003.

The Labour Government and the Conservative Opposition, 1997–2003

Empirical analysis here focuses on the attempts by the two major parties to utilise the MOP approach from 1997 onwards, referring to the key implications already identified.

Being major parties both aim for electoral success. Their market is now very flexible, and the party is a complex product; because it includes leadership, membership, professionals, policies, conferences, therefore there is plenty of scope for party leaders to apply marketing to party behaviour.

The Labour Party is a successful MOP struggling with the delivery stage. The Conservative Party, led during this period by William Hague (1997–2001), Ian Duncan-Smith (2001–3) and Michael Howard (since the autumn of 2003), has battled to make an impact. Our analysis utilises secondary sources covering political marketing and parties generally; primary data from formal interviews with local and national officials from the two main parties and from the Liberal Democrats;[1] and informal conversations between the authors and various party figures in Scotland and London. Evidence is also drawn from party documents, websites and opinion-poll data.

The Conservative Party: marketing in opposition, 1997–2003
The Conservative Party, once the pioneer of political marketing, has struggled since losing power in 1997. Although there was significant recognition that the party had to change (Lees-Marshment and Quayle 2001), initiatives to that end have been hindered by internal division similar to those experienced within the Labour Party in the 1980s. One key difference is that since 1997 they have commissioned substantial market intelligence, its leaders have spoken publicly of the need to listen to voters rather than return to an ideological and elitist approach, and it has engaged in market-oriented activities, including the attempt to devise policies congruent with voter opinion.

Nevertheless, public support for the Conservatives has remained largely low, despite a decline in Labour's support. This poor performance is due to, among other factors, problems it encountered in trying to carry the MOP through all aspects of its behaviour. This has a resulted in a political product that is far removed from voters' image of an ideal opposition party. The story of the Conservatives is one of a party trying to be market oriented, but failing to do so.

Leader approach The party has had three leaders since 1997: William Hague, Ian Duncan-Smith (IDS) and – elected in the autumn of 2003 – Michael Howard. Howard has spoken of the need to reach out to voters, and endorsed IDS's policy reform, but in early 2004 he sent out a statement entitled 'I believe' to party members and the media in a move which does not appear to be particularly market oriented, though it could be based on market intelligence suggesting that voters want a clearer idea of party ideology. Howard quickly established himself as leader and has overturned Blair's lead, for the first time since 1997 (YouGov/Daily Telegraph, Jan 2004, www.YouGov.com, accessed 25 January 2004). He also created a new marketing department at Conservative Central Office (see Lees-Marshment 2004b for further details), but whether this will influence the core product in time to obtain electoral support is debatable.

Both of his predecessors suffered from an inability to lead the party. William Hague, a young leader from a management background, was keen to bring the Party into closer touch with the public, and under his leadership the necessary organisational and constitutional changes were initiated to lay the foundations for a responsive party organisation. Hague, however, failed to obtain positive assessments from the public in polls or focus groups, his efforts hampered by his poor media image (see Lees-Marshment 2004a; Lees-Marshment and Quayle 2001).

The situation was not dissimilar for IDS (see Lees-Marshment and Rudd 2003), elected after the Conservatives' 2001 election defeat on a platform of change designed to make the party re-electable. IDS, from the right-wing of the party and less popular with the public and youth than other contenders such as Michael Portillo, was selected because he was considered more acceptable to party members than rival Kenneth Clarke – a pro-Europe moderate (Bell 2001). IDS did, however, speak of the need to get back in touch with voters, appointed the party's first woman chairman, Teresa May, and pursued a strategy of reaching out to the vulnerable in order to win back middle England. Like Hague, he suffered from poor public evaluation, not just of the public but of Conservative voters (see www.mori .com/digest/2002/c021101.shtml accessed February 2002). He developed market-oriented policies, but internal opposition regarded him as the obstacle to voter support despite his laying the groundwork for a market orientation (Hastings 2003).

Use of market intelligence and initial product design Both Hague and IDS commissioned opinion polls and focus groups, as well as internal party consultation exercises. Hague initiated the 'Listening to Britain' exercise (Conservative Party 1999), designed to reach out to voters (Dykes 2001; Francis 2000; Lansley 2001a). However, they were criticised for not learning the lessons from Labour (Seldon and Snowdon 2001) and relying on the members to make policy. The resulting report (Conservative Party 1999) did identify key voter concerns and fed into the design of policy guarantees in October 1999 (see box 2.1).

Box 2.1   *Conservative Party guarantees, October 1999*

* A parents' guarantee giving them the power to change school management that fails to provide adequate standards.
* A patients' guarantee giving a fixed waiting time based on the need for treatment.
* A guarantee ensuring that taxes will fall as a share of the nation's income over the term of the next Parliament under a Conservative Government.
* A 'can work, must work' guarantee ensuring that benefit claimants who can work will lose their dole if they do not.
* A sterling guarantee that the Tories will oppose entry into the single currency at the next election as part of their manifesto.

Hague also tried to move the overall focus of the party away from taxation to public services, in response to evidence that this was the area about which voters were most concerned. Organisational changes were made in response to internal and external market intelligence, including attempts to broaden the membership and make candidates reflective of the wider society. The 'Fresh Future' reforms and other initiatives included: voting rights for members; the creation of the Conservative Network to attract young professionals into the party; the development of a cultural unit to forge more positive relationships between the party and ethnic minorities (Mannan 2001; Norris 2001); a mentoring programme for women candidates (Dykes 2001); and calls for a socially inclusive party tolerant of people of all sexual orientations.

YouGov conducted polls and the Party's policy unit sought intelligence from think tanks, businesses, relevant professionals and the Conservative Policy Forum. IDS initiated a major policy review and made the 'strategic choice when [he] took over as leader of the Party to concentrate on the public services'; he adopted the theme of protecting the vulnerable (interview with: John Tait; senior Conservative official, 2003; senior figure in the Scottish party leadership, autumn 2002) and made a high-profile visit to Easterhouse council-house estate in Glasgow. In October 2002, the party launched *Leadership with a Purpose: A Better Society* (Conservative Party 2002) that set out five goals targeting all sections of society, not just traditional Conservative voters.

Within the party organisation, further attempts were made to broaden the candidature. The party made the first stage of assessment more professional, testing a matrix of modern skills and favouring women and men equally (Dykes 2003; see also Silvester 2003). As key aspects of the product, all candidates should be professionally selected and fully trained in order to generate a perception of competence and communicate change. Communication staff, however, seemed to dismiss its

importance (interview with senior Conservative official involved with the campaign, 2003; Tait 2003). As Dykes (2003) observed, some still think 'political parties
offer policies, full-stop. The idea they have to offer a shape of a party is new.' Both
Hague and IDS failed to get this accepted.

Problems within the party: the product adjustment and implementation stages
Developmental work was thwarted as the party began to proceed through stages 3
and 4 of the model. Hague's organisational changes and initiatives and statements
by both Hague and IDS about the need to modernise the party had little impact.
Membership did not increase, and although some younger members were attracted
into the party the number of women and ethnic-minority candidates barely
increased. The problems were related to the party's history, culture and membership,
particularly the semi-autonomous Conservative Associations which select candidates and have substantial influence over party messages and the way in which
campaigns are run. Women met unfair barriers during selection processes (see
Lees-Marshment and Rudd 2003): one applicant recalled being asked what would
happen were she to go into labour when there was a three-line whip (*Daily Telegraph*,
2 September 2000). Even after 2001, under IDS, women were put off coming forward
and even single young men felt the process was biased against them because they
were not yet married with children. The party itself became the problem: Steven
Norris (2001), Tory candidate for the post of mayor of London, noted how Hague
'inadvertently had managed to create the impression . . . that the Tory Party was full
of people who were vaguely xenophobic and vaguely homophobic'.

Policy development was also affected. Hague's attempt to focus on public services led to an internal row – partly the result of a failure of internal reaction analysis (Lees-Marshment 2004a). His new policies received little attention, and had not
been checked for achievability until Michael Portillo was re-elected as MP and
became shadow chancellor. A panicked reaction to the results of support analysis
led the Tories to focus on their core voters, and in 2000–1 Hague's initial product
design was abandoned in favour of the themes of asylum, Europe and crime, which
appealed to those voters and were criticised for being 'populist.' As Kenneth Clarke
later commented, the party pursued the wrong strategy for the election: 'from
about half-way through the Parliament we stopped trying to broaden our appeal –
we narrowed it' (BBC 1 *Question Time*, 5 July 2001). This moved the party away
from a market-oriented strategy. Indeed, Lansley (2001a) later conceded that 'it
would have been a damn site better if we'd stuck closely to the "Listening to Britain"
outcome and to the "Common-Sense Revolution" policy document rather than
allow ourselves to be drawn on to other things'.

IDS's 'compassionate Conservatism' and self-proclaimed image as 'the quiet
man' were received with much cynicism by the media. His political programme
had little impact on voters, overshadowed as it was by the challenges to his leadership which finally forced him to quit at the end of 2003. Michael Howard appears
to have made some impact in terms of support, though these are early days, still,
and the party seems ill-prepared for an election that could be as little as a year away.

Communication and campaigning   It is always difficult to communicate, let alone sell, a less than coherent unpopular product. Under Hague, despite the creation of a unified professional campaign pack supplied to local parties and novel attempts to gain media attention (such as Hague wearing a baseball cap at a theme park), party communications suffered from poor organisation, high staff turnover and lack of an overall theme (see Lees-Marshment 2004a; Lees-Marshment and Bartle 2002; Lees-Marshment and Rudd 2003). The party seemed unable to counteract the media focus on Hague's youthfulness and inexperience, while the campaign itself focused on issues which voters considered unimportant. One candidate recalled conflicts of opinion on the doorsteps over the programme he was being forced to adopt by the constituency association. He noted: 'It was symptomatic of the party: the people wanted better health care, I was talking about the euro. Were we out of touch? Were we ever!' (Lilleker interview, March 2002).

The situation was little different with IDS, who also struggled to gain media attention to his new policy agenda 'Believing in Britain'. Images of IDS and David McLetchie in Glasgow hit the headlines and grabbed media attention, completely challenging the stereotype of the Tory agenda. They used slogans such as 'No Child Left Behind' to convey the new approach, borrowed from the US Republican Party (interview with John Tait 2003). New technologies were explored, the 2003 New Year message from the leader being sent out in DVD format to constituency associations. However, the idea that the party could both help the vulnerable and not increase taxes, as staff themselves pointed out, was 'harder to explain' (Tait 2003). Interviews with Conservative communication staff suggested that they were well aware of the vulnerability of their policy, that 'people are sceptical of it' (interview with senior Conservative official 2003), but they had little idea as to the solution to the problems.

In summary, the consequences of failing to implement political marketing were evident in the 2001 election, for, despite the changes Hague made, the party gained only one additional seat and little on its overall vote share. Furthermore, all other indications – polls, focus groups, public debates, membership – suggested low public support for the party. A poll published in October 2002 (YouGov/Telegraph, 6 October 2002) indicated that only 10 per cent of voters thought the Conservatives looked like a government in waiting. The strategy to re-position the party had had little impact, with 70 per cent still regarding the Tories 'the party of the rich'. It is to be doubted that Michael Howard can make the necessary difference in what could be as little as twelve months. Polling results are mixed, and the lead found by YouGov, but not by MORI (www.mori.com/ pubinfo/mag/mixed-news-for-michael-howard.shtml, accessed 20 January 2004), is in the context of Blair forcing the controversial Higher Education Bill through Parliament and expecting, though not receiving, criticism over the Hutton Inquiry report. The Lees-Marshment model was useful in predicting that, unless certain guidelines are followed, an MOP approach will not be implemented. However, the Conservative case shows culture, history and ideology to be crucial to political parties, and it is almost inevitable that they get in the way, giving rise to questions about the utility of the MOP model.

Marketing in government: Labour 1997–2003

In contrast, New Labour's problem was in completing the final stage of the MOP model: delivering on promises and communicating delivery. The challenge for any party in power has been to maintain a market orientation in government. While it has continued to solicit market intelligence, its true efficacy and its influence on product design can be questioned, as can Tony Blair's adherence to the idea of a market orientation. Labour won another landslide in the general election of 8 June 2001, continuing its market-oriented focus on public services. Blair enjoyed unusually high levels of popularity until 2001, but since then has exhibited an increased willingness to go against country and party on issues of conviction. This suggests a decline in responsiveness similar to that shown by Margaret Thatcher.

The Labour case therefore raises many questions for the comprehensive utility of the MOP approach. This section focuses on key aspects of Labour Party behaviour, namely: delivery; the internal and local dimensions; and the move towards a leadership-driven product and superficial consultation.

Delivery   Creating a market-oriented, workable, implementable, realistic product design is simple compared to the final stage of delivery, which remains controversial but is crucial to the success of an MOP. To the party's credit, Labour exhibited an awareness of the need to deliver and be seen to deliver, investing heavily in government communication and even issuing annual reports listing achievements. It succeeded in creating a Scottish Parliament and a Welsh Assembly; maintaining good economic management and low taxation; and introducing a national minimum wage and adopting the Social Chapter.

Political delivery does not, however, equate to satisfaction. This was particularly evident with public services – the key concern of voters. While Labour increased public expenditure on the NHS, education and transport, voters have remained unconvinced that Labour is meeting its pledges (see table 2.1).

The media have played a significant role in highlighting failures, leading to conflict between the Government and the Fourth Estate, Labour resorting to media management – spin – and the relationship breaking down. This has exacerbated an already low level of public trust in politicians generally and, in particular, trust in the Blair Government.

The internal and local dimensions   Problems within the party were evident from 1997, if not before. The leadership resorted to 'Stalinist' methods attempting to block Rhodri Morgan's candidacy for the leadership of the Welsh Assembly and Ken Livingstone's for mayor of London. Party membership slumped from 420,000 after the 1997 election to just 320,000 by mid-1999 and many of those who remained were 'de-energised' (Lilleker 2005; Seyd and Whiteley 2002).

Table 2.1   *Voter perception (2001) of Labour's delivery on its 1997 key pledges*

Responses to question: has Labour kept its promises?

	Yes(%)	No(%)	No opinion(%)
Cut NHS waiting lists	30	59	11
Get 250,000 under-25s off benefit and into work	34	38	28
Not increase income tax, cut VAT on heating by 5 per cent and keep interest rates and inflation as low as possible	51	39	10
Introduce fast-track punishment for persistent young offenders	17	62	21
Cut class sizes to 30 for 5–7-year-olds	32	34	34

Source: MORI, *Sunday Telegraph*; Base: 1,007 British 18+, 11–13 January 2001.

Labour also 'lost' supporters at election time, not because they voted for another party, but because they failed to vote at all, turnout hitting an all-time low at the 2001 general election. The key problem seemed to lie in Labour's heartland constituencies. Focus groups with Labour loyalists, as opposed to the swing voters Labour were targeting, revealed high levels of detachment and alienation. The party was seen as not representing them specifically, and confusion reigned over whom and what New Labour stood for (Lilleker 2005). Such concern may be the result of adopting an MOP approach, for such a strategy can result in a hollowing out of the internal core of a party, which, while yielding short-term electoral success, generates long-term problems.

Furthermore, a gulf between national and local levels became clear. In 2001, the campaign was unexciting, the election's result being viewed as a foregone conclusion. Primary research (Lilleker and Negrine 2004) found an emerging level of political marketing at the local level. Evidence suggests that candidates who 'marketed' themselves as *the* local representative, fighting for the concerns of local people and building themselves a strong local media profile received a swing in their favour of the vote share and a concomitant increase in turnout (Butler and Collins 2001; Lilleker 2005; Lilleker and Negrine 2004). Labour candidates attempted to tap this reserve of support by linking national achievements to real-life examples, and one sitting MP listed on his campaign flyer the many ways his constituency had benefited under Labour. Local marketing could, nevertheless, diverge from the national design, sometimes producing conflict and indicating flaws in a centralised MOP model.

Move towards a leadership-driven product and superficial consultation   Labour has utilised substantial market intelligence since its success in 1997, employing focus groups, polls, surveys and also public consultation – commissioned by both the Government and the party. At the governmental level, in May 2000 Labour organised a national consultation on priorities in health, while The People's Panel continually monitored attitudes towards public services. As for the party, Labour created a project entitled 'Forethought' to encourage participation in relaunching the whole New Labour product and in the autumn initiated The Big Conversation to identify public priorities.

The Forethought policy research centre was designed to facilitate interaction with 'the wider community', although the latter was defined so as to include a variety of academics, MPs and specialists, but few voters. However, Blair's launch speech (18 February 2003) highlighted the themes of the election campaign and indicated a market orientation.

> The Labour party won the big arguments on the economy, on our public services, the kind of country we want to be . . . But we can't afford to be complacent . . . our Party needs constantly to be generating fresh ideas, testing them rigorously and developing practical policies. (www.labour.org.uk/forethought, accessed 20 February 2003)

It was from discussions in Forethought that the notion of The Big Conversation emerged: it was 'a way of re-engaging the public with the big questions, not the trivia, not what is most important, but actually how we go about fixing some of these problems the country has that have been problems for decades' (Labour MP interviewed by Lilleker, December 2003). Its launch in a party political broadcast on Wednesday 26 November 2003, following the Queen's official opening of Parliament, represented an unprecedented change in governmental communication. Subsequent discussion implied a much closer link with the electorate in policy development in the future. Government figures stressed that the feedback received could change party policy (Peter Hain, speaking on *Newsnight*, BBC2 26 November 2003).

For market intelligence to engender a market-orientation, however, it is not enough to carry it out or be seen to be doing it: it needs to influence and inform the product design, including Government policy and prime ministerial behaviour. In 2001, Labour produced popular pledges in areas voters cared most about (see table 2.2), suggesting that it was acting responsively.

Nevertheless, since 2001 the party's market-oriented behaviour has declined. While Labour adjusted its communication as a result of public demonstrations and unfavourable polls, few policies have been market tested in the same way as prior

Table 2.2 *The salience of Labour's pledges, 2001*

	Important(%)	Not important(%)
Cut NHS waiting lists	96	3
Get 250,000 under-25s off benefit and into work	94	4
Not increase income tax, cut VAT on heating by 5 per cent and keep interest rates and inflation as low as possible	91	7
Introduce fast-track punishment for persistent young offenders	90	7
Cut class sizes to 30 for 5–7 year olds	84	12

Source: MORI/*Sunday Telegraph*; base: 1,007 British 18+, 11–13 January 2001.

to 1997. Market intelligence exercises such as The Big Conversation have been criticised by media and political commentators for being little more than a gimmick. Sparrow (2003) argued that it is clear 'where the Prime Minister would like the conversation to end up'.

A brief survey of the website on the 3 and 5 December 2003 did suggest bias. Though consultation and feedback with the public are known to produce more negative than positive comments, statements by members of the public placed on the website did appear over-congratulatory of the party, such as this from 20-year-old salesman Mark Sunoukuntz, from Ilford, Essex:

> I am so proud to have voted Labour with my first ever vote a few years ago. Everywhere I look I see new cars, wealth, opportunities, investment and most favourable mortgage rates. Being disabled life is not very easy and the money which this government put into special units is wonderful. I may not agree with every tax that Labour charge but they certainly have the balance of charges correct. The United Kingdom is much better off with the new Labour Party, you have my vote. ('Your stories and pictures', www.bigconversation.org.uk, accessed 3 December 2003)

Although criticism of the sensitive issue of top-ups for student grants received blanket media coverage, nothing appeared within The Big Conversation. Any criticism that was allowed related to relatively minor issues such as government support of the car culture or lack of uniform provision for recycling. The only message posted that offered real criticism began: 'After 10 years teaching I gave up because I was fed up with the lack of support from headteachers, parents, governors and government.' But Dave, from South Wales went on to argue that: 'We need to get away from a welfare state culture and start rewarding people who are prepared to work towards a better society and who help others, whilst penalising lazy people' (www.bigconversation.org.uk/index.php?id=678, accessed 5 December 2003). This is only slightly divergent from the rhetoric of 'the Third Way' expounded by Tony Blair himself.

One-sided commentary does not make a conversation. Despite Blair's introduction to *A Future Fair for All*, a document billed as a 'conversation starter', acknowledging that the challenge for politics is 'to create a better dialogue between politicians and the people' (Labour Party 2003: 2), it appears unlikely that the exercise is designed to gather public opinion. Some questions the public are asked to consider are too complex and are likely to close, not open up, discussion. For example: 'Can we streamline regeneration funds and cut unnecessary bureaucracy – for example by putting them under the control of the high performing local authorities or local neighbourhood councils?' (Labour Party 2003: 26). The answer, surely, is 'I don't know!' Similarly, the chapter on tackling poverty and inequality, written largely in legal-speak, provides no information on which to base an informed response. The goal seems to be to provide contexts for soundbites, rather than actually engaging with voters. The connection with the voter fails to emerge because discussion does not engage with the big issues, such as trust in politicians, tuition fees, the relationship between the BBC and government, delivery, government communication and spin; the causes of disconnection of voters from politics are ignored rather than faced. Therefore, although Blair claims that The Big Conversation is the only way to have an 'honest, serious debate about the future' (Launch speech, Newport, 28 November 2003, available: www.labour.org.uk/speeches/bigconversation281103, accessed 29 November 2003), critics are more sceptical, and with some justification.

Indeed, Tony Blair's second term of office represents a move away from a market orientation which suggests that any market intelligence will struggle to impact on party/government behaviour. Blair has appeared increasingly unresponsive, becoming a conviction politician, and, as a result, his public standing has declined. A MORI survey in June 2003 indicated that 58 per cent of the electorate think him untrustworthy (www.mori.com/polls/2003/notw_030627.shtml, accessed 20 January 2004), a sharp decline from previously positive figures. Two policy examples illustrate the changed approach: the Iraq war and student top-up fees. Blair has spoken of conviction and belief in regard to both, adopting a sales-oriented approach. For example, on tuition fees he argued:

> It is going to be a big struggle, there are a lot of people still to persuade, but there will be absolutely no retreat on the principles of this at all . . . the job of political leadership is to try and turn people round on that. (Tony Blair, press conference, 2 December, www.number-10.gov.uk, accessed 12 December 2003)

Blair has been subject to significant criticism by the media on this issue and has had to fight internal battles to get the proposal through Parliament, prompting some to suggest his leadership was at stake. A poll conducted by ICM/*Guardian* suggested that 59 per cent of voters opposed the introduction of top-up fees (http://politics.guardian.co.uk/polls/story/0,11030,1107797,00.html, accessed 20 January 2004), but according to a poll conducted by Populus 44 per cent of Labour voters agreed with the principle of repayable fees, while 64 per cent of the 1,006 sample agreed that it was a fair policy (Riddell and Webster 2003:1). So Blair may yet win the argument. But in late 2003 and early 2004, Labour appeared to be engaging in product adjustment to some degree, making changes to the proposed legislation in response to criticism, holding meetings within the party, and engaging in media debates (for example, on *Newsnight*, 19 January 2004), all of which appears, however, to be still more of a sales than a market orientation.

To step back from the particular Labour case for a moment, this problem may be seen also to be a necessary constraint on government and, as such, one that questions the utility of the MOP approach beyond serving the needs of an oppositional party seeking to win an election. As one Labour MP pointed out:

> The public [sees] the future of education as a problem, they want us to fix it. We can't then say OK, how? We are the Government; we have to meet the needs in a way that is equitable to all. That's what we're doing. Some don't agree with the policy. That is their right. Interestingly, they haven't come up with a better solution to paying for education (Lilleker interview, December 2003).

Nevertheless, while Blair may introduce a solution that in the long-term becomes acceptable to broad swathes of the public, he may lose because of the divisions within the party and his authoritarian style of leadership. Certainly, governing and maintaining a market orientation at the same time is not easy – being seen as a strong leader but one who is also responsive is not an easy task.

Consequences for performance: a return to sales-oriented politics? While the 2001 general election appeared to vindicate Blair's strategy it also demonstrated a growing public disaffection with the political process. Turnout at the election dropped to 58 per cent and, while this is the result of a number of factors (Whiteley *et al.* 2001), it seems clear that the marketing employed after the 1997 election victory was no longer working: membership is down, as is personal support for Blair. Since 1997 a negative perception of the Labour Government has developed, and in turn marketing, especially spin has slowly descended into poor public relations (Lilleker and Negrine 2004). We should, however, question whether this is justified. Although Blair has developed a more sales-oriented – at times a product-oriented – stance, placing himself foremost as a conviction politician, does this indicate the death of the MOP in the Labour Party?

Blair was the product of the party's adoption of a market orientation, but he has now positioned himself as the cornerstone of that product. He is both product and salesman rolled into one. As Michael Foley (2000) argued in his study of the prime minister, Tony Blair's, power rests on a personalisation of politics, along with presidential-style government and communication. This has become more pronounced since 2001 as Blair has openly staked his reputation on the success of policies such as the war on Iraq and student fees' reform. The original New Labour brand is in decline (White and De Chernatony 2002) and the Blair leadership brand has taken over with the move away from a market orientation.

We could view this as temporary, supposing that a market orientation will reassert itself at the next general election. That, however, may depend on the strength or weakness of the Conservative Party. Without an effective opposition, Blair can afford some measure of complacency, seeing himself as a product that no longer requires marketing, thereby suggesting that the maintenance of an MOP in government is dependent on the performance of competing parties within that system. Certainly Thatcher's decline into similar conviction – product-style – politics occurred while Labour was struggling to use political marketing effectively.

Alternatively, we could argue that the market orientation is an untenable approach for a party once elected to government. A party that follows the whim of opinion, particularly when it is derived from polls, would be characterised by the public and the media alike as weak and unfit to govern. Blair was certainly criticised for being a follower of fashion; a leader without principles prior to 2001. There is, however, another possibility: it could be argued that he is taking a truly market-oriented approach to government. A market orientation is not simply about giving people what they want; it is about responding to their needs and demands. Blair might claim to be offering a market-oriented leadership whereby he follows where possible, but is realistic when it comes to issues such as university finance, producing policies that will be beneficial in the long term – and declaring war when necessary. Whatever one's stance, a number of issues, both practical and ethical, need further consideration.

Problems for political marketers in the UK

Studying the use of political marketing by the Conservative and the Labour Parties from 1997 onwards, we have found a number of difficulties in practice which need to be considered. Some questions are practical, others are more philosophical and contribute to the general concern about the implications of political marketing for democracy.

The local political market

The MOP model seems at first glance to be a move towards the centralisation of political debate. However, Denver and others (Denver and Hands 1997; Denver *et al.* 2002) have suggested that there is a direct link between campaigning effort and actual votes cast. A similar project shows a link between constituency service, to quote Butler and Collins (2001), and support for an incumbent MP (Cain, Ferejohn and Fiorina 1987). Studies of political marketing have focused almost exclusively on the macro-political level. While that is where the decisions are made, it is not always where they are implemented. Implementation is an important activity in its own right, because parties exist at all levels, and to have a new product design adopted at the local as well as the national level would take time and effort.

The value MPs place on their constituency service activities (Lilleker and Negrine 2004), and the successes of the Liberal Democrats' targeting strategy, nevertheless highlight the importance of localisation to voters. This proved successful for Conservative candidate Andrew Rosindell who, against all national trends, gained a 12 per cent swing in 2001 after conducting a populist local campaign. This strategy could become of greater significance if the public continue to grow cynical of national party politics.

Political marketing practice, as thus far identified, appears to force centralisation on to the electioneering process. The overall product is designed from the results of market research, at a national level, leaving little scope for an individual candidate to have input. Candidates themselves claim that they need to go against this at times in order to represent the demands of their constituents: a nationally designed product makes it more difficult to deliver locally responsive politics. Many incumbents and their challengers have stated that they were torn between the constituency and the party. This was particularly the case in Labour's target seats in 1997 and 2001 where the party machinery moved in to take over the campaign (Denver and Hands 1997). One Liberal Democrat MP noted the problem with centralisation: 'If the party came to here from Cowley Street they would not understand what was necessary to win here. Fancy leaflets, balloons, all the stuff Labour use, won't work if there are real issues. I won by meeting the issues head on' (Lilleker interview with Liberal Democrat MP, 2002). Labour's MOP approach has possibly exerted too much control at the local level, where candidates need to respond to local concerns. The MOP model needs to be adjusted to include appropriate and reasonable local divergence, even though allowing this could result in a perception of disunity if exploited by the media.

Internal democracy and organisation

The internal aspect of party marketing clearly needs greater consideration. From the Conservative perspective, association-level power has prevented modernisation and hindered the adoption of a market orientation. Even the market-oriented candidates were pressured to adopt more ideological and member-driven policies: 'The constituency association chair called me in and told me if I didn't oppose asylum seekers and the Euro they would soon find someone who would. I support the Conservative Party, but it needs to evolve. I needed to get elected to help that process' (Lilleker interview with Conservative candidate, 2002). Between 1999 and 2001 internal divisions were healed through running a member-driven, not a voter-driven, campaign, but one that prioritised policy areas irrelevant to the mainstream voter.

Labour has overcome such obstacles, but have disengaged loyalties, leading to a reduced turnout in the heartland constituencies (Seyd and Whiteley 2002). Members have not been integrated within stages 1–3 of the MOP; they feel that they had little access to the policy-making process and that when they were invited to comment little value was attached to their opinions (*ibid.*). They feel alienated also from the New Labour project: they argue the party was more interested in pandering to the whims of the 'business types who live around London in the big posh houses' (Barnsley focus group member, 2001; see Lilleker 2005). MPs similarly feel marginalised, and dissent has grown (Cowley, 2001). Controversial policies, such as those on Iraq and tuition fees, have exacerbated this trend, resulting (in the case of the latter) in the parliamentary vote on the Higher Education Bill being won by 5 votes, despite Labour enjoying a 166 majority.

The question for political marketing remains whether any leader will ever achieve a market orientation, win a general election, and still have the support of the majority of the party's members and MPs/candidates. The alternative is that both Labour and the Conservatives achieve a market orientation nationally and externally, but are reduced to parliamentary organisations with no grass roots. In the UK that would be fatal, as the parties are already poorly funded and can ill-afford to run constituency campaigns. It would also reduce political participation and therefore have negative consequences for representation.

Political marketing in power: the emergence of a market-oriented government?

Delivery is as much a part as an end of marketing. We have already shown that delivery is not easy, even where there is the strength of will to succeed, as in the case of New Labour. We can argue that party leaders have a tendency to become less responsive once in government, though we need to be careful in stating that a market-oriented *government* (MOG) is impossible.

An MOG as opposed an MOP may take a longer perspective, recognising that the constraints of government are starkly contrasted to the freedom of opposition. An MOG would have to be realistic, producing achievable policies and behaviour, while operating within an environment subject to significant change. During his period in power Blair has had to respond to the post 9/11 world order and the renewed threat of terrorism. Several military interventions have diverted funds away from areas which had been key voter concerns, making delivery extremely difficult. A prime minister must, however, respond immediately to events; to waver is a sign of weakness.

Additionally, on issues such as the finance of university education, it could be argued that New Labour's Government is taking a long-term perspective, laying the foundations for a policy that will prove effective – and popular. Political marketing has been criticised for taking a short-term perspective, yet we posit that it should be used to identify long-term solutions, rejecting the criticism that political marketing is merely 'following fashion'. Blair might argue that by making the case for a workable policy on financing students' education he is looking to the longer term. We suggest therefore that an MOG may take unpopular but necessary decisions to respond to the long-term needs and demands of the public. This suggests that there is room for leadership within the MOP model, and indeed within all forms of market-oriented political behaviour. However, for a market-oriented form of government to work, a very capable individual is necessary, one who can lead without being overly dominant or arrogant and avoid the trap into which: Thatcher fell becoming too remote, unresponsive and losing support both internally and externally. Labour and Blair must learn the lessons of history if they are to avoid problems in the future and make political marketing truly effective in government.

Issues arising from UK political marketing

Political marketing and participation: the problem of falling turnout in the UK
Concerns about the sudden fall in turnout in the 2001 election generated much activity by organisations such as the Electoral Commission and in particular papers on the potential link between political marketing and (non-)participation (see for example Bannon 2003; Dermody and Hammer-Lloyd 2003). The overall wider effect of the use of political marketing on the electorate is difficult to quantify and research offers only mixed conclusions. In theory the dominance of the MOP approach should lead to a higher level of interest from the electorate. If the marketing mix is designed correctly the MOP should be able to mobilise its core support as well as persuade a significant section of the broader electorate to mobilise in its favour. This happened in 1997, but not in 2001.

There is more than one reason for this. Firstly, the greater the use of targeted marketing techniques, such as voter segmentation, the more likely is it that non-target groups are demobilised. Telephone canvassing has replaced the once-popular activity of 'knocking up' whereby candidates and activists visited as many houses in the constituency as possible, encouraging the owners or tenants to vote for them.

The use of telephone calls allows individual swing voters to be reached and calls are often followed up with a visit and direct mailing. Targeting means that voters in safe seats experience a lack of attention at campaign time, which can also have a negative effect on turnout.

Secondly, there are many other factors which could account for low turnout (Whiteley *et al.* 2001), all *unrelated* to the use of political marketing, not least of which was the perception that Labour could not lose and there was consequently only a low level of excitement produced by the contest. However, turnout was markedly down in Labour's safe seats, often a reduction of 40 per cent from 1997. This was less than the reduction average of 10 per cent in Conservative safe seats, while the Liberal Democrats saw a drop of only 2 per cent, claiming that this is because they make their voters feel important in between elections, not just during a campaign. Labour voters, and even some party workers, regarded Labour's failure to retain its core vote as a result of the party's courting only the more affluent swing voters (Lilleker 2005).

It could, however, be argued that turnout was low because of the products on offer, not because of the marketing. Labour might suggest that the low turnout was a sign of satisfaction with its product, though it could equally well be taken as signifying dissatisfaction with the alternative – the Tory product. That turnout fell most in safe Labour seats, however, suggests a link with Labour's performance. It could simply be that Labour supporters were happy with the product the way it was, saw no need to replace it, thought there was no threat to its continuance, so that there was little to be gained from going out to register a vote of support. But the general feeling of disengagement between the public and the politicians remains one for political marketing to consider – either because marketing may be in part responsible for it or because it might offer a solution.

Marketing and the business of governing

Some decisions may be sufficiently complex as to be beyond the reach of public influence. Leaders in both Australia and New Zealand are facing the question of whether to follow opinion or their own judgement (Lees-Marshment 2003a–c). The public may set the priorities but only a government can decide how to allocate funding; equally only a government can decide how to respond to the unexpected. Post-9/11, such arguments are more prescient. However, other areas such as health and education, once the domain of the elite, now incorporate public opinion into discussions. Yet tough decisions have to be made, and only governments can decide how to prioritise resources. This can mean that governments have to resort to 'selling' solutions, rather than use market intelligence to develop them. Given the vague nature of the promises, for example, to cut NHS waiting lists, offered by MOPs, perhaps this is a natural corollary.

Leadership within an MOP

The role of leadership within a political marketing framework is another area requiring further discussion, by practitioners as well as academics, in all areas of politics (Lees-Marshment 2004a). As already noted, the development of a new policy on university funding by the Labour Government may be explicable in terms of the leadership responding to the needs of society in a way that will satisfy voters in the long term. The balance between the rights of the political consumer and the responsibilities of political and public leaders and professionals is an area that will become more important in political marketing research in the next decade, being one with which all political elites are currently struggling as they try to respond to an ever-demanding political consumer. It relates to classic questions about the nature and organisation of democracy. Some might argue that on certain issues leadership and professional judgement can serve the public interest, but there is a fine line between responsive market-oriented leadership and arrogant product-oriented authoritarianism.

Conclusion: the limits for political marketing

While political marketing has offered UK parties clear advantages, there are also potential costs and unresolved issues, such as how to deliver a political product, integrate the local dimension into a national design, manage opposition from internal party culture, while at the same time maintaining internal party democracy. Political marketing seems to be here to stay, but not all questions about its practice have been answered by this analysis, suggesting that while the Lees-Marshment model is a useful framework for generating discussion on an important phenomenon, it needs further development. Moreover, we expect that further issues will be raised by the chapters of this book that analyse the use of political marketing in the electoral systems of other countries.

Note

1 D. G. Lilleker's interviews with MPs were funded as part of ESRC Project R000223540 'MPs and the media: a study of prefessionalisation in political communication'; further research within Labour's heartland constituencies was funded by the Barnsley College 'Partnership with the community' scheme. The majority of interviews by Lees-Marshment were funded by the Carnegie Trust as part of a project 'Marketing the Conservatives 1997–2001'. The support from Carnegie is gratefully acknowledged here and Lees-Marshment would also like to thank the MPs and the staff who agreed to be interviewed both in London and Edinburgh. Further interviews were conducted with Conservative Central Office staff in London in 2003. Attempts were made to interview Michael Portillo and William Hague but were unsuccessful.

Bibliography

Allender, P. (2001), *What's Wrong with Labour? A Critical History of the Labour Party in the Twentieth Century*, London: Merlin.

Bannon, D. (2003), 'Electoral participation and non-voter segmentation', Paper presented at the Political Marketing Group panels at the Political Studies Association Conference, April.

Bell, Alexandra (2001), 'Newspapers are divided on the best candidate', *Daily Telegraph*, 23 August.

Butler, P. and Collins, N. (2001), 'Payment on delivery: recognising constituency service as political marketing', *European Journal of Marketing*, 35(9–10): 1026–37

Cain, B., Ferejohn, J. and Fiorina, M. (1987), *The Personal Vote: Constituency Service and Electoral Independence*, Cambridge, MA: Harvard University Press.

Conservative Party (1999), *Listening to Britain: A Report by the Conservative Party*, London: Conservative Party (autumn).

Conservative Party (2002), *Leadership with a Purpose: A Better Society*, London: Conservative Party (October).

Cowley, P. (2001), *Revolts and Rebellions: Parliamentary Voting under Blair*, London: Politico's.

Denver, D. and Hands, G. (1997), *Modern Constituency Electioneering: Local Campaigning in the 1992 General Election*, London: Frank Cass.

Denver, D., Hands, G., Fisher, J. and MacAllister, I. (2002), 'The impact of constituency campaigning in the 2001 general election', in L. Bennie, C. Rallings, J. Tonge and P. Webb (eds), *British Elections and Parties Review 12: The 2001 General Election*, London: Frank Cass, pp. 80–94.

Dermody, J. and Hammer-Lloyd, S. (2003), 'Exploring young people's trust in politicians and political parties: towards a research framework', paper presented at the Academy of Marketing Conference, Aston University, September *Academy of Marketing Conference Proceedings* (CD-ROM).

Foley, Michael (2000), *The British Presidency*, Manchester: Manchester University Press.

Gould, P. (1998), 'The Labour campaign', in I. Crew, B. Gosschalk and J. Bartle (eds), *Political Communications: The General Election Campaign of 1997*, Cambridge: Cambridge University Press.

Hastings, Max (2003), 'We must dump IDS or say farewell to power', *Daily Telegraph*, 5 October.

Ingram, Sir Bernard (2003), Speech in the debate at the Political Marketing Conference, Portcullis House of Commons, London, September.

Ingram, P. and Lees-Marshment, J. (2002), 'The Anglicisation of political marketing: how Blair out-marketed Clinton', *Journal of Public Affairs*, 2(2): 44–56.

Labour Party (2003), *A Future Fair for All*, available online: www.bigconversation.org.uk (accessed December).

Lansley, A. (2001a), 'Image, values and policy – from here to the next election', Address to the Bow Group, Conservative Party Conference, London, 9 October 2001.

Lansley, A. (2002), 'Conservative strategy', in J. Bartle, S. Atkinson and R. Mortimore (eds), *Political Communications: The General Election Campaign of 2001*, London: Frank Cass.

Lees-Marshment, J. (2001), *Political Marketing and British Political Parties*, Manchester: Manchester University Press.

Lees-Marshment, J. (2003a), Marketing UK Political Parties: The Potential and Limitations of Political Marketing, Staff–student seminar, Politics Department, University of Otago, New Zealand, 13 August 2003.

Lees-Marshment, J. (2003b), 'Marketing British political parties from Thatcher to Blair: the potential and pitfalls of political marketing', talk given to the National Europe Centre, Australian National University, Canberra, Australia, 5 September.

Lees-Marshment, J. (2003c), 'New Labour, new danger: the pitfalls of political marketing in the UK', talk given to the Public Relations Institute of Australia, Press Club, Canberra, 5 September.

Lees-Marshment, J. (2004a), *The Political Marketing Revolution: Transforming the Government of the UK*, Manchester: Manchester University Press.

Lees-Marshment, J. (2004b), 'Marketing the Tories in 2004: from Hague to Howard', *Political Quarterly*, 81 (October–December).

Lees-Marshment, J. and Bartle, J. (2002), 'Marketing British political parties in 2001: an impossible challenge?', Political Marketing Conference Proceedings (pamphlet), University of Aberdeen.

Lees-Marshment, J. and Lilleker, D. G. (2001), 'Political marketing and traditional values: "Old Labour" for "new times", *Contemporary Politics*, 7(3): 205–16.

Lees-Marshment, J. and Rudd, C. (2003), 'Political marketing and party leadership', Paper presented at the 2003 PSA Conference, Political Marketing Group panels, Leicester, 15–17 April.

Lees-Marshment, J. and Quayle, S. (2001), 'Empowering the members or marketing the party? The Conservative reforms of 1998', *Political Quarterly*, 72(2): 204–12.

Lilleker, D. G. (2003), 'Is there an emergent democratic deficit in Britain? And is political marketing the cause?', paper presented at the Political Marketing Group panels at the Political Studies Association Conference, April.

Lilleker, D. G. (2005), 'Political marketing: the cause of a democratic deficit?', *Journal of Non-Profit and Public Sector Marketing*.

Lilleker, D. G. and Negrine, R. (2004), 'Not big brand names but corner shops: marketing politics to a disengaged electorate', *Journal of Political Marketing*, 2(1): 55–74.

Negrine, R. and Lilleker, D. G. (2002), 'The professionalization of political communication: continuities and change in media practices', *European Journal of Communication*, 17(3): 305–23.

Negrine, R., and Lilleker, D. G. (2004), 'The professionalisation of media-based campaigning in Britain 1966–2001: the rise of a proactive media strategy', *Journalism Studies*, 4(2): 199–212.

Riddell, P. and Webster, P. (2003), 'Voters swing behind Blair on top-up fees', *Times*, 9 December.

Scammell, M. (1995), *Designer Politics*, Basingstoke: Macmillan.

Seldon, A. and Snowdon, P. (2001), *A New Conservative Century*, London: Centre for Policy Studies.

Seyd, P. and Whiteley, P. (2002), *Labour's Grass Roots*, Basingstoke, Macmillan Palgrave.

Silvester, J. (2003), 'Occupational psychology and political selection: a diversity challenge', *People Management*, 9 January.

Sparrow, A. (2003), 'Blair's one-sided conversation', *Daily Telegraph*, 29 November.

Thomas, H. (1989), *Making an Impact*, London: David & Charles.

Ward, L. (2002), 'LibDems look to marketing techniques', *Guardian*, 7 December.

White, J. and de Chernatony, L. (2002), 'New Labour: a study of the creation, development and demise of a political brand', *Journal of Political Marketing*, 1(2–3): 45–52.

Whiteley, P., Clark, H., Sanders, D. and Stewart, M. (2001), 'Turnout', *Parliamentary Affairs*, 54(4): 775–88.

Interviews

Chambers, P., head of direct marketing (2001), interviewed by J. Lees-Marshment, Conservative Central Office, London, 18 October.

Dykes, C., head of development (2001), interviewed by Jennifer Lees-Marshment, Conservative Central Office, London, 18 October.

Dykes, C., head of development and candidates (2003), interviewed by J. Lees-Marshment, Conservative Central Office, London, 19 February.

Francis, Rachel, Listening to Britain officer, Conservative Party (2000), interviewed by J. Lees-Marshment, 11 April.

Hogue, Stuart, campaign officer, the Common Sense Revolution, Conservative Party (2000), interviewed by J. Lees-Marshment, 11 April.

Lansley, A. (2001b), interviewed by J. Lees-Marshment, Porticullis House, House of Commons, London, 18 October.

MacDonald, M., head of research (2001), interviewed by J. Lees-Marshment, Scottish Conservative Party Central Office, Edinburgh and (2 August).

Mannan, S., head of the cultural unit (2001), interviewed by J. Lees-Marshment, Conservative Central Office, London, 2 August.

Norman, A., former Tory chief executive (2001), interviewed by J. Lees-Marshment, Porticullis House, House of Commons, London, 18 October.

Norris, S., former London mayoral candidate (2001), interviewed by J. Lees-Marshment, Citigate Public Affairs, London, 19 October.

Senior Conservative official (2003), interviewed by J. Lees-Marshment, Conservative Party Central Office, London, February.

Tait, J. (2003), Conservative Party policy unit staff member, interviewed by J. Lees-Marshment (20 February).

Turner, S., director of the Scottish Conservative Party (2001), interviewed by J. Lees-Marshment, 2 August.

Walter, D., communications director for the Liberal Democratic Party (2002), interviewed by D. G. Lilleker.

3

American political marketing:
George W. Bush and the Republican Party

Jonathan Knuckey and Jennifer Lees-Marshment

The most recent political marketing scholarship has focused on the use of political marketing within British party politics (see, for example, Lees-Marshment 2001a). Research has shown that British parties utilise political marketing to determine not just their campaign strategy but the way they design the political product to be sold. This chapter applies the political marketing framework to the USA, focusing on the 2000 presidential campaign of George W. Bush and the Republican Party. The chapter has five principal concerns. First, it provides a brief overview of the national political context in relation to a brief history of the scope of political marketing in the USA. Second, it provides an analysis of George W. Bush's campaign for the Republican Party (GOP) nomination and the presidency, considering the extent to which Bush and the GOP followed the MOP model. Third, use is made of exit polls from the 2000 presidential election as well of as data from the 2000 American National Election Study to examine the voting behaviour of key groups – or market segments – in the presidential election, as well as voter attitudes to the parties and their candidates. Fourth, some preliminary evidence on the extent to which the Bush presidency has been able to deliver on campaign policies is reviewed. Fifth, we speculate on the future use of political marketing in the USA, highlighting aspects of this case study that may more generally illuminate political marketing as a theoretical framework for use in the study of political parties, campaigns and elections.

American political marketing: national context and history

American political parties and candidates are widely acknowledged to have pioneered many of the techniques that now pervade modern election campaigns in most major democracies. However, the application of the comprehensive political marketing framework – with its attention to the design of the product, not just how it is sold – has not been as widely utilised as in Britain. In part at least this is due to the national political context. For example, in their comparison of

Tony Blair's New Labour and Bill Clinton's New Democrats, Ingram and Lees-Marshment (2002: 54) suggested that 'systemic differences between the . . . UK and USA . . . substantially condition the scope, focus and application of political marketing'.

Like the UK, the USA is dominated by two major parties, the Democrats and the Republicans. It is a presidential system, however, and elections are candidate-centered (see, for example, Wattenberg 1991 and 1996), so that the presidential candidate is a prime aspect of the product. Furthermore, because of the decentralised nature of American party organisations national party leaders have significantly less ability to control and change their parties. Additionally, the USA is substantially larger than the UK, and consists of states with distinct political cultures and legislation. It is more difficult for a leader to implement a market-oriented approach within a US party than it is for a British counterpart. Furthermore, the separation of executive and legislative powers in the US political system, and the ensuing problems of policy co-ordination, even when the president's party controls both houses of Congress, makes the delivery component of the marketing model somewhat less feasible than in a parliamentary system with strong and cohesive legislative parties.

The assumption encountered in the literature, therefore, was that marketing was used by US political parties only to sell a product already designed, and the majority of studies naturally focused on the utilisation of techniques (see, for example, Newman 1994; Niffenegger 1989; O'Shaughnessy 1990). However, the historical record suggests the presence of elements of a market-oriented approach. For example, Ronald Reagan who became Republican president in 1980, conducted formal market intelligence and the product on offer was broadly designed to suit the majority of the electorate, promoting policies to reduce the power and cost of government, to lower income tax and to create general economic prosperity with strong leadership, especially on foreign affairs. The product attracted broad electoral support, in a way similar to Thatcher's product in the UK (Lees-Marshment 2001a: 217–18). Indeed, British politicians have often gone to their US counterpart for ideas. A Conservative Party delegation visited the USA in 1991 to gain advice from the Reagan campaigns in preparation for the 1992 British general election. Similarly, New Labour's advisor, Philip Gould, worked on Clinton's successful Democratic Presidential campaign in 1992; and Tony Blair and Gordon Brown visited Clinton's advisors in January 1993 (Gould 1998). There are remarkable similarities between the development of New Labour in the UK and the new Democrats in the USA under Clinton in 1992 (Lees-Marshment 2001a: 17). The impact of the national political context, Clinton's failures in delivery and the lack of cohesiveness of the party, however, led commentators such as Ingram and Lees-Marshment (2002) to conclude that political marketing might never be used as comprehensively in the USA as in the UK. This chapter tests that proposition more fully, applying the MOP model in full to the case of George W. Bush, who was elected Republican president in 2000.

Marketing a different type of Republican: case-study of George W. Bush

In focusing on the use of marketing by George W. Bush to become Republican president, we consider a single party in order to enable a detailed analysis of each stage of the entire model, rigorously exploring its applicability to the US context in a way that previous studies did not. The case study utilises a wide range of sources, including party documents, secondary academic analysis and primary statistical analysis of election data, mainly from the period 1998–2000. The Republican Party is one of two main parties in the USA and its prime goal is therefore winning control of government. It is the USA's 'conservative' party – though ideology has never been strong there – and its market is traditionally the white-collar professional middle classes. Although it had enjoyed significant electoral success in the 1980s, it lost two presidential elections to Bill Clinton and the Democrats in 1992 and 1996 while extensive internal debates continued about the direction of the party in the post-Reagan era.

The incentives to adopt a market-orientation to renew its electoral appeal were therefore very strong, particularly after the 1998 mid-term elections. The scandals surrounding President Bill Clinton and the Democrats provided a clear opportunity for the Republicans to make ground; nevertheless, in elections to the US House of Representatives the Democrats actually *gained* seats. This encouraged significant self-criticism, and many in the Republican Party blamed the aggressive and confrontational style of the congressional leadership, especially Speaker of the House Newt Gingrich. The potential candidature of the then Texas Governor George W. Bush, eldest son of George H. W. Bush, the forty-first president, became clear when, against this national downturn in party fortune, Bush achieved a landslide re-election as governor, winning 69 per cent of the total vote. Moreover this vote was due to support attracted from outside of the GOP's traditional white conservative base, including such segments as the Hispanic vote, the black vote, Democrats/liberals and women.[1] Significantly, Bush had offered a product developed in response to public demands and criticisms of other Republican approaches: educational reform alongside tax cuts under the overall banner of compassionate conservativism. This set the foundations for a market-oriented strategy that would guide the 2000 presidential campaign. What follows is an in-depth analysis of Bush's campaign for the Republican presidential nomination and the presidency, applying each stage of the MOP process.

Market-oriented Republicanism? An in-depth analysis

Stage 1   Market intelligence: understanding the US electorate
The Republican Party conducted the usual formal market intelligence, using focus groups and polls, and engaged in internal discussions about its strategy and potential presidential candidate. It also analysed previous electoral results to guage party weaknesses.

Adopting the market-oriented concept, the aim was to select a Republican candidate who would appeal to the electorate and, significantly, the party as well. This is important to ensure unity and successful implementation, but parties – particularly those who are or have been unelectable and out of touch – often have difficulty finding a candidate who can do both. However, George W. Bush, with the advantage of name recognition due to his parentage, a proven successful implementation of the market-oriented concept at the state level and – to give him some credit – a product vision that incorporated elements which appealed to both the wider electorate (education) and party (tax cuts), was a clear contender. He could unite the economic and socially conservative wings of the Republican Party, and appeal externally to Independents and Democrats. He could also 'de-Gingrichize' the Republican Party. In 1998–99 he was encouraged to stand by key figures at all levels of the party. Bush was supported by other governors who had also enjoyed electoral success by adopting a more market-oriented Republican vision with a positive role for government, among them John Engler in Michigan, Tom Ridge in Pennsylvania, George Pataki in New York and Tommy Thompson in Wisconsin.

One weakness was the lack of an independent institutional source of market intelligence, such as a policy think-tank. The new Republican movement in 2000 stood in contrast to the new Democratic movement in 1992: Bush was left to develop the product himself, and perhaps as a consequence only partially satisfied the electorate. Political consumers in the USA wanted a more issue-specific campaign. More comprehensive market intelligence was needed to help the politicians design all aspects of the product at an earlier stage: a weakness not of the model's theory but of its application. The basic market-oriented approach of *responding* to the electorate was, however, clearly adopted by both the party and the presidential candidate.

Stage 2   Creating the political product: the evolution of compassionate conservatism

Presidential candidate   George W. Bush was selected with clear party support, as was evident from the primaries, his endorsements and ability to raise money, and the lack of success by other contenders (see Ceaser and Busch 2001: 49–76 and Corrado 2001: 92–124), the only exception being Senator John McCain, to whom Bush reacted by making a subtle adjustment to the product. Bush's 'anointment' was arguably a market-oriented choice by the GOP – the candidate who could appeal both to swing voters and the Republican base. Bush's candidacy did have weaknesses, which included doubts about his skills in public speaking and his competence on foreign policy issues. Overall he was a potentially popular candidate and portrayed himself as a distinctive type of Republican – a compassionate conservative – and as a different kind of politician – a uniter not a divider.

Vice-presidential selection   Dick Cheney was chosen as vice-presidential nominee to reinforce Bush's compassionate conservative message. Cheney held a consistently conservative voting record as a member of the House of Representatives but like Bush projected an image as a pragmatist, had good relations with congressional Democrats and experience of government. Cheney also counteracted potential weaknesses of Bush with experience in the realm of foreign and defence policy.

Policy Policy substance behind the compassionate conservative theme was developed somewhat late, arguably due to a lack of the debate that normally occurs during the primaries when there is more than one clear contender. This was a major weakness, because market intelligence indicated that voters wanted a clear policy agenda. The product was the outcome not so much of design as of process over the course of the primary campaign through the Republican Party National Convention, possibly the consequence of a more decentralised party system in the USA (Ingram and Lees-Marshment 2002).

Bush did, however, focus on issues in the 2000 election that opinion polls showed to be of paramount concern for most Americans, including those on which the Democrats have traditionally had an advantage – education, social security and health care – marking a dramatic departure in Republican strategy at the presidential level. Bush continued to include traditional Republican themes such as tax-cuts, smaller government and a stronger military, but by talking about public services he gave emphasis to the new Republicanism.

Symbols and slogans The compassionate conservative slogan remained central to Bush's campaign, so as to reinforce the message to the electorate that Bush was a type of Republican different from the congressional brand that was not popular with the electorate.

Republican National Convention National party conventions play an important role in setting out the themes that candidates wish to stress in the general election (Ceaser and Busch 2001: 143). The party used its convention to set the new product design, emphasising compassionate conservatism.

> *Stage 3 Sensitive crafting to suit practical reality and ideology:*
> *product adjustment*

Achievability The more experienced vice-presidential candidate Dick Cheney helped Bush to appear serious about delivery after the election campaign.

Internal reaction Bush responded to internal criticism when he lost the first-in-the-nation New Hampshire primary to Senator John McCain, a right-wing conservative, by adjusting his product to increase his own conservative credentials, in order to obtain support McCain might otherwise garner. Bush branded McCain a liberal, temporarily replacing the compassionate conservative image with that of a reformer after results: his appearance at Bob Jones University, an institution that banned interracial dating and whose website referred to the Roman Catholic Church as a cult, received considerable national media attention. Bush therefore tried to stress traditional conservative Republican themes, reiterating his belief in limited government (see, for example, Ceasar and Busch 2002: 77–107; Pomper 2001: 15–45; Sabato and Scott 2002).

There was obviously an attempt to be more responsive to internal reaction to the proposed product design, rather than the electorate at large. The balance between internal and external markets is a difficult one for leaders to manage, however, and although Bush beat McCain and then sought to move back towards the centre for the remainder of the GOP primaries, it left a lingering concern among moderate and independent voters that Bush was, after all, a captive of the religious Right element of the Republican Party.

Competition   Bush's strategy in response to the competition, Vice-President Al Gore, was to attack Gore, who had presented himself as the populist champion of the 'working family', as an 'Old Democrat' whose 'big government' programmes and taxation plan showed that he did not trust the people. Gore's emphasis at the Democratic Party Convention on representing 'the people verses the powerful' was in many respects a throwback to the more populist Democratic themes evident in the 'New Deal' era and in the campaigns of Franklin D. Roosevelt and Harry S. Truman. The perception of the Bush–Gore contest thereafter became one between a 'New Republican' and an 'Old Democrat', arguably a market more favourable to Bush.

Support analysis   An attempt was made to target new market segments. Bush made the most concerted effort by a Republican presidential candidate to address the interests of minorities, including blacks and especially the growing Hispanic vote – already a significant voting group in California, Florida and Texas (Judis and Teixeira 2002: 57–9). This targeting was evident during the Republican National Convention and throughout the general election campaign. Positive ads were also targeted at three other markets among the white electorate: women, moderates and independents.

Many aspects of product adjustment were carried out, but interestingly much of it took place during the primary season, prior to the more public post-nomination stages. The central themes were clearly established in the now-adjusted Bush product:

- to return to the compassionate conservative theme;
- to neutralise the Democratic advantage on the issues of education, health care and social security; and
- to portray Bush as a president who was ready to govern.

Stage 4   *Keeping everyone on message – implementation*

The ease with which Bush secured nomination was indicative of a party ready to move to a market-oriented approach and made implementation relatively straightforward. As with all parties, however, there was some internal criticism. The overall tone of the Republican Convention had given rise to concern: as one commentator observed,

> what [conservatives] sense is that, at a level of politics deeper that the fortunes of the political parties, the ground is shifting away from them. What they have not noticed

is that the 2000 election is shaping up to be a ratification not of conservatism but of Clintonism – and will be so even if the Republicans win. (Ponnuru 1999: 37)

The desire to win back the White House, however, united the conservatives and ensured that they were prepared to give Bush latitude in reshaping the party's image, just as liberal Democrats had done with Bill Clinton in 1992. Overall, Bush succeeded in uniting the party, and implementation was therefore broadly successful.

Stage 5   Building a long-term relationship dialogue with voters – communication
The Republican Party began to try to communicate its new compassionate conservatism at the Republication Convention (Sabato and Scott 2002: 31). Bush (quoted in Dionne 2000: A19) argued that Republicans needed to 'put a compassionate face on our conservative philosophy [because] people think oftentimes that Republicans are mean-spirited folks. Which is not true, but that's what people think.' Each night of the Republican Convention had a theme that was designed to convey the new product to a wider audience.

- 'Opportunity with a purpose: leave no child behind' (Monday).
- 'Strength and security with a purpose: safe in our homes and in the world' (Tuesday).
- 'Prosperity with a purpose: keeping America prosperous and protecting retirement security' (Wednesday).
- Bush's acceptance speech: 'President with a purpose: a strong leader who can unite the country and get things done' (Final night).

These themes were deliberately non-partisan, as were the platform speeches, and avoided blatant attacks against the Democrats. Bush's convention speech stressed his compassionate conservatism and his positions on some key Republican issues such as abortion, tax cuts, military readiness and retirement savings. He received a 'bounce' in the post-convention polls, suggesting success in consolidating the Republican base, while at the same time reaching out to moderate and independent voters.

From the end of the convention until Labour Day, the official start of the general election campaign, the party's communications reinforced the convention message. Bush fought much of the general election on education, social security and health care, emphasising also traditional Republican themes, specifically tax cuts and the need for a strong military. It was market-oriented in responding to the issues voters thought were most important, but also reflected internal reaction analysis, indicating the importance and influence of all stages of the MOP process.

Bush also used communication to reach new target markets. The convention was used to demonstrate a new and inclusive Republican Party, with the three co-chairs consisting of an African-American, J. C. Watts (R–OK), a woman, Jennifer Dunn (R–WA) and an Hispanic, Henry Bonilla (R–TX). Additionally, there were several minority speakers over the four nights of the convention, including Colin Powell and Condoleezza Rice. In July 2000 Bush also addressed the National Association for the Advancement of Coloured People's convention.[2]

Stage 6   *Last chance to sell the product – the campaign*

The campaign officially started on Labour Day. Bush continued to fight on the issues that the wider electorate viewed as most important, together with selected Republican themes. The television advertising campaign is central to communicating to the electorate in presidential elections in the USA. Bush commissioned mostly positive ads with only 2 negative and 4 comparative. According to Mark McKinnon, creative director of Maverick Media, the advertising agency used by Bush for the campaign, the positive content of these ads was designed to communicate that Bush was a Republican of a different kind: 'after a decade, the Republican Party had developed a partisan face and a perception that it was mean – that it wanted to tear down government, that it was against everything and not for anything' (quoted in Devlin 2001: 2345). The positive ads were also designed to appeal to the other target groups (women, moderates and independents) because market intelligence indicated that they were repelled by negative advertising.

The focus of campaign events also reached out to target markets. One television advertisement had Bush speaking of an 'educational recession' under Clinton–Gore, proclaiming that the reading ability of schoolchildren was a 'new civil right.' The Bush campaign also produced six television ads in Spanish, one of which featured his nephew George P. Bush, son of Florida Governor Jeb Bush, to appeal to the Hispanic segment. Another ad was about *trust*, and featured Bush talking on camera about personal responsibility, social security, education, the budget surplus and tax cuts. The word 'trust' was used six times, and the ad ends with Bush saying: 'He [Gore] trusts government – I trust you' (quoted in Devlin 2000: 2345).

The campaign was organised effectively. Individuals who had worked on Bush's state campaign in Texas also headed the presidential campaign team, and provided stability. They included: Karl Rove, who had served as chief electoral strategists in each of Bush's state election campaigns; Joe Allbaugh: gubernatorial chief of staff to Bush in Texas and his campaign manager in 1994; and Karen Hughes, his director of communications. Even at moments of 'crisis', such as McCain's New Hampshire primary win, or when Gore opened up a lead in the first three weeks of the general election, the Bush campaign remained focused on its core compassionate conservativism message. The campaign evinced an effective use of staff as well as good implementation of product design.

Stage 7   *Choosing the product – the election result*

The foregoing analysis indicates that Bush used political marketing to a significant degree, but the question remains as to whether it had any effect on his support? Or is the market-oriented model just a theory which, when applied retrospectively to behaviour appears convincing, but for which there is no statistical evidence? In this section the vote choices of some key groups – market segments – in the electorate are examined as well as attitudes toward the parties and candidates in the 2000 election.

Bush won the White House with a 271 to 266 Electoral College vote over Al Gore, and the Republican Party narrowly retained control of both houses of Congress. It was the first time since 1954 that the GOP controlled the presidency and both houses of Congress. However, the presidential result was famously publicly and legally challenged. Bush also narrowly lost the popular vote to Gore, 48.4 per cent to 47.9 per cent. Indeed, Bush actually ran *behind* the much-maligned congressional Republicans in terms of total votes cast.

We could therefore question the efficacy of the market-oriented approach. However one party does not work in isolation from the competition, and although it is beyond the scope of this chapter to conduct a full analysis of the Democratic use of political marketing, we can reasonably assume that the campaign of Al Gore similarly also followed an MOP. If both parties are market-oriented, then voters may have difficulty choosing between them. Nevertheless, we also conducted a more detailed analysis of the vote and of attitudes and perceptions of the candidates and of the two main parties to investigate the dynamics of the 2000 presidential election in greater depth.

The group bases of the 2000 vote   As table 3.1 shows, there was little vote defection from either party's traditional base. Bush did *slightly* better than Gore in this respect, receiving 11 per cent of the vote from self-identified Democrats compared to the 8 per cent that Gore received from Republicans. The partisan nature of the election is also indicated at the aggregate level when one inspects the states won by each candidate. Bush swept the south and border south states, as well as winning the traditionally Republican prairie and mountain west states. Gore carried the north-east, upper mid-west and Pacific coast states. Overall, Bush won the states that he *should* have won; Gore won the states that he *should* have won (see, for example, Erikson 2001).[3]

Examining the vote choice of selected groups in 2000 reveals that Bush's attempt to create a new image for the Republican Party had mixed success. In terms of the vote by race, despite the attempt to be inclusive, Bush received just 9 per cent of the African-American vote. Bush also gained only 35 per cent of the Hispanic vote, and in only one state, Florida – with its traditionally Republican Cuban American vote – did Bush receive more of the Hispanic vote than did Gore. This suggests that the compassionate conservativism message did not resonate particularly effectively with non-white voters. Targeting the Hispanic segment is a dramatic change in Republican behaviour which, like any new strategy, may need to be continued in government in terms of policy delivery and be included in the renewed product design for the next election, if it is to be convincing enough to win the support of such voters.

Bush's strategy did, however, succeed in narrowing the gender gap in 2000. Gore ran ahead of Bush by 11 percentage points, although when one controls for race the white female vote split down the middle, with Bush receiving 49 per cent of the vote from white women compared to Gore's 48 per cent. Bush also remained competitive among two other crucial swing groups of voters: independents and moderates. Among the independents, Bush led Gore 47 to 45 per cent, and while Gore had an advantage among moderates of 52 to Bush's 44 per cent, it was much closer than in 1996.

Table 3.1   *2000 presidential vote choice, by selected groups (%)*

	All	Gore	Bush
Gender			
Men	48	42	53
Women	52	54	43
Race by sex			
White men	48	36	60
White women	52	48	49
Race			
White	81	42	54
Black	10	90	9
Hispanic	7	62	35
Party identification			
Democratic	39	86	11
Republican	35	8	91
Independent	27	45	47
Ideology			
Liberal	20	80	13
Moderate	50	52	44
Conservative	29	17	81
1996 presidential vote			
Clinton	46	82	15
Dole	31	7	91
Perot	6	27	64
Other	2	26	52
Did not vote	13	44	52

Source: Voter News Service Exit Poll, 8 November 2000.

This suggests that political marketing may have been successful only at the margins in the 2000 presidential elections, although in such a close contest success at the margins may have made the difference between victory and defeat.

Issues and candidate characteristics in 2000   Table 3.2 shows the vote by those issues and candidate characteristics viewed as important by the electorate. On 5 of the 7 issues, Gore was preferred over Bush. Only among those voters who viewed taxes and world affairs as the most important issues was Bush preferred. However, there is evidence that Bush's strategy of campaigning on Democratic issues was successful. For example, among those voters perceiving education as the most important issue, Gore led Bush by just 8 percentage points. Clearly, had the 2000 presidential election been about issues only, Gore would have defeated Bush. Table 3.2 shows also, however, that candidate characteristics mattered in 2000. Bush led Gore on four of the candidate attributes that voters said mattered. Most importantly on the honesty–trustworthiness characteristic,

Table 3.2   *2000 presidential vote choice: issue and candidate characteristics (%)*

	All	Gore	Bush
Issues: which mattered most?			
World affairs	12	40	54
Medicare/Rx drugs	7	60	39
Health care	8	64	33
Economy/jobs	18	59	37
Taxes	14	17	80
Education	15	52	44
Social security	14	58	40
Characteristics: which mattered most?			
Understands issues	13	75	19
Honesty/trustworthiness	24	15	80
Cares about people	12	63	31
Has experience	15	82	17
Likeable	2	38	59
Strong leadership	14	34	64
Good judgement	13	48	50

Source: Voter News Service Exit Poll, 8 November 2000.

which 24 per cent of voters said mattered most, Bush led Gore by an overwhelming 80 to 15 per cent. This suggests that Bush was successful because voters liked him than because they were embracing a re-branded Republican Party. The presidential nominee is a vital part of the product in the US context and may therefore be one of the key reasons for Bush's success and the utility of the market-oriented perspective.

Attitudes to the candidates and parties   We examined perceptions of the political parties in 2000 and the extent to which those perceptions differed from previous presidential election years, using questions that have been consistently asked by the American National Election Studies.[4] To gauge the emotional attachment to both the Republican Party and Bush, 'feelings' thermometers' were utilised. Respondents were asked to place both on a scale ranging from zero (feeling most cold) to 100 (feeling most warm), with 50 denoting a neutral perspective. To put these in perspective we include mean feelings' thermometer scores since 1980, and also include the thermometer items for the Democratic Party and its presidential candidates. Mean feelings' thermometer scores for the presidential candidates and the parties are reported in figures 3.1 and 3.2 respectively.

Figure 3.1 shows that Bush was evaluated a little more positively than Robert Dole in 1996 and G. H. W. Bush in 1992, but this rating was *lower* than that of G. H. W. Bush in 1988 and Ronald Reagan in 1984. Moreover, in 2000 the mean thermometer score for Bush and Gore were almost identical. Thus Bush's campaigning as a different type of Republican did not appear to have a substantial impact on his overall evaluation. This is also confirmed in figure 3.2, which shows that the overall rating of the Republican Party was unchanged from 1996.

Figure 3.1   *Feelings towards Democratic and Republican presidential candidates, 1980–2000*

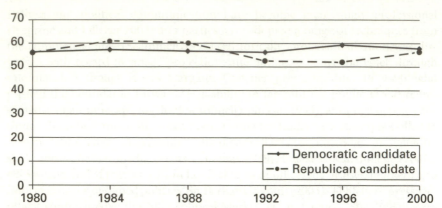

Source: American National Election Studies (1980–2000), available: www.umich.edu/~nes/.
Note: Ratings are the mean scores taken from feelings' thermometers that ask respondents to place each candidate on a scale ranging from 0 to 100.

Figure 3.2   *Feelings towards the Democratic and Republican Parties, 1980–2000*

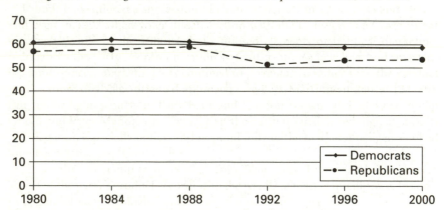

Source: American National Election Studies (1980–2000), available: www.umich.edu/~nes/.
Note: Ratings are the mean scores taken from feelings' thermometers that ask respondents to place each party on a scale ranging from 0 to 100.

Another measure of how Bush and the Republican Party were evaluated in 2000 is the affect index. This is constructed by subtracting the number of dislikes about the Republican presidential candidate or the Republican Party from the number of likes (tables 3.3 and 3.4).[5]

Table 3.3 shows that while 34.8 per cent of respondents viewed Bush positively, 36.0 per cent had a negative perception of him. Indeed, while Bush was liked more than Dole in 1996 and G. H. W. Bush in 1992, this evaluation was still lower than

Table 3.3 *Affect towards Republican presidential candidates, 1980–2000 (%)*

	Strongly like	Moderately like	Neutral	Moderately dislike	Strongly dislike
Reagan, 1980	7.5	25.1	28.0	27.4	12.0
Reagan, 1984	17.3	22.4	21.1	21.4	17.7
Bush, 1988	11.7	24.6	32.5	19.6	11.6
Bush, 1992	9.9	19.6	21.8	26.6	22.0
Dole, 1996	12.1	17.6	29.9	25.1	15.3
Bush, 2000	13.1	21.7	29.3	22.1	13.9

Source: American National Election Studies (1980–2000), available: www.umich.edu/~nes/.
Note: Candidate affect is measured by subtracting the number of dislikes from the number of likes. This produces a score from −5 through +5: strongly like, +3 to +5; moderately like, +1 through +2; neutral, 0; moderately dislike, −1 to −2; strongly dislike, −3 to −5.

Table 3.4 *Affect towards Republican Party, 1980–2000 (%)*

	Strongly like	Moderately like	Neutral	Moderately dislike	Strongly dislike
1980	4.1	19.1	52.0	20.6	4.2
1984	6.9	18.3	48.6	19.5	6.7
1988	7.0	22.3	44.2	18.9	7.6
1992	3.5	15.6	44.8	26.6	9.4
1996	6.5	19.7	41.1	23.4	9.4
2000	7.3	20.8	41.4	21.5	9.0

Source: American National Election Studies (1980–2000); available: www.umich.edu/~nes/.
Note: Party affect is measured by subtracting the number of dislikes from the number of likes. This produces a score from −5 through +5: strongly like, +3 to +5; moderately like, +1 through +2; neutral, 0; moderately dislike, −1 to −2; strongly dislike, −3 to −5.

those received by the last two successful Republican candidates, G. H. W. Bush in 1988 (36.3 per cent) and Reagan in 1984 (39.7 per cent). With regard to affect towards the Republican Party, table 3.4 shows that Bush's campaign had little impact, with 28.1 per cent either strongly or moderately liking the Republican Party and 30.5 per cent strongly or moderately disliking the Republican Party. These figures are not significantly different from those in 1996.

Ideological perceptions of the candidates and the parties Finally, to what extent did Bush succeed in positioning himself and the Republican Party at the centre of the political spectrum in 2000? Figure 3.3 shows the mean ideological placement, on a seven-point scale, of the electorate and the Republican and Democratic presidential candidates, while figure 3.4 shows the same information for the electorate and the Republican and Democratic parties. Both figures show that in terms of ideological placement, both Bush and the Republican Party were considered to be to the right of the electorate.

Figure 3.3   *Ideological placement of the electorate and the Republican and Democratic presidential candidates, 1980–2000*

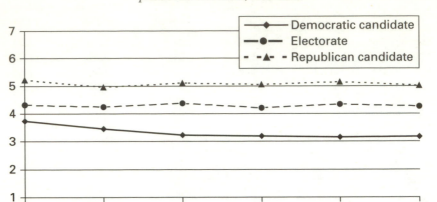

Source: American National Election Studies (1980–2000), available: www.umich.edu/~nes/.
Note: Respondents were asked to place themselves and the presidential candidates on a 7-point scale from 1 (most liberal) to 7 (most conservative).

Figure 3.4   *Ideological placement of the electorate and the Republican and Democratic Parties, 1980–2000*

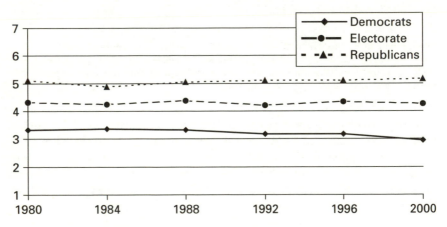

Source: American National Election Studies (1980–2000), available: www.umich.edu/~nes/.
Note: Respondents were asked to place themselves and the parties on a 7-point scale, from 1 (most liberal) to 7 (most conservative).

From this perspective, the evidence is mixed as to how effective political marketing was in changing attitudes about the parties and their candidates. Despite running as a compassionate conservative, Bush and the GOP were nevertheless placed by the electorate to the right of the ideological scale, exhibiting little difference from previous elections. The same point holds for the overall likes/dislikes about the party and candidate.

Stage 8   Stand and deliver – compassionate conservatism as a governing strategy
Evaluating delivery by the Bush presidency is problematical in the light of the terrorist attacks on the World Trade Centre and the Pentagon on 11 September 2001. Essentially, this constituted the demarcation line between two very different Bush presidencies. Prior to 11 September, Bush's ability to deliver and to govern as a compassionate conservative was mixed. For example, his first priority as president was to push through his tax cut, a traditional conservative Republican item. At the same time, the Bush administration was roundly condemned for rolling back some of the environmental regulations introduced by the Clinton administration. In May 2001, moderate Republican Senator Jim Jeffords left the Republican Party to become an Independent, caucusing with Democrats, and in so doing giving control of the Senate to the Democrats. The complaint Jeffords made was that as a moderate he could no longer find a home in an increasingly conservative Republican Party.

Bush has, however, demonstrated that his claim to be a different type of Republican was more than just campaign rhetoric, signing an Education Reform Bill on which he worked closely with Senator Edward Kennedy and publicly acknowledging Kennedy's work. Indeed, as Republican strategists looked ahead to the 2002 mid-term elections, key figures were urging the party and its candidates to re-focus on education legislation. Although education has traditionally been a Democratic issue, this was clear evidence that Bush and the Republicans hoped to permanently stake out ground on the issue. Bush also signed a Campaign Finance Reform Bill into law, sponsored by his GOP primary rival John McCain. The White House website in autumn 2003 listed four main priorities, two of which were focused on compassionate conservative issues: 'Strengthen and Improve Health Care' and 'Encourage Acts of Compassion' see www.whitehouse.gov/president, accessed 11 November 2003). On balance this blending of traditional Republican themes with those not usually associated with the GOP may indicate that compassionate conservatism is more than just a label. It may actually be the first identified example of a complete use of a market orientation, and the MOP model, where a party does not simply ditch ideology, as happened with the New Labour design in Britain, but adjusts mainstream policies to mix them with a party's history and ideology.

Most fundamentally, political marketing is concerned with the ability of political parties to reap electoral success by utilising the market-oriented concept and associated activities. The 2002 mid-term elections, where the Republicans increased their majority in the US House and regained the Senate, certainly were perceived as a personal triumph for George W. Bush. The president had both helped in recruiting quality candidates in key Senate races and then vigorously campaigned for them. Of course, one might argue that the Republican gains in 2002 reflected more of a desire on the part of the electorate to embrace a war president than it did a desire to buy the Republican product. War is, however, part of the political product, and parties in government have to adapt to circumstances as they arise. Yet there is still concern that compassionate conservatism was exceptionally conspicuous by its absence during the 2002 elections, either in terms of substantive issue discussion or of campaign rhetoric, the main focus being domestic terrorism and foreign policy.

On the other hand, the downfall of Senator Trent Lott as Senate majority leader in December 2002 – after making remarks at former South Carolina Senator J. Strom Thurmond's hundredth birthday celebration that were deemed to be racially insensitive – seemed to suggest that many Republicans were serious about re-branding the party's image. Bush himself, along with many conservative commentators, were roundly critical of Lott's remarks, and Lott's eventual replacement Senator Bill Frist was widely regarded as demonstrating a more compassionate brand of conservatism in tune with that of Bush. This has been further underscored by Bush's signing a Medicare Reform Bill into law in December 2003, capturing a potential key strength from the Democrats ready for the 2004 presidential election. The president needs to continue to define its governing agenda if the Republican Party is truly to be recast in his image. This is a stage in the marketing of a new Republican Party – and a possible long-term realignment favouring the GOP – that Bush neglects at his peril. History has shown that voters will not repeat-buy a product they perceives to be unable or unwilling to deliver and thus live up to its election promises.

George W. Bush: a political marketing success?

This chapter has provided an analysis of the extent to which George W. Bush utilised political marketing in order to be elected president. Bush clearly did follow aspects of a market-oriented approach, making significant changes to the Republican product – its policy themes and issue foci – in response to the results of market intelligence, but adjusted it to suit party principles. Political marketing was also used to inform the development of the product rather than simply in the communication and campaign stages.

Therefore, in answer to our original questions: yes, the market-oriented approach informed the behaviour of the Republican Party and of Bush for the 2000 presidential election; yes US political marketing is as broad in scope as it is in the UK and is not simply concerned with the communication or selling of the product. In applying the MOP model in full detail we have been able to provide a clear illustration of how political parties in the USA can use it as comprehensively as do those in the UK, and as the model suggests. Implementation was important and there was a communication stage beginning with the primaries that was separate from the official campaign. Furthermore, adjustment was a vital part of the development of a product acceptable to both internal and external markets. Although US parties are perceived as looser coalitions, lacking ideology and formal membership, Bush still found it necessary to adjust his behaviour to respond to traditional Republican Party views.

The one main difference in applying this UK-based theory to the USA is that systemic differences do influence behaviour in so much as the leader is a more important aspect of the product in the US presidential electoral marketplace. Nevertheless, US parties can and do use all eight stages of the MOP process and both major parties are striving to utilise the MOP approach.

Furthermore, Bush's use of political marketing has provided a blueprint for the Republican Party in future elections. Although Bush has never abandoned his conservative convictions, his ability to address issues that Republicans had hitherto avoided and to stake out ground on Democratic issues is proving significant in that Republican candidates are now talking about education and health care. It appears that the days of issue ownership in US politics are over, with both main parties moving onto each other's terrain. This suggests that political marketing is likely to be increasingly used by political parties around the world.

Difficulties for and questions about the use of political marketing

Two points can be highlighted from the case study of George W. Bush and the Republican Party in the 2000 presidential election which give rise to significant questions for political marketing scholarship to consider. First, the 2000 presidential election may have been the first contest in which two market-oriented parties and candidates went head-to-head with each other. Indeed, one journalist referred to the 2000 election as being a contest between two 'test-marketed candidates' whose images conform to voters' desires in the 'near-perfect feedback loop' provided by focus groups and endless tracking polls (quoted in Weschler 2000). So, what does happen when both major parties adopt and follow the market-oriented approach? Are there any answers to the potential difficulty of stalemate that parties could use to avoid such a close electoral result? Does a party take the risk of staking out new ground on an issue, in an attempt to win more support, or might such a move alienate as many, or perhaps more, of the electorate?

Second, an important assumption of political marketing is that traditional voter loyalty to the parties is in decline, and that a large number of voters are up for grabs at each election. On the evidence of the US case, this decline in voter loyalty, or more generally *de-alignment*, may be somewhat exaggerated (see, for example, Bartels 2000; Miller and Shanks 1996). This prompts the question: just how much of the electorate is actually susceptible to market-led changes in political party behaviour? In this case, there was little statistical evidence to show that voters abandoned their partisanship or their perceptions of the ideological placement of the parties and candidates in the 2000 presidential election.

The link between party identification and actual votes is, of course, a major area for debate among voting behaviour analysts. In marketing terms, the relation between votes, party identification (or other sociologically generated consumer behaviour characteristics), voter evaluation of the political product and a party's use of marketing has yet to be fully investigated and tested both qualitatively and quantitatively, retrospectively and prospectively. In any case, when two parties are evenly matched in terms of their underlying support – as with the Democrats and Republicans today – it is even more crucial for one party to target and appeal to the swing voter, independents and soft partisans of the other party. The effectiveness of Bush's targeting and the MOP-based stances on Republican issue may become more evident if Bush is successful in embedding his new vision of Republicanism.

Democratic concerns with political marketing

One further normative issue is raised by this case study, namely that the use of a market-oriented approach and the whole idea of parties and political leaders following, rather than leading, voters' demands, is perhaps becoming unpopular. Politicians like Bush are increasingly attempting to deny their use of focus groups to the extent that the MOP model suggests. During his quest for the presidency, Bush often commented that he did not just follow focus groups:

> I think you got to look at . . . whether or not one makes decisions on sound principles, or whether or not you rely upon polls and focus groups on how to decide what the course of action is. We don't stick our finger in the air trying to figure out which way the wind is blowing. I do what I think is right for the American people.[6]

This suggests a marketing backlash among the public, one indication of which in the summer of 2003 was that the front-runner for the Democratic presidential nomination for the 2004 presidential election was the former Vermont governor, Howard Dean, who appeared to have adopted more of a product-oriented approach, attracting support for standing up for Democratic Party values. Despite the success of the Clinton–New Democrat era, many in the Democratic Party seem to be suggesting that the use of political marketing came at the cost of its soul, not dissimilar to the underlying, if more hidden, problems associated with the loss of ideology within the UK's Labour Party (Lees-Marshment 2001a: 200–7). Political marketing practice, if not its theory, would seem in need of further refinement to ensure it does not damage the overall nature of politics.

One issue that seemed to encourage a return to more idealistic politics of leadership has been the Iraq war in 2002–3, though this was not without problems. Bush was more favourably positioned than Blair in so much as the US public, broadly speaking, stood behind its leader in respect of the war in Iraq. However there was certainly an increase in the questioning of his leadership as a result of the war and this has practical as well as democratic implications. It can also be argued that as US president Bush needs to market both at home and abroad, and war, with the emotions and conflicts it provokes, makes it difficult to pursue a strategy that will satisfy international as well as domestic consumers. At the time of writing (November 2003), the consequences of the war and public opinion about it for the 2004 presidential election remain to be seen, but the overall issue of war, marketing and leadership remains one for further debate.

Overall, this chapter has demonstrated that comparative studies of party marketing help to highlight the utilisation of political marketing in a variety of political systems. It also suggests new issues, however, that political marketing scholarship needs to address in the study of political parties in different political systems.

Notes

1 According to exit polls, Bush received 49 per cent of the Hispanic vote, 27 per cent of the black vote and 31 per cent of the vote from the Democrats and liberals. At the same time, he received 65 per cent of the vote from women, indicating that he could neutralise the 'gender gap' that had become evident in voting behaviour at the presidential level.
2 Despite this appearance, the NAACP mounted a multimillion-dollar campaign, primarily to mobilise the black electorate.
3 Indeed, the state-by-state correlation of the 2000 and 1996 vote was 0.95, the highest between a pair of consecutive elections since the 'New Deal' period.
4 Data were conducted by the Centre for Political Studies of the Institute for Social Research at the University of Michigan. Responsibility for the analyses and interpretations presented here are those of the authors alone.
5 Respondents could name up to five dislikes or likes about the candidate and the party, thus creating a 10-point scale from −5 through +5. This index was then collapsed into five categories: strongly dislike (–3 to –5), moderately dislike (–1 to –2), neutral (zero), moderately like (+1 to +2) and strongly like (+3 to +5).
6 Quoted from the first presidential debate as reported in the *New York Times*, 3 April 2002: A21.

Bibliography

Bartels, L. M. (2000), 'Partisanship and voting behavior, 1952–1996', *American Journal of Political Science*, 44(1): 35–50.

Ceaser, J. W. and Busch, A. E. (2001), *The Perfect Tie: The True Story of the 2000 Presidential Election*, Lanham, MD: Rowman & Littlefield.

Corrado, A. (2001), 'Financing the 2000 elections', in G. M. Pomper (ed.), *The Election of 2000*, New York: Chatham House.

Devlin, I. P. (2001), 'Contrasts in presidential campaign commercials of 2000', *American Behavioral Scientist*, 44(12): 2338–69.

Dionne, E. J. (2000), 'In search of George W.', *Washington Post*, 6 August: A19.

Erikson, R. S. (2001), 'The 2000 presidential election in historical perspective', *Political Research Quarterly*, 116(1): 29–52.

Gould, P. (1998), *The Unfinished Revolution: How the Modernisers Saved the Labour Party*, Little, Brown.

Ingram, P. and Lees-Marshment, J. (2002), 'The Anglicisation of political marketing: how Blair out-marketed Clinton', *Journal of Public Affairs*, 2(2): 44–56.

Judis, J. B., and Teixeira, R. (2002), *The Emerging Democratic Majority*, New York: Scribner.

Lees-Marshment, J. (2001a), *Political Marketing and British Political Parties*, Manchester: Manchester University Press.

Lees-Marshment, J. (2001b), 'The product-, sales- and market-oriented party and how Labour learnt to market the product, not just the presentation', *European Journal of Marketing*, 35 (September–October): 1074–84.

Mayer, W. G. (2001), 'The presidential nominations', in G. M. Pomper (ed.), *The Election of 2000*, New York: Chatham House.

Miller, W. E. and Shanks, J. M. (1996), *The New American Voter*, Cambridge, MA: Harvard University Press.

Newman, B. (1994) *The Marketing of the President: Political Marketing as Campaign Strategy*, Thousand Oaks, CA: Sage.

Niffenegger, P. (1989) 'Strategies for success from the political marketers', *Journal of Consumer Marketing*, 6(1): 45–61.

O'Shaughnessy, N. (1990) *The Phenomenon of Political Marketing*, Basingstoke: Macmillan.

Pomper, G. M. (2001), *The Election of 2000*, New York: Chatham House.

Ponnuru, R. (1999), 'State of the Conservatives', *National Review*, 22 November: 37

Sabato, L. J. and Scott, J. J. (2002), 'The long road to a cliffhanger: primaries and conventions', in L. J. Sabato (ed.), *Overtime! The Election 2000 Thriller*, New York: Longman.

Wattenberg, M. P. (1991), *The Rise of Candidate-Centered Politics*, Cambridge, MA: Harvard University Press.

Wattenberg, M. P. (1996), *The Decline of American Political Parties, 1952–1994*, Cambridge, MA: Harvard University Press.

Weschler, Lawrence. (2000), 'A fluke? A crisis? No, the future', available online: www.salon.com/politics/feature/2000/11/12/middle/index.html, accessed July 2003.

4

Canadian political parties: market-oriented or ideological slagbrains?

Alex Marland

Two questions arise when considering the suitability of Lees-Marshment's product-oriented party, sales-oriented party and market-oriented party (POP, SOP and MOP) models to the Canadian political context. First, how do Canadian national parties fall within these categories (if at all)? Second, to what extent do Canadian parties follow the stages of the political marketing process? This chapter attempts to address these questions by profiling the marketing activities of the major political parties in the 2000 Canadian general election.

The Canadian political context and marketing features

Canada is a highly decentralised federalist state. The Federal Government is responsible for national matters, such as defence, but its dominance has eroded as Canadians have placed greater importance on health, education and welfare services. These areas are the jurisdiction of the ten provincial units, such as Quebec, which operate their own elections and whose political parties are often largely autonomous from their federal counterpart. Each province has its own political culture, though Canadians, as a whole, share many demographic similarities with residents in other Western societies. Formal education levels have been increasing, traditional family units have modernised, and multiculturalism characterises growing city centres. Cynicism regarding government has receded somewhat since the early 1990s, but it and declining elector turnout continue to fuel concerns about the vibrancy of Canadian civic society. One outcome has been that turnout among registered electors aged 18 and over has been consistently declining, reaching a record low of 61 per cent in 2000; this is comparable to the USA and the UK. Yet, Canadians are more socialist, less religious and not as transfixed by racial issues as are Americans, and compared to the British Canadians are less class oriented, less partisan, and are larger consumers of broadcast media.

Canada's parliamentary system acknowledges the British monarch as its head of state; the queen vests her authority in the appointed governor-general, who oversees formal procedural matters and undertakes ceremonial tasks in a largely statesmanlike manner. In practice, political power rests with the indirectly elected head of government, who is the prime minister by virtue of being the leader of the party with the most seats in the House of Commons. Only two Canadian parties have ever formed government, although a number of fledgling product- and sales-oriented organisations have enjoyed intermittent success. Electoral rules are British-inspired and have lately faced constitutional challenges under an US-styled Charter of Rights and Freedoms.[1] In federal elections, the parties operate 36-day official campaigns in which each focuses on a leader who embodies its political product, and they defer to their constituency associations (where they exist) to organise in the 301 electoral districts.[2] These associations have considerable autonomy, though the five major Canadian parties and their figureheads retain a relatively broad influence over their members of parliament (MPs) and electoral candidates. Party discipline, which is comparable to Britain's, facilitates the implementation of a marketing programme in which presenting the party product as a unified 'team' is a time-honoured tactic.

As with the UK, Canadian electoral regulations limit campaigns' electoral contributions and expenditures; there are also partial reimbursements for election expenses and tax credits for small political donations. All told, US political marketing has influenced both countries (the UK by consultants imported from the USA, Canada by osmosis), and transporting UK political marketing practice to Canada is feasible because the countries have highly similar political systems and customs. The systemic differences between the two – such as the absence of political broadcast advertising in the UK – are not major conceptual barriers.

Canada's most notable political characteristic is perhaps the prevalence of language and regional market segments. The Canadian federation has experienced English, French, and aboriginal identity stresses, while an influx of other ethnicities has increased the presence of multiculturalism. More notably, the nation's socio-economic structure has contributed to the five distinct regions of Atlantic, Ontario, Prairies, Pacific, and especially Quebec. Regionalism has been historically exacerbated by the fact that Ontario and Quebec together have more than half of the seats in the House of Commons. This persists in a country of 30 million residents scattered across one of the world's largest boundaries and has considerable political marketing implications. Cairns's 1968 observation that the single-member plurality electoral system exaggerates the support of regional parties at the expense of seats for national parties is still accurate.

In recent years, parties that have reflected the interests of geographically clustered electors have enjoyed considerable success, and Canada no longer has a traditional two-party system. The Liberal Party has formed the government most often, due to its mass-marketing of a centralist platform that alternatively balances socialism with fiscal conservatism. In comparison, the Conservative Party, known as the Progressive Conservative Party (PCP) since the 1930s, has enjoyed only intermittent success, and has had more difficulty in generating mass appeal. Until recently, the socialist New Democratic Party (NDP) has enjoyed enough electoral support as a moral protest group for it to be Canada's third major party. Historically, smatterings of regional party movements that have responded to the demands of local markets (for instance, Prairie farmers, Quebec nationalists) have been absorbed by the major parties. While minor parties exist – the Green Party, Marijuana Party, Natural Law Party, these niche organisations receive only negligible levels of support.

Canadian party politics changed significantly with the 1993 federal election, when regional movements succeeded in fracturing the country's party system for the third time in its history. The governing PCP was reduced to just two seats because its coalition of regional segments disintegrated and its product no longer reflected market demands. Protest votes that had traditionally benefited the NDP also evaporated and the Liberal Party resumed its so-called role as Canada's 'natural governing party'. Two new regional parties succeeded, each winning dozens more seats than the PCP and the NDP combined, based on concentrated vote support. One was the Bloc Québécois (BQ), a special-interest party dedicated to Quebec's independence, which was formed in 1990 by a PCP cabinet minister and immediately attracted support of Quebeckers unhappy with failed constitutional amendments. The other was the Reform Party, a grassroots bastion for frustrated ('small-c') conservatives and disenchanted western Canadians. The result of the 1997 election was quite similar.[3]

Canadian campaigns emphasise leadership, and entering the 2000 election, Liberal leader Jean Chrétien continued his 'little guy from Shawinigan' ticket that had allowed him to exceed expectations. By comparison, the other four major parties had switched leaders since 1993's pivotal election and were largely regional rumps. The oligopolistic party politics that exist in the USA or the UK, and which used to fit Canada, had seemingly been replaced by a Liberal monopoly amid a divided opposition.

A brief history of political marketing in Canada

Historically, the Liberals have been the most noticeable investors in emergent political marketing, in part because they formed government for much of the twentieth century. The party imported from the US George Gallup's opinion research methods in the 1940s (Robinson 1999), and by the 1960s was emphasising polling, strategic advertising and branding philosophies even in some of its constituency campaigns (Land 1965). Its commitment to professionalised electioneering bloomed in the 1970s, when leader Pierre Trudeau's centralised electioneering helped build his image, and the party created an in-house advertising agency. In fact, in the 1984 campaign, commercial marketing consultants were so eager to help the Liberals that *two* pollsters provided strategic guidance, which paradoxically contributed to the party's electoral defeat (Clarkson 1988). Nevertheless, the Liberals are an excellent example of a market leader that can afford the financial outlay of being market oriented. Since 1993, careful monitoring of opinion polls has facilitated the party's managerial style of governance, and it has been careful to dodge policy decisions that could spur regional dissention.

The PCP has also been something of a Canadian electioneering trendsetter despite its intermittent electoral success. It worked with an advertising agency in the

1917 election (Kline *et al.* 1991), sponsored some of the first radio attack advertising in the 1935 campaign (Ward 1999), and emphasised leadership in the first Canadian televised elections in the late 1950s (Spencer 1994). However, as recently as the 1968 campaign, the party still lacked employees with marketing research knowledge, and it was only in 1984 that it finally mastered the use of rolling opinion poll data to develop political strategy (Perlin 1988). In 1988, as the governing party, it commissioned focus groups just to develop ideas for a new party logo, and then again to test logo concepts (Krause 1989). The party also authorised over 200 opinion surveys in the 15 months prior to the 1993 election (Guy 2001). However, it suffered a colossal research failure in 1993, when it focus-group tested attack ads mocking Chrétien's facial paralysis, but public backlash was such that they rank among the greatest blunders in modern electioneering (see Soderlund *et al.* 1999).

Conversely, the Reform Party has been a political communications innovator in facilitating its grassroots philosophy and sales-oriented approach. Its product was initially populism, which influenced the party's experiments with telephone referenda, online meetings, tele-voting and mail questionnaires (Barney 1996). By the 1997 campaign, Reform was moving away from being a POP to a SOP. It aimed to expand its share of the targeted right-wing market segment, and so Reform began to change its homogeneous image. It recruited ethnic and Québec candidates; discouraged caucus members from making unnecessary public statements; and changed the party leader's physical image (including voice lessons reminiscent of Margaret Thatcher's). Although it made some limited electoral gains, as former PCP pollster Allan Gregg commented before that campaign, Reform was still perceived by many as 'a bunch of ideological slagbrains' (Bickerton, Gagnon and Smith 1999: 141). To improve its chances of securing the mass support needed to form government, in 1998 Reform undertook a bolder re-branding exercise to market its product to conservatives east of Manitoba, and to 'unite the right' within a single conservative party. The result of many high-profile gatherings was a re-packaged product with a new name – Canadian Alliance Party [CAP] – a new logo, new members, a new leader in the telegenic Stockwell Day and somewhat more moderate conservative policies.

By comparison, the NDP remained an organisation that shunned the image change needed for mass appeal. It has always been a sales operation due to internal and external pressures not to stray from its ideological foundations. The NDP's small market segment of leftists have been scattered across the country, which makes it difficult to elect candidates, and pollsters have had little incentive to offer their expertise to an unbending organisation. For example, their pollster in the 1984 pre-campaign faced 'operational problems' that inhibited market intelligence, such as the party executive disagreeing with his recommendations (Morley 1988); an US pollster replaced him, who in the next campaign had to supervise party staffers analysing his own data (Whitehorn 1989). It is also telling that, towards the end of the 1993 and 1997 campaigns, in an attempt to save money the NDP reduced its polling to regions and electoral districts where they believed the party could win (Whitehorn 1994 and 1997).

Even less of a marketer has been the BQ, which has been content to offer an ideo-logical product to geographically segmented electors. Because it fields candidates only in Quebec's seventy-five electoral districts it acts as an elected pressure group with the unique objective of promoting the interests of Quebec, specifically the views of Quebec nationalists and disgruntled federalists. At its inception, the BQ was a conventional POP that drew on its linkages with the provincial Parti Québécois, and has not been known for any noteworthy marketing innovations.

In general, the quality of insights obtained from market intelligence has improved over the years as the parties have moved on to a selling or marketing orientation. Canadian pollsters consistently use top-of-mind awareness questions to identify campaign issues, to assess which party is on-message and to define the ballot question. In preparation for the 2000 campaign, they used polling to identify target ridings, to test advertising language, and to monitor party strengths and weaknesses. Research data are also used to respond to regional variations by adjust-ing messages in different parts of the country (see Carty *et al.* 2000). A brief look at the 2000 Canadian election suggests, however, that SOPs were prevalent, and that marketing intelligence was used predominantly for communications (rather than product) decisions.

Case study of the 2000 Canadian election

In the late summer of 2000, many pundits speculated that a federal election, which was required by June 2002, might occur as early as spring 2001. With no burning issue to debate, and determined to suppress a party coup of his leadership, Prime Minister Chrétien surprised many, even in his own caucus, when he announced that a general election would be held on 27 November 2000.

This case study provides an overview of the political marketing activities of the five major parties in that election. In mid-2002, I conducted depth interviews with political strategists from all 5 parties, 6 media pollsters, the leaders of 2 minor parties and 6 constituency campaign managers from different types of electoral district.[4] The qualitative insights derived were combined with knowledge from existing literature, news media coverage of the campaign and quantitative data such as campaign expenditure figures filed with Elections Canada. Collectively, these interviews bolstered conventional wisdom that the 2000 election was largely forgettable except for its air of negativity, and suggested that the major Canadian political parties provided an offering that reflected mostly existing party members' demands, rather than those of the electorate at large.

Some distinctions fundamentally guide how Canada's major parties gathered their research intelligence and structured their offering or promotions. The govern-ing Liberals and fifth-place (in terms of seats) PCP were mass-market parties, because they offered a product designed to appeal to as many electors as possible. To achieve widespread support, there was a need to 'broker' national and regional inter-ests, and to be responsive to cross-country intelligence. By comparison, the fourth-place NDP (left-wing) and second-place CAP (right-wing) were ideological parties that placed much emphasis on designing a product to appeal to the segment of the electorate that shared their philosophical ideals, although the Alliance had attempted to morph into more of an MOP. These two parties practised segment marketing by focusing on the support of a large cluster of like-minded electors. The third-place BQ, however, was unique as a micro-marketing party that targeted a geographically concentrated niche of electors. This special-interest party used intelligence to help improve a product confined to the defence of Quebec's interests. Segment- and niche-marketing parties like the NDP and BQ operated knowing that their unique selling propositions lacked the requisite scope to translate into the number of seats sufficient to form government; at best they could hope to form the official opposition.

Canadian parties' use of political marketing

Liberals: mass marketing   The Liberal Party entered the 2000 campaign maintaining its considerable lead in public opinion polls. It has had a modern history of governing for prolonged periods, such as 1935–57 and 1963–79, with short Conservative Party interludes, and so it appeared that Canadian politics was in the midst of yet another period of Liberal dominance. The party's monitoring of the electorate continued to indicate that its leadership, symbols, policies and candidates were known commodities that many electors generally preferred over the alternatives. While governing, it had adjusted its product in response to elector demands for increased social spending, particularly in the area of health care, and had appeased others in a pre-election 'mini budget' with a small tax cut. Yet, the strong probability of another majority victory reduced the value that the Liberal organisation placed on being a MOP.

   The thinking was that the Liberals needed to do little more than preserve their existing brand positioning. There would be no bold initiatives or inspiring visions; just the continued positioning as the only viable pan-Canadian party. Conspicuously little emphasis was placed on defining what the Liberals had to offer, as illustrated by the party's manifesto, which included fuzzy phrases such as 'A new Liberal government will champion community action on illness prevention, health promotion, and wellness' (Clarkson 2001: 38). This contrasted with its product in the two previous elections. In the 1993 campaign, the Liberal 'Red Book' had outlined the party's policy proposals in considerable detail, and was followed by a somewhat less precise 'Red Book II' in 1997. The party's initial advertising was also vague, and promoted feel-good messages about health care commitments, the budget surplus, multiculturalism, reduced taxes and the quality of the Liberal 'team'. These, too, were markedly different from earlier versions of the Liberal product, which had provided alternatives to policies of the then-governing Conservatives or emphasised Chrétien's leadership.

   Devoid of a justifiable reason for calling an election just over three years into a mandate, the Liberals diverted attention from their product and sought to define that of one of their *opponents*. This type of aggressive counter-branding is surely unique to the political arena, and the strategy may have military origins (Marland

2003). Engaging in competition analysis within stage 3 (product adjustment) of the MOP model, the Liberals understood from their light tracking polling data that the CAP's Stockwell Day was attracting enough support in English Canada as to pose a potential threat to another Liberal sweep of Ontario seats. If the Liberals could position the contest as a two-way race, many PC and NDP supporters would likely vote Liberal in a bid to stop the eastwards expansion of the CAP. Before they could be attacked, the Liberals would initiate a pre-emptive defence marketing strategy that involved directing guerrilla-like messages at their principal threats (box 4.1). In Quebec, this was the BQ; in the rest of Canada, it was the CAP and its leader. The Liberals would help shape how electors and journalists perceived Day, a federal neophyte, in particular his character and leadership capabilities. The objective was to position the election as a decision between the Liberals' socialist centralism and the CAP's right-wing 'values'.[5] In other words, they would use marketing intelligence to develop messages which would define the CAP's product before that party could.

Box 4.1 *Jean Chrétien's pre-emptive comments illustrating the Liberals' defensive marketing strategy, 2000 campaign*

- 'Mr Day dared me to call an election ... [and there are] two crystal clear alternatives' (Canadian Broadcasting Corporation, 23 October).
- '[There are] two very different visions' (*National Post*, 27 October).
- Alliance represents the 'forces of darkness' and the 'dark side' (*Ottowa Citizen*, 30 October).
- 'The Reform Alliance party would have a country where the interest of the few will take priority over the well-being of the majority' (*National Post*, 30 October).
- 'We ask them [the Alliance] to be honest with the Canadian people. What is their real agenda?' (*Globe & Mail*, 4 November).
- 'The proposition of Stockwell Day is to destroy Canada' (*Globe & Mail*, 11 November).

In classic SOP fashion, the Liberals aimed to denigrate the youthful Day brand in a semi-civil manner to diminish electors' trust in him, rather than renew their own product, which was led by an aging Chrétien. One Liberal strategist confided that the plan was to 'hobble' Day as he was entering the leader debates, by 'breathing life' into a perception of him as a political villain, while taking care not to 'destroy' him too early. This required investigative research by war-room operatives and daily monitoring of the electorate's views. The party certainly had access to a plethora of primary research data: for example, its daily rolling cross-country opinion polls had an impressive sample of 20,000 respondents. Strategists used geo-demographic software to analyse seventy-five sets of regional polling numbers in pinpointing seats and segmenting electors demographically.[6] These data were supplemented with qualitative insights obtained from daily focus groups across the country and exit interviews at party meetings.

Party strategists proceeded to position the CAP as a home for politically incorrect intolerants. Liberal spokespersons diluted the CAP's new symbols by stubbornly referring to the renamed party as the 'Reform Alliance'. Researchers exposed Day's creationist religious beliefs according to which humans and dinosaurs coexisted. Collectively they undermined CAP policies and their neo-conservative 'hidden agenda'.[7] The sum of these activities fueled public suspicions about the CAP's leadership, candidates and supporters. Only towards the end of the campaign, when opinion polls indicated that the PCP was attracting some soft Liberals, did Chrétien and his entourage specifically target another party to solidify their likely majority. One result of this strategy was that Stockwell Day was perceived by a number of electors to be too extreme. Although this alone does not explain the Liberals victory (Blais *et al.* 2002), by reducing the salience of the CAP brand the Liberals indirectly increased their ability to reflect the needs and wants of electors. Although this MOP had declined on the product lifecycle into a vague SOP, it was nevertheless rewarded with an even larger majority in government.

The Liberals provided an unchanged product designed to meet the most basic needs of mass markets by brokering issues near the middle of the political spectrum. This required significant investments in formal market intelligence and a realisation that they were likely to win with only some negligible product adjustments. The Liberals apparently governed electors so well during the inter-election period that the party's product sold itself amid a splintered opposition. This suggests that the party was largely market oriented; however, rather than re-align itself to meet electors' desires (e.g. for new leadership), the organisation employed sales' tactics to promote its existing offering. As part of a pre-emptive defensive strategy, the Liberals used conflict communications in an attempt to persuade electors that the party met their needs. Their 'values' discussion de-emphasised product dialogue, increased the importance of imagery and reduced the party's long-term delivery accountability. A true MOP would not take this approach, and the Liberals' stagnant product required governance by opinion polls.

PCP: mass marketing   The PCP had won majority governments in 1984 and 1988, but upon its electoral collapse in 1993 the party became concerned about its very survival. In 1998, the party held a leadership campaign won by one-time prime minister Joe Clark, who stubbornly professed the importance of retaining the existing product without change, ostensibly because it was already more palatable to a greater number of electors than the right-wing Reform–Alliance Party. Yet, in response to the Reform–Alliance re-branding exercise, many PCP members, backroomers, and potential candidates publicly abandoned the party in favour of the CAP bandwagon; some of its MPs also crossed the floor to other parties. Amid this commotion, PCP delegates voted on a brokerage type of election platform (Woolstencroft 2001), which was finalised by the party executive and caucus. Underlying this SOP behaviour was that the PCP was too disorganised,

underfinanced and organisationally challenged during this hectic period to enter-
tain notions of being a MOP.

Because the party product was lacking in positive differentiation from that of the
Liberals or the CAP, the PCP had little option but to weaken the brands of these
opponents. Their pollster began preparing for the election just five weeks before
the writ drop and was given a second role as campaign manager. Having already
designed the current offering, party officials were content to delegate their pro-
motional authority; according to one senior strategist, they told the pollster:
'You're the pro . . . you tell us what to do, and we'll do it. Just don't spend money
that we don't have.' He was quickly bogged down by an array of organisational
details and was generally 'responsible for everything'. The party's pre-campaign
polls indicated that the Liberals could win in a landslide, and the PCP commissioned a handful of focus groups, which identified Clark's chief advantage as his
trustworthiness. These insights were used to design the party's advertising, which
masked negativity with humour, and the ads' impact was tracked in just two-dozen
constituencies during the campaign.

It is interesting that the PCP's campaign strategy planned to take jabs at the
Liberals, just as the Liberals had planned against the CAP. The PCP's research intelligence indicated that it was the second choice of many Liberal supporters, and so, in
addition to targeting soft right-wingers, its strategy was to attract soft Liberals by
weakening the trust these voters had in the governing party. From the campaign's
outset, the PCP engaged an offensive marketing strategy that sought to destabilise its
primary opponents by means of unexpected tactics. Clark repeated that Chrétien was
'arrogant', suggested that he should be criminally investigated for some dubious constituency behaviour and questioned the trustworthiness of the CAP (box 4.2). The
party ran low-budget ads designed to incite anger about the Liberals' costly election
call and its 'greatest lies'. According to the PCP's pollster, he was not trying to 'sell a

---

Box 4.2   *Joe Clark's attacking comments illustrating the PCP's offensive
marketing strategy, 2000 campaign*

- 'The prime minister has already acted with unparalleled arrogance in quit-
  ting his job halfway through his term' (Canadian Broadcasting Corporation,
  23 October).
- The Alliance is 'scary . . . dangerous . . . narrow . . . a party of exclusion . . .
  that pits the have regions against the have-not regions' (*National Post*,
  30 October).
- Chrétien 'did lie. He lied to Canadians about the GST, he lied about the free
  trade agreement' (*Globe & Mail*, 6 November).
- The Alliance is 'not a party you can trust. It creates a very real question
  of what it is they would do with power if it ever came' (*Globe & Mail*,
  10 November).

product', but rather 'trying to destroy a product' (Heinzl 2000: A8), and a strategist confided that the party was 'like a little guerrilla group'. The party's resource limitations also meant that it had to target regions where it might do well (such as the Atlantic constituencies) and ignore others altogether (such as the Saskatchewan constituencies). Despite a strong debate performance by Clark and some late campaign momentum, the PCP barely retained official party status, with just twelve seats.

CAP: segment marketing   The CAP's challenge in the 2000 campaign was to convince electors that its aforementioned re-branding from the Reform Party had involved a product improvement rather than mere re-packaging. True, the 'new' party was still the official opposition, had been rising in opinion polls, had received more donations, was enjoying favourable media coverage and had been publicly recruiting disillusioned PCP members. However, in 1997 it had infamously run television advertisements decrying Quebec politicians, and all of its seats were won in the Pacific and Prairie regions. Could this SOP complete its transformation into a MOP?

To woo Ontario voters, the CAP needed to undertake more of a mass-marketing approach. Some previously vocal ideologues continued to disapprove of the watering down of party principles and party members had a history of being wary about making policy decisions based on opinion research (Ellis and Archer 1994). Consistent with this transition difficulty, the strategist interviewed complained about pressures to monitor support for Conservative issues, rather than to explore those that mattered to the masses. These implementation problems were probably linked to a lack of marketing knowledge among some decision-makers or other partisans, according to Lees-Marshment's description (2001). Drawing on her proposals, it can be said, what the CAP experienced is usual among sales-oriented parties that aim to become market oriented, because insufficient internal reaction analysis contributed to a poor understanding of how to obtain buy-in from party candidates and members.

The communication and election campaign stages of the MOP process were big problems for the CAP in 2000. It was critical that the redesigned offering generate favourable brand positioning for the party and its leader. That is, however, one area where the paths of commercial and political marketing diverge slightly, because in commercial marketing it is uncommon for a corporate figurehead to be part of the actual product available for purchase. The commercial equivalent of a party leader might be a high-profile chief executive officer, such as Virgin Enterprises' Richard Branson, except that Branson is only a figurative part of an airline flight or music recording. When a party leader's personal beliefs interfere with the implemented product, a collapse can occur that research intelligence failed to avert. The upheaval surrounding Martha Stewart Living Omnimedia demonstrates that this can occur within the commercial realm, and the leadership of Stockwell Day in the 2000 campaign is a political example.

As already mentioned, the Liberals shrewdly highlighted Day's shortcomings during the campaign. Journalists scrutinised his social conservatism, and his many publicity stunts seemed to increase the legitimacy of perceptions of him as an intellectual lightweight (see, for example, Ellis 2001). Possibly compounding the problem was that Day often ignored his strategists' pleas that he communicate negative messages as part of a broader attack strategy; instead, he publicly insisted that he would campaign under an 'agenda of respect' that would focus on policy ideas and leadership (Ellis 2001). This forced the party, unilaterally, into a defensive strategy that restricted its ability to attract opponents' softest supporters (box 4.3). For example, in his speeches Day ignored hard messages directed at Chrétien by his speechwriters, and so would end up having to address his competitors' attacks. It was only at the mid-point of the campaign that he accepted his advisors' strategy. Eventually the party broadcast advertisements that suggested Chrétien had broken multiple promises; Day called Chrétien a liar several times during the leaders' debate; and later he maintained that Chrétien had been involved in criminal actions. However, by then only the size of the Liberal majority was in doubt, and even though the CAP would go on to gain a dozen seats (though predominantly in western Canada), journalists were speculating on Day's political future a week before election day.

Box 4.3   *Stockwell Day's position comments illustrating the CAP's defensive marketing strategy, 2000 campaign*

- '[I]f he [Chrétien] gets some particular joy out of going after me, then I feel better that I made him feel better' (*Ottawa Citizen*, 26 October).
- '[T]he only thing I can hope for, of course, is that the electorate will deal with that type of low-level approach in a campaign that does not dignify a response' (*Globe & Mail*, 15 November).
- 'This is a new low in the level of attack ads, personal attacks and scare tactics. Jean Chrétien, call off your dogs and tell them to stop with these inaccuracies and slurring activities' (*Globe & Mail*, 16 November).
- 'I will not throw back a slur because one was thrown at me. Let's stick to the strategy' (*Toronto Star*, 24 November).

The CAP failed to fulfil all stages of the MOP process. In re-branding itself, it drew on considerable formal and informal intelligence; redesigned a product to appeal to more electors; experienced some minority resistance to implementing a marketing orientation; communicated and campaigned in a positive manner; and, having come second in the election, had no opportunity to deliver on promises. An argument could be made that the party was a good example of a MOP that had faltered, though that would be to overlook the party's underlying ideological constraints and to overemphasise its campaign failures. Opponents' attacks during the campaign revealed that the CAP was in fact just a dressed-up sales' operation whose core product had not sufficiently adjusted.

NDP: segment marketing   The NDP's offering in the 2000 campaign was very similar to the 1997 version and there were no pretences that the party would finally form the official opposition. The party had the same low-profile English leader in Alexa McDonough, continued to promote democratic socialist policies and was seemingly content to target a small segment of the Canadian electorate while keeping other parties in check. At best, it could hope to win key seats that would allow the party to continue its role as Parliament's so-called 'moral conscience'. Privately, party operatives were braced for the possibility that their seat total would plummet to 1993 levels. Their primary goals were to win McDonough's seat and to maintain official party status, so, like the PCP, the focus was on survival rather than achieving a breakthrough. Although Canadians' number one policy priority was the NDP's bread-and-butter issue of health care, the other parties also championed the topic, and the party's SOP approach (with a platform that was developed by a series of committees) precluded any electoral growth.

NDP strategists drew on market intelligence, rather than market-driven activities, to persuade the electorate. One of the top strategists confided that although they often monitored the electorate's views through telephone polls and focus groups, he and other NDP decision-makers were sceptical of over-emphasising marketing strategy, and so placed more emphasis on day-to-day campaign logistics. Like the PCP, the NDP was financially stressed, overlooked by the news media, had lost some MPs to other parties, turned to amateurs in positions of high responsibility, and concentrated resources where the party believed it had a chance of winning a seat. Given the circumstances, it is not surprising that they likewise embarked on a campaign strategy that involved guerrilla attacks. Their advertising communicated the socio-ideological themes of health care, the environment and the taxing of elites, and only briefly mentioned the party (Whitehorn 2001). Throughout the campaign, McDonough criticised the Liberals' record on social programmes, raised alarms about CAP ideologues, and was often shrill in her name-calling (box 4.4). On Election Day, the party barely achieved its minimalist objectives with 13 seats.

Box 4.4   *Alexa McDonough's attacking comments illustrating the NDP's offensive marketing strategy, 2000 campaign*

- 'What Chrétien has done is to display unspeakable arrogance again and again' (*Globe & Mail*, 27 October).
- Alliance policies are 'mean-spirited . . . based on blame . . . based on hatred . . . based on the notion that it's each person for themselves' (*National Post*, 30 October).
- Chrétien is 'smug . . . arrogant . . . self-serving' (*Globe & Mail*, 20 November).
- Stockwell Day is 'a cockroach' (*Globe & Mail*, 24 November).

BQ: niche marketing   The BQ entered the 2000 campaign as a dying force. The Liberals had largely avoided the constitutional debates that had plagued the country under the Conservative Government and had led to the BQ's rise. Quebeckers' support for another sovereignty referendum had also been weakening in the late 1990s. In 1997, the BQ had lost seats under new leader Gilles Duceppe, and support for the party continued to slip in part because its niche market was smaller and because the party did not successfully redesign its offering. A harbinger of its waning relevance was the limited public outcry against the passage of the Clarity Act, which requires the involvement of the Supreme Court in any future sovereignty referendum. There were also elector frustrations with the BQ's sister party, the Parti Québécois, which was a tired provincial government. The BQ would have to be an aggressive SOP or the party would face a further erosion of seats.

In 2000, the BQ prepared a programme that was similar to 1997's and was devised through consultations with forty organisations (Bernard 2001). The party maintained its policy of refusing corporate donations; with only modest research capabilities, BQ strategists monitored issues that mattered to Quebec electors, and responded by promoting policy ideas that reflected provincial concerns (such as biker gang laws). The Liberals were the only federalist party with much relevance in the province, and so, while the rest of the country was considering a Liberal–CAP race, Quebeckers braced for another federalist–sovereigntist contest. During the campaign, BQ targeted Quebec nationalists in a flank attack marketing strategy that isolated those least likely to be federalist (box 4.5): for example, it ran French-only advertising that displayed electors expressing detachment from federal politics. Its blue-and-white colours (Quebec flag), when contrasted with the Liberals' red and white (Canadian flag), once again served as subliminal policy surrogates (Kucharsky 2000). But, with reduced public interest in the BQ's *raison d'être* of promoting another referendum on sovereignty, the party was somewhat directionless and lost a half-dozen seats.

Box 4.5   *Gilles Duceppe's attacking comments illustrating the BQ's offensive marketing strategy, 2000 campaign*

- Chrétien's career 'was built on thrashing and belittling Quebec' (*National Post*, 30 October).
- Chrétien's is 'the worst attitude' towards Quebec (*Ottawa Citizen*, 30 October).
- Chrétien has 'spent his career trying to diminish Quebec' (*Globe & Mail*, 8 November).

Difficulties translating UK practice to Canada

The POP–SOP–MOP framework is constructive for Canadian political study. Encouraging students of Canadian politics to look at inputs (such as using market intelligence to design a political product) rather than just outputs (promotion of the designed product) is fundamentally important in understanding political behaviour in the country. Some flexibility is evidently necessary with any typology, and the Canadian case suggests that in a multiparty first-past-the-post system it would be inefficient for all parties to be MOPs. In a classic two-party system, both can be MOPs because failure means forming the chief opposition. But the inability to translate votes into seats in a multiparty, single-member, simple plurality environment can mean cataclysmic failure. A clear example of this once again is the 1993 PCP, which by then was a tired MOP, and obtained just 2 seats on a 16 per cent vote share spread across the country. Conversely, in that election regionally segmented parties were able to concentrate their vote, and so a POP became the official opposition (the Quebec-based BQ won 54 seats on 14 per cent of the national vote). Meanwhile, the western Canada-based Reform Party earned 50 seats on 18 per cent of the vote. Similar results in the 1997 and 2000 elections demonstrate that some parties can be more successful as market segmenters than they would be as pure MOPs. It is the same in commerce. Corporate history is littered with examples of profitable sales-oriented niche businesses that went bankrupt attempting to overtake an established market leader. The Canadian political case shows that an electoral system can regularly result in exaggerated electoral rewards for a narrowly focused POP or SOP. There is room in the model to reflect the significant electoral advantages of not being a MOP.

A breakdown of each party's activities at each marketing stage in the 2000 Canadian election suggests that the parties can be cautiously slotted in to the Lees-Marshment typology. This provides a useful basis for discussion. Although the governing Liberals followed the eight-stage marketing process, theirs was a mass MOP which recognised that it could get re-elected with a sales campaign. The other three mainstream parties were confined by ideology and/or a lack of resources and so were primarily sales oriented. The CAP was able to finance its visible transformation from a segment MOP, but this makeover crumbled in the election campaign when it was revealed as a sales' operation. Conversely, the PCP was once a mass-market party, but nearly a decade removed from government was still too disorganised and cash-poor to present much even of a sales' campaign. The NDP was also financially restricted, but its use of market intelligence and ideological principles to target its market segment was a classic manoeuvre of a SOP. Conversely, one major party was a POP even though it attempted to move away from this orientation: the BQ sought to build on its softening niche market of Quebec nationalists by representing provincial interests as a whole; however, it was confined by its unique selling point of a separatist ideology. These examples show that slotting parties into the POP–SOP–MOP model is a useful, if subjective, exercise; they demonstrate also that being fully marketing oriented is difficult because failing at just one or two marketing stages disqualifies a party from being a MOP.

Difficulties or issues arising from the use of political marketing generally

It is not a problem so much as a reality check to learn that Canada's top political strategists were generally unfamiliar with the term 'political marketing'.[8] Even the most successful strategists considered the terminology to be academic language that ignores the multidimensional complexities of an election campaign. One high-profile pollster, for example, explained that Canadian political strategists 'would look at you sideways if you used the term'. This lack of awareness may simply suggest that Canadians use different vocabulary. Alternatively, it may help explain the narrow marketing orientation that can exist throughout a party organisation, because one indicator of the pervasiveness of a marketing philosophy is the extent to which senior and junior personnel embrace it. Indeed, Canadian parties' inner circles closely guarded their strategies and campaign staff tended to be informed of intelligence on a need-to-know basis. One Liberal strategist noted: 'Anybody else in the campaign follows orders . . . whether they buy into it or not, I couldn't give a damn'. The disparity between senior and junior ranks was exacerbated when the party caucus was populist, ideological or fundamentalist, because there was a greater likelihood of MPs believing that they intuitively understood their constituents' wants and needs. A pollster who transforms all party followers into holding a needs-oriented ideology would no doubt guide a more exemplary MOP than exists in Canada.

But there is the problem that political marketing is expensive and is the domain of only richer parties or candidates that already hold seats in the House. Financial challenges have long been a problem for major opposition parties in Canada (see Perlin 1988) and persist with the public subsidising of electioneering expenses. In the 2000 campaign, the Liberals benefited from considerably more free advertising than did their opponents, even though they also spent three times what the downtrodden PCP did (see table 4.1). The gap widens without such state subsidies. For example, each opposition party held at least one leadership convention since the Liberals formed government in 1993, but none of them matched the annual dollar value of contributions received by the market leader. Moreover, the Liberals' abrupt election call successfully thwarted the CAP's ability to continue its transformation into a MOP.

Organisational capacity for primary research does not always matter: recall that the PCP had focus-group tested the disastrous Chrétien 'face' ads in 1993. Nevertheless, one may consider the presence of political consultants as a barometer of the level of Canadian parties' political marketing activity. The governing party is

Table 4.1 *Liberals' broadcast and expenditure advantages, 2000 general election*

Party	Free broadcast ads (minutes)	Broadcast ads at lowest price (minutes)	Campaign expenditure limit ($)	Campaign expenditure as % of limit
Liberal Party	115	113	12,710,074	98.5
CAP	59.5	60	12,638,257	76.5
BQ	40	40	3,383,175	58.2
NDP	40	40	12,584,911	50.3
PCP	49	48	12,352,405	32.2

Source: Elections Canada data.

likely to employ throughout the legislative session a handful of commercial marketing specialists who are concerned primarily with information quality. An underfunded major party will retain, on short notice, a professional or two whose research is determined foremost by budget limitations and who regularly multitask (attending to daily internal issues). Bank loans and fundraising campaigns may take precedence over planning; moreover, the media polls that the governing party scoffs at may be a source of invaluable information for these less-wealthy parties. At the other extreme, for a minor fringe party it may be an accomplishment just to pay the party's campaign manager. Under such circumstances, it is difficult to imagine how these parties can compete with governing parties by restructuring their political product to meet the electorate's wants and needs.

Political marketing also begs some public policy attention because of weaknesses associated with the transfer of commercial practices to politics. This limitation has been discussed elsewhere (see, for instance, Scammell 1999), and the point is well taken that the media intensity, the brevity of the campaign, a winner-take-all environment, a fixed public decision day and public debate of governance issues are just some of the features that are peculiar to politics. In Canada, the 2000 campaign demonstrates that public policy changes are necessary to better control some of the negativity that occurs in the communication and campaign phases of the political marketing process. The parties are specifically exempted from commercial guidelines, such as the 'distasteful' provisions of the 'Canadian Code of Advertising Standards' which specifies that advertisements shall not 'demean, denigrate or disparage', 'discredit', 'attack', or 'exaggerate the nature or importance of competitive differences' (Advertising Standards Canada 2003). The absence of restrictions, combined with a lack of finance, may have the effect of dragging a potential MOP down to the level of the SOP.

Democratic implications of political marketing

An MOP is responsive to electors because, in many cases, responsiveness wins seats, and this type of party *should* better satisfy electors. My case study of Canadian parties in 2000 has, however, illustrated that if the only MOP is already in government then there is little pressure for that organisation to remain an MOP. An environment of multiple SOPs may turn nasty, because political actors have little incentive to avoid destroying an opponent's image or even the brand category. Market intelligence is not used to identify only benefits for electors, but also negative messages that can be used as part of a conflict marketing strategy. Attack offence and pre-emptive defence communications seem likely to prevail over kinder approaches, resulting in lower trust in politicians and increasing numbers of dissatisfied electors. Moreover, if SOPs seek primarily to weaken electors' confidence in their opponents as a means of selling their own product, there is a reduced ability to hold the winner accountable after the election.

As a result, the Liberal Party delivered a different type of product than that for which Canadians voted in 2000: it was market oriented insofar as the party continued to govern by making many decisions guided by opinion poll data, although a growing number of caucus and party members were vocal that the Liberals were reflecting Canadians' desire for leadership change – and product renewal. In 2000, Chrétien had managed to interrupt this dissent by calling an early election, but faced again with those pressures he announced in mid-2002 that he would retire by February 2004. This led to the architect of these internal rumblings, Paul Martin – Chrétien's former leadership rival and erstwhile finance minister – becoming the party leader in November 2003. In between, Chrétien uncharacteristically moved on a range of divisive legislation that was not discussed in the election campaign, such as the decriminalisation of small quantities of marijuana and the recognition of same-sex marriages. Although an activist product had been sorely lacking for some time, the party had received no specific mandate for such decisions, or for many of the policy changes introduced after Martin became prime minister in December 2003. All of this illustrates the trend that the longer a government goes unchallenged by another MOP, the further it can descend into a SOP, or even a POP, and the less democratic accountability exists for its decision-making. It also suggests that even for a successful governing party there are clear electoral benefits in being sales oriented rather than market oriented.

There are signs that the Liberal hegemony is waning unless Martin returns the party to being a MOP, and competitive pressures may force him to do so. Some dissident CAP MPs briefly formed a coalition with the PCP after the 2000 election, and by mid-2003 both parties had new leaders. The month before Martin became Liberal leader, CAP leader Stephen Harper and PCP leader Peter MacKay agreed in principle that their parties would merge into a new entity called the 'Conservative Party'. The Conservative Party once again presents a single government alternative to the Liberals and stands to reduce the success of the Liberals' SOP approach. There is also renewed vitality for the NDP, which has a new (more flamboyant) leader in Jack Layton, and the party should benefit from the Conservative realignment. All of this repositioning is more market oriented than has been seen since the 1993 campaign and it presents Canadians with seemingly better offerings.

The lone exception is Quebec, where the BQ has continued to strive for relevance since the 2000 vote. However, Paul Martin's Liberals were dogged in the first half of 2004 by a major scandal involving the misappropriation of government monies by Liberal-friendly Quebec advertising agencies. Support for the Liberals and the new prime minister declined in public opinion polls and, with increasing numbers of electors voicing a need for change, all three major opposition parties experienced bumps in support. By happenstance rather than by merit, the BQ suddenly led the Liberals in Quebec polling. The newfound support for a POP like the BQ is a reminder to political marketers that a public scandal can quickly trump the most professionalised of parties.

It appears that at least one more electoral cycle will be needed before an MOP alternative to the Liberals emerges. History suggests that this will be a more centralist Conservative Party that will have to attract disaffected BQ supporters. Until such a renewal occurs, the opposition parties will likely once again rely on guerrilla-style tactics that will draw all into conflict marketing. It also seems that, even after the liberal minority government outcome of the June 2004 election, political communicators and ideological slagbrains will generally continue to command more influence than will their political marketing counterparts.

Notes

1 The courts imposed some limits on parties' advertising spending in 1995 and restrictions on interest groups' campaign spending in late 2002.
2 Scheduled to increase to 308 seats in 2004.
3 The major difference was that Reform claimed the official opposition title from the BQ, while the NDP and the PCP regained official party status after winning slightly more than the minimum of twelve seats.
4 Although this case study does not scrutinise the minor parties, it should be noted that they appear to have passed through only three of the marketing stages (product design – campaign – election).
5 These 'values' tended to surround issues such as abortion (Marzolini 2001). However, Blais *et al.* (2002) have determined that within Quebec the value cleavage was sovereignty, and in the rest of Canada the value that most impacted voter choice was the free-enterprise system.
6 It is revealing that the NDP and the PCP strategists interviewed were completely unfamiliar with geo-demographic software.
7 Almost half (47 per cent) of Canadians believed this claim by the mid-point of the campaign (Adams 2000).
8 This is somewhat similar to what O'Cass (1996) found in Australia.

Bibliography

Adams, P. (2000), 'Liberals slip after debate as voters "take a look"', *Globe & Mail*, 13 November.
Advertising Standards Canada (2003), 'Canadian Code of Advertising Standards', available online: www.adstandards.com, accessed 7 August 2003.
Barney, D. D. (1996), 'Push-button populism: the Reform Party and the real world of teledemocracy', *Canadian Journal of Communication*, 21(3): 381–413.
Bernard, A. (2001), 'The Bloc Québécois', in J. H. Pammett and C. Dornan (eds), *The Canadian General Election of 2000*, Toronto: Dundurn Group: 139–48.
Bickerton, J., Gaguon, A. G. and Smith, P. (1999), *Ties that Bind: Parties and Voters in Canada*, Toronto: Oxford University, Press.
Blais, A., Gidengil, E., Nadeau, R. and Nevitte, N. (2002), *Anatomy of a Liberal Victory: Making Sense of the Vote in the 2000 Canadian Election*, Peterborough, Ontario: Broadview Press.
Cairns, A. C. (1968), 'The electoral system and the party system in Canada, 1921–1965', *Canadian Journal of Political Science*, 1: 55–80.
Carty, R. K., Cross, W. and Young, L. (2000), *Rebuilding Canadian Party Politics*, Vancouver: UBC Press.

Clarkson, S. (1988), 'The dauphin and the doomed: John Turner and the Liberal Party's debacle', in H. Penniman (ed.), *Canada at the Polls, 1984*, Durham, NC: Duke University Press: 97–119.

Clarkson, S. (2001), 'The Liberal threepeat: the multi-system party in the multiparty system', in J. H. Pammett and C. Dornan (eds), *The Canadian General Election of 2000*, Toronto: Dundurn Group: 13–57.

Ellis, F. and Archer, K. (1994), 'Reform: electoral breakthrough', in A. Frizzell, J. H. Pammett and A. Westell (eds), *The Canadian General Election of 1993*, Ottawa: Carleton University Press: 59–77.

Ellis, F. (2001), 'The more things change . . .: the Alliance campaign', in J. H. Pammett and C. Dornan (eds), *The Canadian General Election of 2000*, Toronto: Dundurn Group: 59–89.

Guy, J. J. (2001), *People, Politics and Government: A Canadian Perspective*, 5th edn, Toronto: Prentice-Hall.

Heinzl, J. (2000), 'Cheesy ads turn off the public', *Globe & Mail*, 18 November. A8.

Kline, S., Deodat, R., Shwetz, A. and Leiss, W. (1991), 'Political broadcast advertising in Canada', in F. J. Fletcher (ed.), *Election Broadcasting in Canada*, Ottawa: Royal Commission on Electoral Reform and Party Financing and Dundurn Press: 223–302.

Krause, R. (1989), 'The Progressive Conservative campaign: mission accomplished', in A. Frizzell, J. H. Pammett and A. Westell (eds), *The Canadian General Election of 1988*, Ottawa: Carleton University Press: 15–25.

Kucharsky, D. (2000), 'Bloc leads the ad charge in Quebec', *Marketing Magazine*, 20 November, 105(46): 4.

Land, B. (1965), *Eglinton: The Election Study of a Federal Constituency*, Toronto: Peter Martin Associates.

Lees-Marshment, J. (2001), *Political Marketing and British Political Parties*, Manchester: Manchester University Press.

Marland, A. (2003), 'Marketing political soap: a political marketing view of selling candidates like soap, of electioneering as a ritual, and of electoral military analogies', *Journal of Public Affairs*, 3(2): 103–15.

Marzolini, M. (2001), 'The politics of values: designing the 2000 Liberal campaign', in J. H. Pammett and C. Dornan (eds), *The Canadian General Election of 2000*, Toronto: Dundurn Group: 263–76.

Morley, J. T. (1988), 'Annihilation avoided: the New Democratic Party in the 1984 federal general election', in H. Penniman (ed.) *Canada at the Polls, 1984*, Durham, NC: Duke University Press: 120–36.

O'Cass, A. (1996), 'Political marketing and the marketing concept', *European Journal of Marketing*, 30(10–11): 45–61.

Perlin, G. (1988), 'Opportunity regained: the Tory victory in 1984', in H. Penniman (ed.), *Canada at the Polls, 1984*, Durham, NC: Duke University Press: 79–96.

Robinson, D. J. (1999), *The Measure of Democracy: Polling, Market Research, and Public Life 1930–1945*, Toronto: University of Toronto Press.

Scammell, M. (1999), 'Political marketing: lessons for political science', *Political Studies*, 47(4): 718–39.

Soderlund, W. C., Hildebrandt, K., Surlin, S. H. and Gosselin, A. (1999), 'Quantitative assessment of advertising effects: survey data', in W. I. Romanow, M. De Repentigny, S. B. Cunningham, W. C. Soderlund, and K. Hildebrandt (eds), *Television Advertising in Canadian Elections: The Attack Mode, 1993*, Waterloo, ON: Wilfried Laurier University Press: 117–31.

Spencer, D. (1994), *Trumpets and Drums: John Diefenbaker on the Campaign Trail*, Vancouver: Greystone Books.

Ward, I. (1999), 'The early use of radio for political communication in Australia and Canada', *Australian Journal of Politics and History*, 45(3): 311–30.

Whitehorn, A. (1989), 'The NDP election campaign: dashed hopes', in A. Frizzell, J. H. Pammett and A. Westell (eds), *The Canadian General Election of 1988*, Ottawa: Carleton University Press: 43–53.

Whitehorn, A. (1994), 'The NDP's quest for survival', in A. Frizzell, J. H. Pammett and A. Westell (eds), *The Canadian General Election of 1993*, Ottawa, Ontario: Carleton University Press: 43–58.

Whitehorn, A. (1997), 'Alexa McDonough and Atlantic breakthrough for the New Democratic Party', in A. Frizzell and J. H. Pammett (eds), *The Canadian General Election of 1997*, Toronto: Dundurn Press: 91–109.

Whitehorn, A. (2001), 'The 2000 NDP campaign: social democracy at the crossroads', in J. H. Pammett and C. Dornan (eds), *The Canadian General Election of 2000*, Toronto: Dundurn Group: 113–38.

Woolstencroft, P. (2001), 'Some battles won, war lost: the campaign of the Progressive Conservative party', in J. H. Pammett and C. Dornan (eds), *The Canadian General Election of 2000*, Dundurn Group: Toronto: 91–112.

5

Marketing the message or the messenger? The New Zealand Labour Party, 1990–2003

Chris Rudd

This chapter provides an in-depth case study of the New Zealand Labour Party and how it attempted to use political marketing to revive its flagging electoral fortunes in 1999 after suffering its worst election defeat since 1931. In 1993 the party's nationwide share of the vote fell further even though it increased it seats. It needed to act quickly, especially given the introduction of a new mixed-member proportional (MMP) electoral system later that year which would not award so many seats from a lower percentage vote share. The Labour Party did respond: in 1993 it selected a new leader, Helen Clark, the first woman to lead a major New Zealand political party. Clark lead the party to power in 1999, when it became the largest party in Parliament, forming a minority government,[1] and in July 2002 it further increased its vote share and seats. This chapter examines the party's response to defeat in 1990 and 1993 within the Lees-Marshment (2001a) political marketing framework, taking account of institutional and cultural differences between the New Zealand and the UK system from which the model is derived (Lees-Marshment 2001b: 220).

New Zealand's political market and the Labour Party

New Zealand has many similarities with Britain, and other countries, in terms of its overall political market environment, including significant demographic, social and economic changes since the Second World War. For example:

- an increase in the numbers of white-collar workers and a decline in the number of blue-collar workers;
- growing numbers of voters whose occupational status differs from that of their parents;
- increases in affluence and improvements in quality of life;
- the waning of class consciousness;
- better educated citizenry, particularly in terms of tertiary education;
- the emergence of television as the main source of information on politics;

- emergent issues such as those involving environmental preservation, promotion of women's equality, and multiculturalism;
- the breakdown of the traditional family structure, especially the growth in number of single-parent households and childless couples.

There has also been a weakening of party identification; a much weaker sociali-sation of partisanship from one generation to the next; and fewer of the electorate voting on the basis simply of social group membership. Voters are now more influenced by a party's position on issues, and by short-term factors such as the performance of leaders and the personality of the local candidate: the actual 'product' on offer. The electoral market is volatile, characterised by weak or non-existent party loyalties. By the mid-1990s New Zealand voters were 'nearly as likely to change their vote as to chose the same party again' (Aimer 1998: 51). At the 1999 election, 50 per cent of respondents to an election survey said that they made their decision about whom to vote for during the four-week campaign – 12 per cent on election day itself (Vowles 2002: 17–18).

The implications for New Zealand parties is that they can no longer take the loyalty of certain social groups for granted. The Labour Party's traditional core support group (the poor, low-income workers) has shrunk to the size of a bottom portion in a diamond-shaped social structure, which will not provide sufficient votes to maintain major party status or win power. Labour has therefore been forced to attract voters from the white-collar segment of society. However the material interests of more upwardly mobile voters vary and conflict, making it harder to craft a comprehensive product to attract a majority than it was in respect of the social group the party could traditionally rely on, a group which had more cohesive demands to satisfy.

Parties can respond to this situation in one of two ways. The first is to try to become more market-oriented, actively chasing voters through the design of a product in response to results from polls and focus groups. However, a party may find that there are so many potential markets, with conflicting and varied values and beliefs, that it is difficult to develop a coherent, detailed and credible policy programme to satisfy all of their demands. A party may therefore choose to empha-sise non-policy aspects of the product, such as the party as a whole ('unified', 'com-petent') and its leader ('trustworthy', 'honest'), that can appeal to a large market segment, and this could be the case in New Zealand.

While there are many apparent similarities between the two, there are a number of contextual differences between the New Zealand Labour Party under Helen Clark and the British Labour Party under Tony Blair, three of which are of partic-ular significance:

- *Ideological* When in government between 1984 and 1990, Labour had imple-mented a New Right policy programme that included a large-scale sale of state assets, downsizing and restructuring of the public sector, and extensive deregulation and liberalisation of the New Zealand economy. In contrast to the situation facing the British Labour Party of Kinnock, Smith and Blair, the New Zealand Labour Party leader had to reposition the party away from the extremist policies of the New Right, not those of the socialist left wing.

- *Re-establishing faith* The Centre-Right policies implemented in government had not been outlined in the pre-election manifestos. The Labour Party had to devise a marketing strategy to re-establish trust with voters and improve the credibility of its own politicians, not simply highlight weaknesses in the competing government in 1999.
- *The electoral system* New Zealand's proportional representation voting system, in place from the 1996 election, impacts on a party's campaigning strategy in two interrelated ways. First, smaller parties in particular are enticed into niche marketing: just 5 per cent of the party list vote is sufficient to win them parliamentary seats. Even large parties may choose not to appeal to a broad range of voters at the risk of aggressively invading the policy space of potential future coalition partners. This leads to the second constraint of a PR system – the need to form coalitions can necessitate a party sacrificing or at least de-emphasising policies that, while attractive to its own voters, are anathema to a potential coalition partner's voters.

Political marketing in New Zealand: a brief history

Up until the late 1970s, political marketing in New Zealand was very limited. New Zealand had a two-party system, the Labour and National Parties, and party polling and use of focus groups had yet to develop. It was not until the 1969 election that the *Otago Daily Times* (one of New Zealand's major metropolitan newspapers) carried a news story on polling during an election campaign. The two parties, Labour in particular, would be categorised as product oriented. Voting was strongly based on class, with two 'large and relatively unchanging blocks' of Labour and National voters 'facing each other across the electoral lines' (Chapman, Jackson and Mitchell 1962: 199). Labour was the party of manual workers, National of non-manual workers and farmers. However, changes in the political market environment, previously discussed, facilitated the rise of new issues in the 1970s that cut across the socio-economic divide, such as the women's movement, Maori nationalism, anti-nuclear protest and environmentalism. Parties had to be more active in identifying and appealing to a more fragmented electorate which encouraged the use of marketing.

In the 1969 election Labour utilised political marketing techniques, hiring the 'hotshot' advertising firm of MacHarman Associates of Auckland, which used new television-based communication methods and changed Labour's logo from the silver fern leaf to a simple graphic 'L'. In 1972 MacHarman commissioned a specialist market research agency and organised in-depth polling in two areas (the key marginal constituencies of Waitemata and Palmerston North) to discover voter concerns and then shape the campaign accordingly. Advertising in newspapers was also targeted for each regional audience and MacHarman designed the memorable slogan 'It's Time. For Labour.' One of the founders of MacHarman Associates, Bob Harvey, stated in an interview in 1973:

> We ... did a complete merchandising job just as if we were handling a commercial client selling, say cars. We sent out an election kit to each candidate . . . . We gave them hints on speeches, what type faces to use in their ads, how they should appear on television, how to have their photographs taken to best advantage, how to make hoardings and so on ... we merchandised the whole thing.[2]

Labour won the 1972 election, and this forced the National Party also to utilise political marketing. Advertising and market intelligence became a fixed part of New Zealand politics. A move to using marketing to influence the product came with the appointment by the National Party of an aggressive young communication firm, Colenso, for the 1975 and 1978 elections. Colenso attempted to find out what New Zealanders wanted prior to designing its product. Michael Wall, one of the founders of Colenso, put it thus:

> All the king's horses and all the king's admen can't put National together again. This will only happen if the boys in blue take a long, hard look at the political market. If they seek to honestly understand the real hopes and fears of the real New Zealanders. *And then rearrange their product to meet those needs.* (quoted in Misa 1987: 65, emphasis added)

Colenso initiated a giant 'listening-in' operation by which party members would go out and find what was worrying people and then frame policy to answer those fears. Questionnaires were used to find out the key issues in each electorate and candidates then wrote position papers outlining their stance on those local issues. Party workers would telephone electors likely to be interested in those issues (derived from the occupational classifications used in the electoral rolls) and explain to them the candidates' position on the issue. If voters were undecided, they would receive a call from the candidate in person.[3] Political marketing in its most comprehensive sense was therefore in New Zealand from 1978 onwards. The use of marketing intelligence has expanded since then, with Labour in 1984 investing heavily in sophisticated attitudinal lifestyle and trend research (Harvey 1992: 106); and in 1987 Labour committing 'sizeable funds into depth polls and qualitative research in order to formulate its key issue stances and advertising formats' (Denemark 1992: 165), while the National Party conducted in-depth interviewing and polling, focus-group research and targeted messages on unemployment, education and pensions. By the 1990 election the National Party had a new president who supported marketing techniques and identified them as a major factor in the party's 1990 victory (Collinge 1991).

The use of political marketing was not without problems: until the 1990s there was opposition to marketing techniques within both major parties; the cost of such techniques and advertising could not always be borne by all parties at all elections and party unity was important to the success of political marketing. If there is disagreement as to the message which is to be communicated as a result of depth interviewing or which groups are to be targeted, then the campaign will end up sending out mixed messages and fail to reach the targeted audiences. This is what happened to Labour in 1990 and to the National Party in 2002. A well-financed and unified party are prerequisite for a successful marketing campaign and it was this in particular that was so important to the revival of the electoral fortunes of the Labour Party under Helen Clark.

Redesigning the New Zealand Labour Party, 1990–2003

The case-study for this chapter now focuses on the use of political marketing by the Labour Party from its defeat in 1990 to later electoral success in producing the first female prime minister in New Zealand within an MMP electoral system. Information is taken from party documents and secondary sources, such as newspaper and magazine articles, and the focus is more on the period since Helen Clark became leader in 1993. It sets the party behaviour against the MOP model but in doing so highlights behaviour that diverges from this framework.

Stage 1   Market intelligence

Following the 1990 election defeat, the party's MPs embarked on internal market intelligence in a way similar to that adopted by the UK's Labour Party in the 1980s and by the Tories in 1997. The MPs initiated a 'Labour listens' process, circulating an 'Aims and values' document to party branches and regional conferences where it was extensively debated. From this came a new broad statement of principles that was endorsed at a full national conference. The process was internally therapeutic, 'drawing people back into the party who might have given up, and attracting some new people' (James 1991: 16–17). In 1993, Labour had established a working party on MMP consisting of extra-parliamentary and parliamentary representatives. The working party sent out questionnaires to all party branches to elicit their views on the process for selecting candidates for a reduced number of electorate seats (from 99 in 1993 to 65 in 1996 in a 120-seat Parliament), and for selecting and ordering the names on the party list. From the responses received, the working party drafted a report which again went out to the branches and regional conferences for discussion before final recommendations were put to the 1994 annual conference for approval. This lengthy process of consultation was in line with the efforts of the party leaders to be seen to be inclusive and to present a unified picture to the electorate at large.

External, the Labour Party began and has continued to use UMR Insight, arguably one of New Zealand's best polling organisations, adding questions to the monthly omnibus poll carried out by UMR to produce quantitative data and commissioning focus-group work for qualitative information on policy preferences and to pre-test words or phrases. Once in government after 1999, the Labour Party has continued to use UMR Insight to gauge public opinion, especially on controversial issues, such as how the Government should respond to the recommendation of the Royal Commission on Genetic Modification and the decision to send troops to Afghanistan in 2001 (O'Leary 2002: 196).

Following an election setback in 1996, Helen Clark redoubled her efforts to 'get out and meet the people'. In 1996–98 she toured the regions, speaking at a large number of meetings, and hammering home the message that Labour could be trusted and would create clear and deliverable promises. Helen Clark was particularly keen to re-establish links with Maori in response to the party's losing all five Maori seats (previously safe Labour seats) to New Zealand First at the 1996 election.[4] Her success in conveying this credibility message was measured by focus groups that perceived Helen Clark as likely to do what she said she would do.

Other market intelligence, in the form of polls, identified a new element in market demands. New Zealanders were looking for a 'positive' party, with 'vision', 'ideas' and did not engage in 'negative whingeing' or 'moaning'. In a 1997 interview Clark said: 'I think we have to communicate that Labour is the party of the big picture, the big ideas for the [twenty-first] century. That it is an outward-looking party. That it wants New Zealand to do well in the global economy . . . ' (quoted in Ralston 1997: 133). This outlook informed Labour's communication, as it ran a positive inter-election campaign, ignoring rather than attacking the opposition. Other market intelligence results informed the development of policies, as will be discussed under stages 2–3 below.

Market intelligence has been continued even after a second successive election victory in 2002. Clark has been assiduous in ensuring that the party does not become distant from its core voters again. In March 2003, Clark and other ministers made visits to various Maori tribal organisations to 'find out what was happening in Maori communities'.[5] These visits were also conducted to ensure that local communities became more aware of the Government's initiatives.[6]

Stages 2–3   Product design and adjustment
In Lees-Marshment's model product design and product adjustment are treated as two distinct stages in the marketing process. In practice, it can be difficult to separate the two stages, given the extent to which they interact, and for the purposes of this chapter both are analysed in this one section.

Party organisation   Re-organisation in various forms was an important founding activity for the party to succeed in using political marketing and regaining office. Labour suffered internally from party conflict. During both its previous period in government (1987–90) and its first period out of office (1990–93), there was significant and acrimonious dissent and debate in response to the New-Right policies of the fourth Labour Government. Members felt the parliamentary party had discarded traditional values, had ridden roughshod over the wishes of the trade union affiliates in particular but also the party at large, and a division between left and right wings became very apparent in the candidate selection process in a way similar to what happened in the UK Labour Party in 1979–83.

Helen Clark worked to heal these divisions both as deputy leader in 1989 (Myers 1989: W3) and overall leader from 1990 onwards. Party conferences became much more unified and manageable – a far cry from the acrimonious conferences of the late 1980s and early 1990s. The party presidency had previously been a 'politicised' position, with occupants coming from the left wing of the party (Jim Anderton, in

1979–84) and/or representing the union movement (Rex Jones, in 1987–88) or the feminist movement (Margaret Wilson, in 1984–87; Ruth Dyson, in 1988–93; Maryan Street, in 1993–95) in contrast to the three most recent party presidents: Michael Hirschfeld (1995–99) was a millionaire businessman; Bob Harvey (1999–2000), founder of an advertising agency; and Mike Williams (2000–) who set up two companies dealing with direct mail and market research.

The party also streamlined its organisation to make it more effective and efficient; there was a centralising of administrative tasks to head office, such as membership and fee collection, and a strengthening of the links between the party executive and the leader's office. Resources for the leader's office were increased as the leader took more professional policy advice.

The process of selecting candidates was reformed: the constitution was changed after 1990 to ensure that voting rights were given only to people who actually turned up to monthly meetings, and the trade unions were no longer given a block vote, making the process more representative of the wider market. Training of candidates was improved and provided on areas such as party policy and campaigning techniques, particularly important after the introduction of the new MMP electoral system in which the performance of candidates in all electorates would be relevant and not just candidates in the marginal electorates as under the first-past-the-post system.

Policies   In 1993, the Labour Party drew up its first strategic plan with the help of business experts. Six corporate objectives were included in the plan, and performance on them was regularly assessed. The results of market intelligence helped the party flesh out the details of policy in certain key areas identified as of particular importance to voters. In-house polling showed that a major concern of voters was the insecurity and uncertainty surrounding issues such as health, pensions, jobs, and law and order. These poll findings were fed directly into the planning of the policy pledges that appeared on a 'credit card' (see below).

In response to market intelligence results, however, the party placed greater emphasis on changing the presentation of policies than on the policies themselves. This suggests that the problem was perceived to be the messenger rather than the message. The party placed greatest emphasis on trying to convince voters of its credibility and trustworthiness. Helen Clark and her advisers combined the refining and redefining of party policies with a strategy of repositioning the party and re-establishing its credibility.

As regards repositioning, Clark lost no opportunity to identify Labour as a Centre-Left party: 'Labour didn't start as a party of the Centre, it has no desire to be a party of the Centre. You can call it a party of the Centre Left . . . its traditions lie in the desire of working men and women' (Legat 1994: 133). Unsurprisingly, perhaps, the New Zealand Labour Party, like its British counterpart, also jumped on the 'Third Way' bandwagon, and Helen Clark with some of her senior ministers and policy advisers have been identified as Third Way advocates.[7] For the 1998 annual conference, the party brought over Robert Reich to promote the Third Way concept.

Regarding the desire of the electorate for stability and credibility, Clark stated that she would lead a government with an achievable set of policies – no surprises, no further restructuring, no more policy blitzkriegs as in the 1980s. During the 1999 campaign the Labour Party pushed this theme and offered a few clear-cut promises that could be kept. Hence the credit card – a gimmick borrowed from the UK Labour Party – which contained seven pledges (see box 5.1).[8]

Box 5.1   *New Zealand Labour Party's credit-card pledges in 1999*

- Create jobs through promoting New Zealand industries and better support for exporters and small business.
- Focus on patients not profit and cut waiting times for surgery.
- Cut the cost to students of tertiary education, starting with a fairer loans' scheme.
- Reverse the 1999 cuts to superannuation rates. Guarantee superannuation in the future by putting a proportion of all income tax into a separate fund which *cannot* be used for any other purpose.
- Restore income related rents for state housing so that low income tenants pay no more than 25 per cent of their income in rent.
- Crack down on burglary and youth crime.
- No rise in income tax for 95 per cent of taxpayers earning under $60,000 a year. No increases in GST (i.e VAT) or company tax.

The 1999 pledges indicate that the party engaged in achievability and targeting. The pledges were designed to be easy to implement or were worded in such terms that it would be relatively easy to produce evidence of their delivery and to suit the target markets to which the Labour Party was trying to appeal. Pledge 1, on government assistance to business, for example, was clearly designed to address the business community's known apprehension about the prospects of a Centre-Left government, though it was unhappy with the rather dogmatic non-interference approach of the opposition National Party. Pledges 2–5 concerned social welfare, which polling showed was of major concern not just to disadvantaged and low-income groups but to middle-income New Zealanders. The tough stance on crime (pledge 6) had overtones of Blair's 'Tough on crime, tough on the causes of crime', and reflected Clark's own judgement that this is what wage-worker voters wanted even though many Labour MPs had reservations over such a hard-line stance (James 2001: 204).[9] The final pledge, on taxation, also indicates an element of competition analysis and differentiation. The tax increases affected very few voters and, not surprisingly, did not raise that much extra revenue. Nor did the tax increases go anywhere near to off-setting the tax cuts that had occurred in the 1980s under the fourth Labour Government and in the 1990s under the National Party. But it was symbolically a very important pledge, given that it helped set Labour apart from its main rival, the National Party, which was proposing *cutting* taxes even further.

This effort at product differentiation was part of the repositioning of the party away from the New Right and ensuring that the Old Left (which wanted substantial tax increases) did not out-flank the party. There was a link to the credibility issue here, with Labour arguing that its proposed modest increases in spending on, for example, health were fiscally responsible, as they would be funded by the tax increases. Incidentally, the tax issue also reflects the sales-oriented approach of Labour. There was little or no evidence that voters desired this policy; rather Labour decided that it would be an issue and aggressively marketed it to a largely indifferent electorate.

The perceived desire for *security* was tied into other Labour policies that did not appear on the credit card but were well debated in the campaign. In particular, there was Labour's promise to re-establish the recently ended monopoly of a state agency over workplace accident insurance, and to repeal the 1991 Employment Contracts Act, which many felt gave too much of an advantage to employers in the field of industrial relations. On this latter point, however, it should be added that Labour did not intend to return to the status quo ante of compulsory unionism, which again reflected its aim of not appearing to lurch to the Left or appear anti-business.

One issue that did not appear on the credit card, and may not have been an election issue as such, was the *nationhood* theme. Polling had shown that the general public was receptive to efforts to promote New Zealand's national identity. Clark made clear her desire to push for more local content on television to promote New Zealand arts and culture (she adopted the portfolio of Arts, Culture and Heritage herself on becoming prime minister). She maintained strong links with organisations such as the Returned Servicemen's Association and during her first year in office made high-profile overseas trips with war veterans to Gallipoli, in Turkey, to commemorate the eighty-fifth anniversary of the First World War Australian and New Zealand Army Corps' landings (the first New Zealand prime minister ever to be at Gallipoli on ANZAC Day) and to Crete for the sixtieth anniversary of the Second World War Battle of Crete.[10]

Leadership   Helen Clark was elected leader by her fellow Labour MPs in December 1993 as someone who could build bridges between the caucus and party organisation, was relatively untainted by the 'rogernomics' that had lost Labour credibility, and was also perceived as the best person to deal with the Alliance and its leader Jim Anderton. While this satisfied internal demands, initially her qualities were much less apparent to the electorate at large. In the months before the 1996 election, Clark was viewed as the preferred prime minister by only 3 per cent of the electorate polled. As one commentator put it, she was seen as a 'childless former academic, political scientist, partner in a DINK marriage to a medical school lecturer, urban liberal, labelled a dilettante socialist . . .' (Roger 1996: 48). Unusually for a party leader, Clark was aware of her image problem and took steps in 1996 to find a solution.

In early 1996 she appointed Mike Munro as her chief press secretary. He was instrumental in helping Helen Clark overcome the suspicion and hostility she had often shown to the media (Clark presented a cold and stilted image on television). During July and August 1996 (and again for the 1999 election) she made use of media trainers Brian Edwards and Judy Callingham. In July she appointed Maggie Eyres, a former artistic director, to be her press officer in Auckland. Eyres revamped the visual image of Helen Clark prior to the 1999 election 'with airbrushed, soft-focus billboards publicly displaying the Labour leader with straightened teeth, heightened cheekbones and just-emerged-from-the-salon hair' (Coddington 2001: 65).

In government she developed a close relationship with the media by the end of her first year, even taking calls from journalists personally, particularly when at home on Sunday afternoons, in order to influence 'the agenda for Monday morning newspapers' (Wellwood 2001, 9). Clark also reinstated formal post-Cabinet press conferences on Monday afternoons and handled them very effectively. By the half-way point in her first term of office, Helen Clark became the most popular New Zealand leader of the modern age.

Stage 4   Implementation

After nearly a decade in opposition and having come agonisingly close to forming a government in 1996, there was a certain degree of pragmatic acceptance within the party of Helen Clark's cautious approach to policy. While the union movement had hoped for a more decisive rejection of the existing industrial relations framework, it had no wish to jeopardise the opportunity to remove the Centre-Right parties from power. More radical demands of the unions regarding paid parental leave and longer statutory holidays for workers were not pushed at this time. Rank-and-file members were also willing to acquiesce to the Third Way as a compromise necessary to both heal divisions within the party and to neutralise potential media hostility over any appearance of a lurch to the Left. However, there is no evidence to suggest that 'new-look Labour' attracted new members or did anything to win back members who had left during the latter half of the 1980s. Implementation was effective at the national level but was perhaps not as effective at lower levels of the party.

Stage 5   Communication

Overall, the 1999 campaign of Helen Clark and the Labour Party was a 'no surprises' undertaking. Two months before the 1999 election date the Labour Party 'tested its campaign committee meeting, media-monitoring, communications, and theme coordinating systems, with senior spokespeople and selected backbenchers campaigning on designed themes around the country' (James 2001: 204). Policies were clearly set out well before the official campaign began. The key policy planks were understandable, credible and achievable. The image put forward was of a stable and united party, one that could be trusted, and one that had a moderate policy agenda – voters wanted change but not radical change, as had been experienced in the past. After the election, Clark reiterated this point when she said of her newly formed government: 'it's got to be a government of moderate change. They've voted for a correction' (quoted in Ralston 2000: 57).

Internal communications were also improved and have helped to create the image of a unified party. The adoption of new technology may be a contributing factor to improved internal communications. The Labour Party president claimed that an 'e-mail project' begun in 2000 had by 2003 provided the party organisation with the e-mail address and online details of 40 per cent of party members.[11] The Labour Youth movement has been a major user of online meetings, though the expectation is that it will be a tool available to all members in having a say on policy-making, especially for those living in rural areas where opportunities for face-to-face meetings are infrequent.

Stage 6   Campaign

The 1993 campaign was witness to a number of incidents that suggested there was still disunity within the party, even if it was less prevalent than before. For example, there were the conflicting statements over taxation made by David Lange (the former party leader) and Mike Moore (the then leader). There were other incidents of candidates from the party's right wing making statements that went against official party policy. The 1996 campaign, while not totally free of internal conflict, was much more of a unified campaign, reinforced by the strong showing of party leader Helen Clark. Unity was extremely high for the 1999 election, exemplified by the 1998 annual conference, at which there was no evidence of factional battles, no controversial remits from the floor, and the election members to several party positions were uncontested.

Although the party used the latest in computerised information exchange in 1999, the main campaign was run around traditional activities such as door-knocking, street-corner meetings and billboards. These are not normally the features associated with a market-oriented party, and they reinforce the impression that the Labour Party in New Zealand has some way to go before it resembles its UK counterpart. Clark, did however, appear in a series of 'Labour is Listening' television advertisements in which she acted as confidante to a number of disadvantaged groups. This culminated in her closing television address on 26 November 1999 when she stated that 'everyone's telling me it's time for a change' (quoted in Ralston 2000: 57).

One final point needs to be mentioned regarding the 1999 campaign. Unlike what happened in the lead-up to the 1996 campaign, the Labour Party and the party of the Old Left, the Alliance, publicly agreed in August 1998 that they would be prepared to form a coalition after the election. Helen Clark had even been invited to attend and speak at the Alliance annual conference in 1998. Both parties had declared that the difference between them was more 'of degree than direction', and this had important consequences for the marketing strategy of the Labour party during the 1999 campaign. In particular, with the Alliance as a potential coalition partner, Labour was able to present itself as a viable alternative government in waiting, something that may have been crucial in winning over wavering supporters.

Stage 7   Election

The image-making and media training of Helen Clark were seen to bear fruit at the 1996 election. Her performance during the leaders' debates is credited by some as instrumental in boosting the support for the Labour Party. In a pre-Christmas poll in 1998, Clark was found to be ahead of the National Party leader on all personality characteristics, including capability, honesty, earthiness and ability to relate to others. This was a significant turnaround of a leader who had been criticised for lacking the common touch.

During the 1999 election campaign, Clark was again seen to do well in the televised leaders' debates. She appeared relaxed and seemed to enjoy the debates, while demonstrating articulateness and grasp of detail (Harris 2000: 81). Most importantly, Clark managed to convey the impression that she and the Labour Party were ready to govern.

At the outset of the 2002 election campaign, Labour was riding so high in the opinion polls that it looked quite possible that the party could win a majority in its own right. All Helen Clark had to do, it seemed, was to conduct another 'no surprises' campaign, this time with the bonus of being able to claim, with some justification, that her Government had delivered on its promises. During the campaign, the party set up a 'virtual Millbank' modelled on the UK Labour Party's media machine housed in Millbank Tower near the House of Commons. Staff had the task of monitoring newspaper, radio and television reports with the aim of 'rebutting damaging claims' before they could gain currency.[12] A similar set-up had existed for the 1999 campaign.

However, the 2002 campaign did produce some surprises for Labour, and highlighted the dangers of focusing the party's campaign around the prime minister and her credibility. First, during week two of the campaign Clark walked out of an interview with an ABC TV reporter.[13] A few days later she reacted angrily during an interview on New Zealand TV about an alleged government cover-up of genetically modified corn being grown in New Zealand.[14] It was widely reported in the media that she subsequently described the interviewer as a 'little creep', and when later reminded of this said: 'The only thing I regret is that I didn't add the word sanctimonious as well.' Clark also publicly denigrated the leaders of nearly all the opposition parties during the campaign, including the spouse of one of the leaders. Finally, during the televised leaders' debates she at times descended to patronising laughter when her opponents were speaking. Overall Helen Clark's poor campaign performance undoubtedly contributed to her party's slide in the polls from 52 per cent at the start of the campaign to just 43 per cent on the eve of the election, while as preferred prime minister Clark had slipped from 53 per cent to 41 per cent. Fortunately for her and Labour, the main opposition party ran a woeful campaign and the vote for the parties to the Left of Labour collapsed.

Stage 8   Delivery

In a way strikingly similar to the UK Labour Party, the New Zealand Labour Party made vigorous efforts to persuade the electorate that it was keeping its election promises. In red bold letters on the credit card containing the seven pledges was written 'WE WILL DELIVER.' Helen Clark was careful to set out a modest and achievable programme, and took every opportunity during her first year in office to stress that that there would be 'no surprises, no ambushes . . . and no hidden agenda'. In an interview in February 2000, Clark stated that 'this government is getting on with what it said it would do. We were open about it. There was no secret agenda. There is no secret agenda. What you see is what you get, and this going to be the style of this government.'[15] In an interview in August 2001 she stressed: 'we have delivered on every core pledge we made. We have delivered and we will keep delivering' (quoted in Quaintance 2001: 51).

The 1999–2002 Government issued progress reports, the first of which, after one year in office, was entitled 'Key achievements in government' and said on its cover: 'it was time for a change . . . and we are delivering that change. We gave our word that we would deliver our commitments to you and your family.' One year after its 2002 re-election, the Government made available on its website a thirty-five-page document which detailed the 'Key achievements of the Labour–Progressive Coalition'.

Delivery was communicated also to members. At the time of the 2001 budget, a message from Helen Clark to party members read: 'Keeping our Word. We continue to deliver on our commitment card pledges.' On the party's website one could download a 'Helen Clark MP reports' newsletter highlighting the achievements of the Government. The website also contained Labour ch@t that allowed visitors to the site to ask an MP or Labour Party member a question, the recipient of which endeavoured to respond online in as close to real time as possible. Another four-page glossy newsletter available from the party headquarters in Wellington was entitled 'Labour Leader . . . We're keeping our word'. At the local level MPs also made known to members the Government's achievements through monthly newsletters.

The Labour Party placed great store in showing that it had a pact with the people and that, unlike previous administrations, it was not going to betray that trust. It deliberately set out modest and realistic goals, ensuring their delivery and thus trying to restore faith and confidence in government once more. In her address at the opening of Labour's 2002 election campaign Clark stated that 'last election we made specific pledges we were determined to keep. I'm proud to say, we kept our word on every single one of them.' She went on to detail each pledge, how the Government had delivered on them and what new commitments Labour was making for a second term in office.

It was interesting to see that the party had made some effort to ensure that its junior coalition partner during 1999–2002, the Alliance, was able to claim credit for certain policies. The two most prominent examples of this were the establishment of the 'People's Bank' as a subsidiary of New Zealand Post and the introduction of paid parental leave. Helen Clark went on record as saying that Labour had to 'make room' for the Alliance and acknowledge that the Alliance was 'entitled to visibility and credit where it's due' (quoted in Clifton 2000: 22).

The obvious problem with having such a modest policy programme is what you do *after* you have 'delivered'. Fortunately, with a short electoral cycle of just three years (and even then the 2002 election was called five months early), the Labour Party was able to complete its first term without giving the appearance of having run out of ideas or pledges to fulfil.

Throughout the second term of office, the Labour Government continued to invest time and energy in its efforts to appear to be an administration that was delivering. After the July 2002 election, a government Communications Unit, the so-called 'Burns Unit', was set up, headed by former newspaper editor Brendan Burns. With a budget of over $300,000 and a full-time staff of five, the main aim of the unit was to 'tailor news to the plethora of lightly staffed provincial and community media outlets in the hope they [would] run "straight" detailed, localised stories overlooked by the cynical lens of the parliamentary press gallery'.[16] A specific idea was for the unit to organise a Smart Growth Day in May 2003 (or 'Day of Spin', according to the opposition parties). Thirty-eight Labour MPs fanned out across the country and handed out a total of $4.75 million to various organisations and businesses identified as making a sustained contribution to the economy.

The danger of setting the achievement of specific goals as a benchmark by which to judge the Government obviously occurs when a government fails to deliver – or in this case, changes its mind about the achievability of a publicised goal. In 2001 Helen Clark had announced the Government's intention to move New Zealand into the top half of the OECD economic league table by 2011 – a vague enough promise and one for which Clark is unlikely to be accountable when judgement day arrived. Yet when Clark fudged the issue as to whether such a goal was feasible in the time-frame set, she came under heavy criticism from other parties and she showed her sensitivity to such criticism for not keeping a promise made.[17]

Conclusions

The overall strategy of the Labour Party from 1990 onwards, but in particular since Helen Clark became leader in December 1993, was to

- overcome the distrust left by the actions of governments and parties since 1984;
- promise little but ensure such promises were kept and make sure voters were aware of this;
- heal divisions within the party; and
- if not to destroy the Alliance as a rival for the Left vote, then at least heal the rift with the Left–Alliance, ultimately achieving the former in the run-up to the 2002 election.

A reflection of Clark's success was succinctly put in an article written just prior to the July 2002 election:

[U]nder Helen Clark, Labour is not an easy target, because it has dispelled the criticisms routinely levelled at it in the past: that it can't manage the economy; that it is beholden to trade union bosses and to its own loony idealists; that it tends to be stupidly ideological and riven by internal conflict. (Campbell 2002, 22)

Comparatively there are remarkable similarities between the experiences of the New Zealand and the UK Labour Party, and this notwithstanding the significant differences in their respective political systems. This suggests that the Lees-Marshment model applies equally well to multiparty as to two-party systems. The New Zealand case does, however, raise some points that are worth keeping in mind in future research in this area. First, it may be that a party cannot be neatly categorised as product, sales or market oriented. At times, an *amalgam* of the sales- and market-oriented models suggests itself. On the one hand, it is clear that on certain major issues, the Labour Party was not poll-driven but instead offered leadership up-front. The main illustration of this was the Labour–Alliance's decision to become more proactive in economic development.[18] In other areas, polling and focus groups may have played a much greater role in raising issues such as cutting hospital waiting lists, reducing the costs of tertiary education, tougher sentencing and stricter immigration controls. Therefore, rather than asking whether a party is product sales or market oriented, it maybe more fruitful to ask what combination of product-, sales- or market-oriented principles reside in a party's marketing strategy at any one period.

A second point to be emphasised is that, when discussing the extent to which a party may follow voter demands, what voters demand may be an intangible, such as strong or trustworthy leadership, rather than a specific policy *per se*. This is certainly provided for within Lees-Marshment's model, but it is worth stressing the point. A market-oriented party following voters' demands for strong, reliable leadership, as was the case with the New Zealand Labour Party 1990–2002, may use tactics that look very much like the spin-doctoring to be expected of a sales-oriented party. Although the original motivations may differ across the two party models, what they actually do to sell their leaders can appear quite similar.

Finally, the nature of the party system may have an impact on the political marketing strategy that a party pursues. In a two-party system – of which there are now few examples – it may be rational/efficient for both parties to adopt a catch-all appeal and use a market-oriented approach to win the all-important 'middle ground'. However, in a multiparty system there are often parties located towards the end of a Left–Right spectrum. The *raison d'être* of such parties is the 'principled' position – the leaders have a 'faith' in their product and are not prepared to 'follow' public opinion. For such niche parties, a product orientation makes sense – perhaps for a minor party even a sales-oriented approach maybe a desirable option if the party does not seek to challenge one of the major parties (see Collins and Butler 1996). However, an important point to note is that there is no logical reason why product- or sales-oriented parties will not make full use of modern marketing techniques: polling, focus groups, use of symbols and logos to develop a brand image, use of electronic newsletters, e-mail, chat rooms and so forth. The *aim* of such techniques may differ – to reinforce and mobilise, for the product-oriented party; to persuade and convert, for the sales-oriented party; to identify and react, for the market-oriented party – but the techniques themselves bear striking similarity.

Notes

1 Electoral 'victory' is less clear under a proportional representation electoral system than it was under first-past-the-post. In 1996, for example, it was widely expected that Labour would form a coalition government with the small Centre party New Zealand First, even though Labour was not the largest party. However, New Zealand First surprised everyone by agreeing to go with the Centre-Right National Party. In 1999, the Labour Party was the largest party and was able to form a minority coalition with the Alliance (with the Greens offering support on confidence issues).

2 Quoted in an interview with the editor of *Management*, 'The Labour Party's 1972 election advertising campaign' (January 1973): 6.

3 Misa 1987: 65.

4 Since 1867 New Zealand has had a number of parliamentary seats for MPs representing the Maori race. This number was fixed a 4 until the 1990s since when it has increased to 7 (for the 2002 election) in line with the increase in the number of Maori choosing to register on the Maori electoral roll.

5 *Evening Standard*, 12 March 2003.

6 Noted by Clark in *Dominion POST*, 21 March 2003.

7 Chris Eichbaum and Peter Harris both became ministerial advisers in the 1999–2002 Labour–Alliance Government. Earlier they had edited a volume entitled *The New Politics: A Third Way for New Zealand*. Steve Maharey (minister of Social Services and Employment) and Phil Goff (minister of Foreign Affairs and Justice) have been identified as 'Third Wayers'.

8 The similarity with the UK Labour Party's 'ten-point contract with the people' launched for the 1997 election is not coincidental. There is a regular exchange of ideas between the two parties, with frequent visits by senior members of each party to each other's election campaigns.

9 The New Zealand Labour Party came out again with a credit card in 2002 listing seven pledges and titled 'The next steps . . . our commitments to you' although its impact the second time around was limited, especially as the opposition parties parodied it. New Zealand First issued its 'Stop the rot' debit card which listed Labour Party 'promises they're not telling you about'; ACT launched its election credit card which listed the 'facts, not the spin' of Labour's seven pledges; and the Alliance labelled it 'Labour's pledge to National voters' because Labour had to tried to attract National Party supporters.

10 After the 2002 election Helen Clark attended the sixtieth anniversary commemorations of the second battle of El Alamein in Egypt.

11 *Otago Daily Times*, 1 April 2003: 21.

12 'The worker bees', *Dominion*, 29 June 2002: 1–2.

13 The ABC reporter had raised the issue of the prime minister having signed a painting she did not paint for a charity auction. This became know as 'paintergate', and although the issue had come to light well before the election campaign the police investigation into the 'fraud' was concluded and reported on during the campaign itself.

14 Currently there is a moratorium on field trials for genetically modified crops.

15 Quoted in *MG Business*, 21 February 2000: 8

16 Vernon Small, ' "Burns unit" latest political spin doctoring move', *Otago Daily Times*, 14–15 September 2002: A10.

17 This was seen in her uncharacteristic and unexpected attack on business leaders at a Knowledge Wave conference in March 2003. Business leaders had let it be known that

they were keen to stick with the commitment made by Clark – adding to her discomfort on this issue.

18 Examples of this were the Government's setting up of a new private sector-oriented agency (Industry New Zealand), the launching of a Regional Partnership Programme and financial backing for a New Zealand Venture Investment Fund.

Bibliography

Aimer, P. (1998), 'Old and new party choices', in J. Vowles, P. Aimer, S. A. Banducci and J. A. King, *Voters' Victory: New Zealand's First Election under Proportional Representation*, Auckland: Auckland University Press: 48–64.

Chapman, R., Jackson, W.K. and Mitchell, A. V. (1962), *New Zealand Politics in Action: The 1960 General Election*, London: Oxford University Press.

Collins, N. and Butler, P. (1996), 'Positioning political parties: a market analysis', *Harvard International Journal of Press/Politics* 1(2): 63–77.

Campbell, Gordon (2002), 'Out for the count?', *Listener*, 29 June: 22–4.

Clifton, Jane (2000), 'The end of the beginning', *Listener*, 16 December: 18–23.

Collinge, J. (1991), 'The National Party: tactics and strategies', in E. M. McLeay (ed.), *The 1990 General Election: Perspectives on Political Change in New Zealand*, Occasional Publication No. 3, Wellington: Victoria University Press.

Coddington, Deborah (2001), 'Spinning, spinning, spinning', *North and South* (November): 61–70.

Denemark, D. (1992), 'New Zealand: the 1987 campaign', in S. Bowler and D. Farrell (eds), *Electoral Strategies and Political Marketing*, London, Macmillan.

Eichbaum, C. and Harris, P. (eds) (1999), *The New Politics: A Third Way for New Zealand*, Palmerston North: Dunmore Press.

Harris, S. (2000), 'Follow the leaders', in J. Boston, S. Church, S. Levine, E. McLeay and N. Roberts (eds), *Left Turn: The New Zealand General Election of 1999*, Wellington: Victoria University Press: 77–88.

Harvey, B. (1992), 'Inventing the truth', in M. Comrie and J. McGregor (eds), *Whose News?* Palmerston North: Dunmore Press: 101–10.

James, C. (1991), 'Labour: getting ready to govern', *Management* (October): 16–17.

James, C. (2001), 'Campaigning', in Ray Miller (ed.), *New Zealand Government and Politics*, Auckland: Oxford University Press: 196–212.

King, A. (ed.), *Leaders' Personalities and the Outcomes of Democratic Elections*, Oxford: Oxford University Press.

Lees-Marshment, J. (2001a), 'The marriage of politics and marketing', *Political Studies*, 49(4): 692–713.

Lees-Marshment, J. (2001b), *Political Marketing and British Political Parties*, Manchester and New York: Manchester University Press.

Legat, N. (1994), 'Helen Clark', *Metro* (September): 132–4.

McMillan, N. (1999), 'Personality, style may decide leader', *MG Business*, 18 January: 10–11.

Misa, T. (1987), 'All the politicians' Men', *North and South* (August): 56–71.

Mughan, Tony (2000), *Media and the Presidentialization of Parliamentary Politics*, Basingstoke: Palgrave.

Myers, V. (1989), 'Meet a woman of substance', *National Business Review*, 27 October: W3 and W17.

Norris, P. (2000), *Virtuous Circle*, New York: Cambridge University Press.

O'Leary, Eileen (2002), 'Political spin', in J. McGregor and M. Comrie (eds), *What News?* Palmerston North: Dunmore Press: 186–98.

Quaintance, L. (2001), 'The prime of Miss Helen Clark', *North and South* (August): 48–58.

Ralston, Bill (1997), 'Politics', *Metro* (August): 132–3.

Ralston, Bill (2000), 'Making of a Prime Minister', *Metro* (January): 50–7.

Roger, W. (1996), 'Helen Clark and the dead cat effect', *Metro* (February): 46–55.

Vowles, J. (2002), 'Did the campaign matter?', in J. Vowles *et al.* (eds), *Proportional Representation on Trial*, Auckland: Auckland University Press: 16–33.

Wellwood, E. (2001), 'Helen shows she's press conference queen', *The Press*, 21 March: 9.

6

Political marketing in Irish politics: the case of Sinn Féin

Sean McGough

This chapter examines the extent to which Sinn Féin has adapted business-marketing concepts and techniques in order to further its political ends in Ireland. The success of Sinn Féin in the Irish Dail elections of 2002 has surprised and confounded many political analysts. The analysis explores whether such success is based on a marketing strategy which Sinn Féin believes will help it win political power and eventually lead to the party gaining majority rule in a thirty-two county Ireland. Many hope this new political behaviour is a confirmation of the end of the links with terrorism and a promise of a future based on peaceful and democratic strategies. Sinn Fein is also an interesting case for political-marketing analysis because while it has moved from a POP, using its ideological purity as the focus of its political appeal to members and voters, to a SOP and being sufficiently aware of the modern electoral arena to recognise the need for contemporary political salesmanship, this does not mean it is heading towards a MOP identity. The MOP is a different political animal from the other types of party, as it depends on the electorate for its ideological and political direction, whereas Sinn Féin continues to follow its own ideological drive. Nevertheless, it is professionalising its election strategy and has adapted tactics of political marketing.

The Irish political context and Sinn Féin

Ireland was partitioned into two separate states by the Better Government of Ireland Act (1920). The six counties of Northern Ireland remained part of the UK, although it was governed under a devolved Stormont Parliament that created a 'Protestant government for a Protestant people'. Ultimate control still remained with Westminster until 1969, when a bitter conflict between Protestant unionists and Catholic nationalists finally ended with the signing of the Good Friday Agreement (1998). The Northern Ireland Assembly was set up as part of the Good Friday Agreement and involves parties from all sections of the unionist and nationalist communities. The Assembly has 108 members representing 18 constituencies, elected through a single transferable vote (STV) form of proportional representation (PR).

In Northern Ireland communities are divided on religious (Catholic v. Protestant), geographical (Northern Ireland–Britain v. Southern Ireland), cultural (Irish v. British) and political (unionist–loyalist v. nationalist–republican) lines. The Protestant unionist community is seen as largely British and wishes to stay an integral part of the UK. The Catholic nationalists are content to see themselves as Irish and believe an eventual unification with the Republic of Ireland is both natural and inevitable. There are therefore distinct, clearly conflicting, market segments, of which any party seeking to use political marketing must take account.

Twenty-six counties of Ireland were given independence in 1921 and eventually became the Republic of Ireland. The Dail (Lower House of Parliament) has 166 members representing 41 constituencies, and elections are also conducted on an STV system of PR. The Irish Republic is predominantly a Catholic state and was formerly very closely aligned with a mode of governance that rested on the strong influence of the Church on the State.

Sinn Féin presents itself as a thirty-two county all-Ireland party which does not recognise the legitimacy of partition. It subsequently competed as a single party in elections on both sides of the border and attempted to develop an election strategy that has continuity and relevance to both parts of the island. The complexities of the political system means that Sinn Féin competes in several distinct markets.

Northern Ireland is part of the UK and is under the control of Westminster (the British government). Political parties in Northern Ireland compete in the UK general elections for seats in Westminster, which is dominated by the competition between the Conservative and Labour Parties. In separate devolved elections, they also seek seats in the Northern Ireland Assembly. However, Sinn Féin also competes as an all-Ireland party in the Republic of Ireland elections, where Fianna Fáil and Fianna Gael are the dominant parties.

In Northern Ireland, Sinn Fein and the Social Democratic Labour Party (SDLP) are the dominant nationalist parties and are faced by the Unionist and Democratic Unionist Parties, which act as the dominant parties for Protestants. Sinn Féin refuses to recognise UK authority over any part of Ireland, declines from entering the Westminster Parliament as elected MPs (abstention) and seeks unification of the two partitioned parts of Ireland. The consequence for political marketing is that Sinn Féin attempts a degree of synthesis between its strategies in all three national elections (Dail, Westminster and Northern Ireland Assembly) and in European elections on the island of Ireland. Strategy and politics differ little across national borders, except in the degree to which Sinn Féin can exercise power once elected. In the Northern Ireland Assembly it can enjoy a dominance of nationalist politics, while the small number of seats it possesses in the Westminster and Dail Parliaments (four in each) means it wields little power in actual decision-making.

Moving from conflict to marketing

Sinn Féin conducts its marketing in a state historically conditioned by conflict and terrorism. The War of Independence and the establishment of the Irish Free State in 1921 led to the formation of a system of government the leading parties of which had their roots firmly set in the Irish Republican Army (IRA). The 'Irish problem' did not end with the formation of the Free State but continued in six northern counties of the island. Sinn Féin was central to the conflict that raged on until the present peace process, which has given all sides an opportunity to settle differences through the ballot box and embrace the democratic process, rather than rely on violence as a means to achieve political goals. Sinn Féin is closely linked to the Provisional IRA, and is fundamental to the process of resolving the conflict in Northern Ireland. Having been condemned as the political voice of terrorism, Sinn Féin is now trying to achieve political goals through the democratic process. The ballot box has replaced the armalite and political marketing has supplanted military strategy. The election strategy developed by the party shows the ways in which political marketing can be used to gain democratic representation. In the aftermath of 11 September 2001 and the conflicts in Afghanistan and Iraq, the 'war on terrorism' will eventually require political and democratic solutions to the problems that communities face. Terrorist groups will eventually have to put the gun aside and seek political representation.

History of Sinn Féin's use of political marketing

Sinn Féin is the historical embodiment of the republican ideal of a united socialist Republic of Ireland, tracing itself back to the movement of the United Irishmen of the 1790s (Lyons 1985: 256). Sinn Féin won a sweeping victory in the general election of 1918, then announced its political separation from Westminster and established a Dáil Eireann (Assembly of Ireland), which has consistently formed the basis of its political claim as the legitimate party of rule in Ireland (see Sinn Fein website: http://sinnfein.ie). However, the IRA was recognised by the Sinn Féin party as its army, and the Irish Civil War and the splitting of the IRA led to the isolation of Sinn Féin and a loss of political power for the first half of the twentieth century. In the 1970s and 1980s, Sinn Féin became the political voice of republicanism. That bond was vocalised in the 1980s by Danny Morrison's call for a Sinn Féin strategy that involved 'an armalite in one hand and the ballot box in the other' (quoted in Patterson 1989: 205–206). The development of the peace process in the 1990s and the Good Friday Agreement provided a means to bury the armalite and use both hands to embrace the democratic process.

Membership of Sinn Féin was boosted by an emotional fundamentalism fostered by the hunger strikes of the 1980s. Amid the H-Block protests, sectarian murders, shoot-to-kill policies and the Westminster and Dáil bans on media contributions by its leaders, Sinn Féin increased its profile and effectiveness as the voice of the northern nationalist Catholics. The party developed a brand name that differentiated it from all other political competitors and it declared itself a socialist all-Ireland party. Despite the restrictions on Sinn Féin taking part in the political process borne of its close association with the IRA, the party grew stronger with each election. It developed an incremental trade-off between its abstentionism and participation in the Westminster and the Dáil (Irish Parliament of the twenty-six counties) systems of governance. Abstentionism (the refusal of elected Sinn Féin representatives to sit in either the Westminster or the Dáil Parliament) had become the party's political mantra, but this policy had to end if Sinn Féin was to partici-pate in government and develop an effective role in the peace process.

Sinn Féin quickly moved into a new arena of the political marketplace, having first ensured that the majority of its support from the product-oriented market of republicanism was safely placated by the essential ideological purity of the party's future direction. It is here that Sinn Féin diversified its electoral strategy, moving into the sales-oriented model of political marketing in order to achieve its goals and appeal to a whole new set of voters.

Case study of Sinn Féin

Sinn Féin is an important topic of study in political marketing as it is a unique case of a party with strong links to terrorism being encouraged to move away from vio-lence and put its trust in the democratic process. This study has concentrated on interviews with party members and pursues the idea that a political marketing strategy, although new to the party, has been embraced at all levels. The crucial period has been from the 1980s to the present.

Research revealed how political marketing came out of the synthesis of all party members' wishes to find an effective alternative to the violence of the 1970s, and take advantage of the political and emotional capital gained from the deaths of the hunger strikers in the 1980s. The party set out to redirect the zealous and concen-trated dedication of republicanism away from terrorism and into democratic politics. Its product was clearly identified as belonging to the history of the Irish struggle for power and independence. The party now needed to package its product into a variety of saleable strategies that appealed to a number of markets in Northern Ireland, the Republic of Ireland and internationally. Political market-ing was the process through which Sinn Féin would now 'win the war'.

The sales-oriented approach was also an opportunity to appeal to a wider elect-orate than just the 'devoted' party members. The aim was to win elections, force the British to leave Ireland and convert the political system into one based on 'old-fashioned' socialism. The most crucial period of this study concerns the party's retreat from links with terrorism and its movement into a central role in the present peace process, which occurred over the period of 1980 to the present. However, an important qualification is that the success of the political marketing strategy is one that depends on a majority of members singing from the same hymn sheet. Regardless of the internal conflicts and disagreements, the party's external appearance must be one of total unity and conformity with agreed basic aims and objectives. Nonetheless, this limitation is also a strength of the study, as the primary research shows a political marketing strategy that has, to all intents and purposes, suffocated opposition within the ranks and presented a united and committed strategy to the electorate. Such a display of discipline and clarity can itself be an important aspect of a successful political marketing strategy, although it also does little to counter the fears that republicanism is still firmly embedded in the militarist antecedents of violent revolution.

Sinn Féin as a marketed product

Sinn Féin identifies the movement of other Irish political parties to the centre ground of politics as one of the reasons for the rise in its electoral fortunes (McNight 2002). The party's list of Dáil Eireann candidates for the May 2002 elections points to an alliance of anti-Sinn Féin rhetoric (Doolan 2002). Sinn Féin candidates claim they are a refreshing alternative to the cynical tabloid politics of their competitors. In the process, Sinn Féin is making an impact on a section of the electorate that is evidentially growing politically disinterested, the youth vote (Little 2002: 8). Sinn Féin claim that other parties are trapped into moving with the tide of mass opinion, and increasingly becoming market-oriented victims of the capriciousness of the electorate. Sinnott (1995: 37) describes how Fianna Fáil conducted a campaign in 1977 in which: 'policies were treated as products to be updated, packaged and marketed and voters were consumers to be captured with all the techniques of marketing – specific policies for specific market niches, loss leaders, brand image, and general media razzmataz'. By 1997, the sales-oriented approach evolved into a market-oriented strategy that included using focus groups and market intelligence to shape party policies into a consumer-friendly product (Coakley and Gallagher 1999; Holmes 1999; Kotler and Kotler 1999). Lees-Marshment (2001a) has tracked the same development in the UK's Labour Party. Sinn Féin is selling an ideological purity and engaging with the electorate in an attempt to make itself an attractive and responsive alternative to the market-driven policies of its competitors (Lawlor 2002). The party's success shows that it is important to wed the marketing of a party to a consistent political identity. Nevertheless, Sinn Féin has incorporated aspects of both the sales and marketing model into their strategy.

The use of political marketing by Sinn Féin: a model SOP?

Sinn Féin has adopted a sales orientation. Although it retains its essential principles and goals, as an SOP it recognises that the ordinary voter may not initially be convinced of the party's aims and methods. Using market intelligence to understand the voters' response to its behaviour, the party employs the latest media techniques to attract voters' support, convincing them that what it offers is the right choice. Market intelligence is secondary to *product design* according to party principles, ideology and history.

Sinn Féin emerged on the electoral stage with an ideological commitment to achieve a united Ireland. It remained committed to its product, and the main policy of unification has remained the basis of all of its political policies and is the brand name to which the party wishes the electorate to relate. Its' supporters' cry of *Tiocfaidh ar la* ('Our day will come') demonstrates the party's aim to achieve an all-Ireland polity by any means. Sinn Féin's role in developing and supporting the Good Friday Agreement, coupled with the IRA's cease-fire, moved the party further towards democratic electoral politics. The IRA would identify its main objective as the establishment and protection of 'a socialist, democratic Republic of Ireland' (McNight 2002). Sinn Féin is the political face of that mission and its relationship with the IRA is an inevitable outcome of the quest to achieve the very essence of the 1916 proclamation. The peace process allows Sinn Féin and the IRA to use political persuasion to show that the *solution* to the Irish *problem* is dependent on the growing electoral strength of Sinn Féin. Political marketing provides the party with an opportunity to move away from terrorist tactics and attempt to achieve its goals through democratic means.

Sinn Féin has broadened its political product to offer socialist-related policies affecting the daily lives of citizens. The panacea of a thirty-two county democratic socialist Republic of Ireland is coupled with the promise of 'radical alternative politics' that will deliver improvements in 'health, childcare, housing, rural re-development, the peace process, and the future of the island, the Nice Treaty and a fairer and more equitable distribution of the wealth' ('Vote no to the Treaty of Nice', Sinn Fein document, available: http://sinnfein.ie; accessed 2 March 2002).

The socialism of Sinn Féin policies is communicated through the egalitarian language of presentation, with manifestos entitled 'The sharing of wealth' and 'An Ireland of equals'. Promises include 'free health care for all' and the investment of the 'unprecedented resources' of the 'Celtic Tiger' into a transformation of the Irish education system (N. Kehoe, 'Irelands education system', public speech at the Sinn Fein Education Centre, Dublin, 10 March 2002). The Sinn Féin 'housing plan' includes the establishment of rent control in the private sector and increases in capital gains tax on speculative owners of multiple dwellings (C. O'Caolain, 'Free health care for all', public speech in Dublin, 10 February 2002). At the launch of Sinn Féin's Election Directorate Women's Committee's policy document, in Dublin on 24 April 2002, Gerry Adams declared: 'It's about changing the balance of power – men have to move over – to make room for women.' Questions about the credibility of Sinn Féin's 'socialist' identity have to be set against the party's 'radical' policies, which demonstrate a traditional 'Left' approach. Its contemporary policy documents read as socialist programmes and Sinn Féin use a political marketing method to understand its market and communicate its message in the most effective way possible.

Market intelligence: understanding and segmenting the market environment
An SOP will use market intelligence to identify two types of voter: those who already support the party and those who can be persuaded to support it. By reaching an understanding of all of the voters' viewpoints, Sinn Féin is able to segment the market and then target its communications to suit each particular group. Sinn Féin is adept in understanding the general political market environment and it has identified six main target segments. It has also sought to break down each area to enable more effective communication and campaigning.

Nature of the political market environment   The Sinn Féin product is manufactured in a divided environment. Ireland's electorate is partitioned into two radically distinct historical, social, political and economic environments. The Anglo-Irish Treaty of 1921 meant that Ireland was partitioned into communities whose experiences, needs and desires were developed in a confrontational climate. The division is between Unionist and Republicans, between Protestant and Catholics, and between Catholics of the south and the north. Many in the northern Catholic population have acquired a cognition of oppression, discrimination and deprivation, whilst the southern Catholics have enjoyed a degree of independence and security, an autonomy that is now jealously guarded. In the *Irish Times,* an article on Sinn Féin TD Caoimhghin O'Caolain emphasised an embedded satisfaction with the twenty-six county republic as opposed to O'Caolain's Ireland of 'Easter Week 1916' (Hennessy 2002: 5). The consistency of attacks in some Irish papers, and Sinn Féin's claims of a cross-party conspiracy, suggest that a section of the Irish population is content to hold on to the present 'republic' and rejects an all-Ireland republic on the grounds that it would foster 'unionist alienation and increase anti-Agreement sentiment', arguing that 'the people of the Republic [twenty-six counties] have absolutely no wish to take on its [the six counties'] burdensome responsibility' (Molony 2002: 24).

Market segmentation and identification of six target   Sinn Féin has conducted signification market intelligence and has identified six target markets; the party has packaged its own identity with a political sensitivity that demonstrates a focus on more than one audience. Peace is offered as a universal good with which Sinn Féin affiliates itself. Whether appealing to the 'besieged' Catholics of the north, the 'prosperous' Catholics of the south or an Irish-American audience, Sinn Féin capitalises on its role as a party of 'leadership' and change. It professes to give more vociferous support to the Good Friday Agreement than does any other party, and then manipulates that supportive self-presentation to address six particular audiences (see box 6.1).

Box 6.1   *The six Sinn Féin target markets*

- Northern nationalist Catholics
- Northern Catholic community
- Alliance and soft Ulster Unionist supporters
- Republic of Ireland voters
- *Ogra Sinn Féin* – the all-Ireland youth wing
- Irish–American/international support

- *Target market 1: northern nationalist Catholics.* The nationalist Catholics feel that Sinn Féin is the political manifestation of their desire for a socialist 32-county Republic of Ireland and make no distinction between socialist goals and a 32-county Ireland. Along with the party's most ardent supporters in the south, they are fanatically faithful to Sinn Féin: the Ard Fheis of 2001 illustrated the fundamentalism of these members, with motion 206 congratulating the leadership of the IRA and motions 207–11 confirming their adherence to the Good Friday Agreement and their perception of it as having a republican agenda.

- *Target market 2: northern Catholic community.* There is a section of the Catholic community in the north which has previously abstained from voting or supported the SDLP and are now deserting the moderate line in favour of Sinn Féin's policies on demilitarisation, policing, loyalist attacks, plastic bullets and Orange parades. Sinn Féin is increasingly seen as *the* nationalist party, and despite the warnings of many observers the SDLP was left 'licking its wounds' after the Westminster elections 2001 (Cowan 2002: 1).
- *Target market 3: Alliance and 'soft' Ulster Unionist supporters.* Martin McGuinness declared in respect of this more contentious target, 'it is vitally important that bridges to the unionist community continue to be built by Irish Republicans' (quoted in O'Hanlon 2002: 8).
- *Target market 4: Republic of Ireland voters.* The strategy in Southern Ireland requires a different approach, taking account of the possibility of Sinn Féin needing to find coalition partners. Motions 197–200 of the 2001 Ard Fheis created great debate as they examined the prickly question of entering into coalition in the 'twenty-six county establishment circle'. The central problem is that Sinn Féin's radical approach to politics demands change, while the STV system encourages compromise and seldom leads to significant change. Sinn Féin's route out of this difficulty is to focus on a list of socialist policies it 'wishes' to follow, rather than contemplating making concessions to competitors: very much a sales-oriented policy rather than a market-oriented approach. This has led to the party being demonised by the media, allowing its competitors to unify in condemning and vilifying its activities.
- *Target market 5: Ogra Sinn Féin.* The youth wing of the party is a vital part of Sinn Féin's success story, given that interest and support from young voters is of increasing concern to all parties. Sinn Féin enjoys an unprecedented level of success in attracting active members aged 18–25. Ogra Sinn Féin has fifteen representatives at the Sinn Féin Ard Fheis (national delegate conference), is represented on the Ard Comhairle (national executive), on all comhairle cuigi (regional executives) and in every comhairle ceanntair (district executive) and cumann (local or work branch). Policies promoted by the youth are evident in the Ard Fheis, as indicated by motion 133 of the 2001 meeting, which called for 'the formation of Youth Provision Councils as a mechanism for enfranchising young people and addressing their specific needs'. This is an example of relationship marketing, with the party developing links with the country's youth in the hope that they will develop into adult supporters of Sinn Féin.
- *Target market 6: Irish–American and international support.* Sinn Féin cannot afford to ignore the Irish–American community, for it has traditionally underwritten the republican cause and its continued support is vital to the success of Sinn Féin in the peace process. The orchestration of Sinn Féin's political programme has required a careful packaging of its international image.

The identification of potential constituencies and continued communication with them is an on-going endeavour for the party. Sinn Féin uses market intelligence to identify a constituency in which it feels its 'socialist agenda' will have resonance, often a marginalised area which other parties have deserted. In unison with its complete informational saturation of a constituency, Sinn Féin assesses the exact make-up of the electorate contained therein. Street maps are marked with the political composition of each road and activists are assigned to campaign in those areas, with strict checks carried out at regular intervals by the director of elections. In the Republic of Ireland, this has been refined to the point that the canvasser often knows whether he is knocking a door to gain a first vote or to attempt to change a person's second preference to Sinn Féin.

Communication and campaigning – selling Sinn Féin

Sinn Féin has used political marketing in its communications in order to sell the Republican product, focusing on a particular market and designing a strategy of communications suited to that individual target. It has developed a distinctive campaign style which it believes separates it from its competitors and bestows a clear advantage in all elections. Three of the six targets just outlined are considered now in terms of communications, following which organisational aspects of the party's campaigning effort are examined.

- *Communication to the north.* In Northern Ireland, Sinn Féin ensures that it remains the voice of a particular type of republican community, promoting a picture of voters as barely free from the chains of conflict and still enduring sectarianism and intimidation from various quarters. If the party is to prevent these supporters from deserting Sinn Féin for other groups, like Republican Sinn Féin, which advocate a more fundamentalist approach, it cannot allow itself to be seen as a separate entity from the IRA. Some nationalist Catholics identify the two as their defence against discrimination and violence and as the instruments necessary for the achievement of a thirty-two county Republic of Ireland. They see the Royal Ulster Constabulary as inactive observers of the steady decline of 'unprotected' Catholic estates and identify IRA units as their own police force.
- *Communication to Republic of Ireland voters.* Sinn Féin has developed an alternative language for dealing with the concerns of the middle class voters of the south. Gerry Adams targets them as the 'people who want change' (Judge 2002: 8). Councillor Arthur Morgan offers them the opportunity for a 'change from the stagnant tweedledum tweedledee politics that have failed to deliver on . . . housing, health care, transport and the environment' (Little 2002: 8). This also resonates with the working classes, yet, Sinn Féin is moving into a wider market where the failure of other parties to offer change is producing disaffection among their supporters. Many have failed to ride on the back of the Celtic Tiger and have been left in pockets of abject poverty.

  Sinn Féin targets the *second-preference* votes of the middle class. The STV system in Ireland allows Sinn Féin to conduct a dual strategy in the south. The conservative pattern of middle class voting in the Republic is so entrenched that the hope of converting the middle class to regard Sinn Féin as their first preference is indeed slim. Nevertheless, Fianna Fail voters, while politically conservative, would identify themselves also as nationalists. Sinn Féin appeals to these people on the basis of a republican agenda and enjoy the bonus of a growing discontent with the 'corruption' of mainstream parties that has dogged the Irish political scene (the McCracken, Flood and Moriarty tribunals). Sinn Féin trumpets its political integrity as an alternative to the unscrupulous politics of others.

• *Communication to Irish-American–International support.* Sinn Féin's political programme has required a careful packaging of its international image. Its role as a prime player in the resolution of conflict is buttressed by policy presentation that 'in its simplest terms means government by the people for the people ('Republican and Labour', Sinn Féin document; available: www.geocities.com). Resonance with the US constitution moves the focus away from Sinn Féin's socialist agenda and points towards the more acceptable aim of achieving self-determination.

However carefully the international image is packaged, the balancing strategy can sometimes compromise the whole of Sinn Féin's election strategy. The arrest of the 'Columbia Three' and the accusations of involvement with the Marxist Revolutionary Forces of Columbia exemplify the extent of the juggling act required. To its traditional supporters in Northern Ireland the issue is one of a 'formidable guerrilla army' resisting the 'treachery of the US and the Colombian elite' (RM Distribution, 'Death of Columbian peace process', 8 January 2002; available: http://irlnet.com). In the south it is presented as a campaign against anti-Sinn Féin rhetoric, with the Columbia Three identified as innocent Irishmen trapped abroad and denied their human rights. Gerry Adams refused to appear before a US committee and President of the Irish National Caucus Father Sean McManus pointed towards an 'Ollie North . . . rogue' who, with 'malicious intent', was trying to involve the IRA and Sinn Féin in US and Columbia politics (RM Distribution, 'The hidden agenda behind the Columbia hearing', 30 April 2002; available: http://irlnet.com, accessed 10 May 2002).

Political marketing communication techniques: continual canvassing   Sinn Féin has made extensive use of marketing techniques in campaigning and communication, and its electoral strategy is based on a policy of continual canvassing, with market intelligence identifying constituencies potentially open to persuasion. As the Sinn Féin election machine goes into action, a practised package of political cajolery saturates the area. The campaign begins with a choreographed display of film, music and speeches: Irish nationalist history and culture are presented in films of graphic violence and suffering; and rebel and traditional music provide the backdrop to scenes of patriotic struggle. The message is that the 'Shinners' (Irish slang for Sinn Féin) are coming.

Long-term approach: merging of the campaign and permanent communication
Sinn Féin displays a degree of mastery of permanent marketing communications, political pressure being applied immediately and then maintained over succeeding years. Rather than the short-term electioneering of the main parties, Sinn Féin makes a long-term commitment to the community involved. The end of an election is not followed by a winding down of the political campaign; rather, the party workers re-double their efforts, immediately investing in the next election and continuing to exercise responsibility for the welfare of the community. For areas and communities that have grown politically apathetic and feel isolated or forgotten, the effect is intense and enduring.

Trained staff, activists and politicians SOPs put most effort into communications, and one aspect of this is the training of staff, activists and politicians. The palpable air of conviction brought by party activists is nourished through intensive training and experience, with prospective Sinn Féin activists undertaking a six-week course of learning and development. The success rate for the completion of the courses of historical, ideological and political learning is 15–20 per cent. Everyone who wishes to become a Sinn Féin activist is expected to successfully complete the training (Lawlor 2002).

A further aspect of the electoral strategy is media training. Early ventures into the political arena were marked by hostility towards all Sinn Féin candidates from the media. Effective communication in interviews was haphazard and improved only through a process of trial and error. The Belfast activist Joe Austin was the first to suggest a more professional approach. A room in the Divis flats was turned over to sessions of mock interviewing and Joe would subject interviewees to a good imitation of a hostile Jeremy Paxman; so good was he that the future Sinn Féin councillor Paddy McManus responded with a tirade of cursing and stormed out of the 'practice' session swearing vengeance. Nevertheless, the training continued and most of Sinn Féin is now more than comfortable with hostile interviewing situations (McNight 2002).

Local organisation Winning the hearts and minds of the electorate through a process of empowerment and the use of local resources is central to Sinn Féin's electoral strategy. Once extensive market intelligence has been conducted the specific concerns of local communities are identified and researched by party activists, after which the party helps local people to organise groups and meetings in which community leaders are identified and appointed. Sinn Féin provides the resources and knowledge needed to promote and maintain a campaign. The party organises leaflets, posters, meetings, marches, pickets and protests, and takes on the responsibility for bringing about change. The advantage to Sinn Féin is that such local organisations become vastly more effective, with the party achieving far more through a process of delegation than it ever could hope to do through direct involvement.

Professionalised operations   The professionalisation and modernisation of Sinn Féin's strategy at election times extends to every facet of its operations, with daily localised assessments of the progress of the party being carried out. Reports in the media, feedback from activists and every other source of opinion, complaint and inquiry are taken into account, examined and acted on. A weekly larger meeting, chaired by the director of elections, is held at which the progression of the election campaign is carefully analysed. Strategies are discussed and nationally co-ordinated. In the earliest stages of becoming politically active, Sinn Féin developed an openness to the use of all possible means of advancement; today, the experience of members as managers, trade unionists, teachers and a variety of other professions is called on. Whatever works in other environments is tried and tested, with the outcome being a unique blend of ideological purity, managerial innovation and practical application (McNight 2002).

Co-ordination and support are central to Sinn Féin's electoral strategy. The responsibility for organising, administrating and assessing the strategy falls upon the local activists, though leaflets, posters and booklets are financed and supplied centrally. Problems are tackled first at the lowest level, while any persistent difficulty is readily transferred to a higher level and swiftly dealt with there.

Election – signs of success

In the six counties, Sinn Féin support has grown from 10.1 per cent in the 1982 Assembly election to an impressive 24 per cent in the Assembly election of 2003. The European election of 1999 saw a total of 205,808 votes cast across Ireland for the Sinn Féin campaign of 'Independence in Europe' (http://sinnfein.ie, www. geocities, 10 March 2002). The success of the party was confirmed in the 2002 Dáil elections, at which it won four TD seats, retained the Cavan Monaghan seat and just narrowly failed to win two more new TD seats. Evidence of the party's appeal to new voters was illustrated by the fact that Sinn Féin won more first-time-voter support than all of the other parties put together (Molony 2002: 27). In November 2003 Sinn Féin became the largest nationalist party in the Northern Ireland Assembly, gaining twenty-four Assembly seats and overtaking the SDLP, its 24 per cent of the vote making it the second most popular party in the province, pushing the Unionist Party into third place. The key to this growth in support has been the legitimising of the party through the Good Friday Agreement and the peace process, allied to a professional and modernised presentation of the parties' policies and candidates.

Sinn Féin is achieving considerable gains in the quest for democratic representation, often in the very areas where other parties are failing. From the increasing membership and the vitality of Ogra Sinn Féin, to the support of marginalised communities, Sinn Féin demonstrates a new effectiveness in winning the electoral votes. This is a warning to all other parties, for failure to professionalise and modernise their electioneering has seen Sinn Féin making significant and growing inroads into its competitors' voting stock. Sinn Féin has transmitted the psychology of the long war to a process of recurrent crusading. The core of Sinn Féin's character is not found in any affiliation to the IRA. Political practice is approached as a war of attrition in which innovative and reactive tactics are applied to a peace-making rationale and the goal of winning power. Political marketing, with a sales-oriented approach and the utilisation of marketing techniques, such as market segmentation and targeting, are vital to this strategy. In many ways the war in Ireland is still as 'hot' as ever, only now it is a political campaign, one which Sinn Féin addresses in much the same way as the IRA carried out its military operations.

Sinn Féin's election strategy and a review of the Lees-Marshment model

Having conducted its market intelligence, Sinn Féin designs and carries out an election strategy that can be seen to fit with the Lees-Marshment model for a SOP. Lees-Marshment (2001a: 1077) describes stage three of the model as including

> the so-called near or long-term campaign but also on-going behaviour. Not just the leader, but all MPs and members send a message to the electorate. Attempts are made to ensure all communication helps achieve electoral success, and to influence others in the communication process.

The campaign is unambiguous and highly effective, and uses a variety of methods to get the message across. The core principles of the party come first, then market intelligence is used to shape the product to the voters responses, using techniques such as market segmentation and target marketing. In the case of an MOP, public demands shape the product, whereas here sales techniques are used to promote the party's own message. Sinn Féin has grasped the sales-oriented concept and the utility of marketing techniques.

The tactics of political marketing comprise a mixture of sales-oriented innovation and product-led lucidity. The electorate is left in no doubt as to what it is voting for, while simultaneously believing that its own issues are being listened to and dealt with. This balance between reactive politics and ideological certainty is achieved through a professional approach to everything that Sinn Féin does. Activists are trained and developed through formalised and competitive teaching that ensures proficient and specialist activists. Constituencies are targeted, surveyed and carefully saturated with the Sinn Féin 'style', which leaves very little to chance and capitalises on the weaknesses of other parties. The party promotes radical change in a political environment increasingly blurred by the insipid offerings of its political competitors. Nevertheless, although an advocate of a popular brand of politics, Sinn Féin is no bargain-basement clear-out. It clearly identifies the likely markets for its product and uses every ploy from the worlds of politics and competitive business to achieve its political goals and win power. This is no short-term exercise, as Daithi Doolan (2002) illustrated in predicting that the present campaign would continue for the next 30–5 years, when the first phase would be completed with the success of a Sinn Féin-led government on the island of Ireland.

Inclinations towards a market orientation

Sinn Féin has adopted a sales-oriented approach to political marketing, though there are also inclinations towards market-oriented politics. For example, Sinn Féin is careful not to promise too much: it has no 'magic wand' and is more comfortable offering to others its know-how and enthusiasm (Doolan 2002). The party's structure is designed to facilitate a highway of communication between itself and the electorate. The cumann, numbering 5–12 members, monitor local issues and are the means by which Sinn Féin weaves itself into the fabric of the community (McNight 2002); the cumann are linked to the next level of authority through representation on the comhairle ceanntair, or district executive, which is at the county level, and the comhairli limisteir, which has regional responsibility for Sinn Féin operations.

The 1980s, with the hunger strikes and the party's successful early ventures into politics on both sides of the border, brought a realisation that terrorism was merely one path to victory. Two factors began to have a significant influence on republicans in general. First was the republican prisoners' recognition of the futility of pursuing a purely military strategy. While some were content to 'free Ireland' through the gun, most recognised the potential of *unarmed* contributions to that end. Whether it was by posting leaflets, carrying banners, running child-care schemes or repairing derelict properties, republicanism developed a multi-faceted approach that enabled everyone to become active. The prisoners, for example, used their captivity to school themselves politically, developing and refining their skills and commitment to the 'cause' by devising ways to gain power through democratic means.

Prison conditions were no harsher than the isolation and deprivation of the families and wives of those incarcerated. Prisoners wives and relatives, who form the second major influence on republicanism, mobilised and demanded change, bringing enthusiasm and novelty to the practice of politics in Ireland. Sinn Féin now has women at all levels of representation; women are predominant in the local offices and their activities contribute significantly into the growing political success of Sinn Féin. Women, the republican prisoners, their families and communities injected a new style into Ireland's politics, including a willingness to both learn from mistakes and seek new ideas on how bring about radical change and electoral success.

The resistance of Sinn Féin to becoming a fully market-oriented model of behaviour is explained in part by its dual strategy of retaining a core ideology and promoting its own brand of socialist politics. Nevertheless, significant changes in its methods of communication and campaigning have moved the party to a sales-oriented position. Sinn Féin's participation in the Northern Ireland Assembly and its prospect of some future role in the governance of the Republic of Ireland are indicative of the party's commitment to a political path to power. The success of that strategy may eventually lead to a full decommissioning of arms and the disbanding of the IRA – the political success of Sinn Féin and the annulment of the IRA are inextricably linked. What will happen, however, should the party's political success begin to wane? Will it return to the methods of the past and seek a military solution, or will it re-double its political efforts? If it opts for the latter course of action the party will be faced with another vital choice – whether to remain an SOP, perhaps never acquiring the support necessary to secure majority rule in

Ireland, or whether to move towards a market-oriented identity, changing their policies to suit the demands of the electorate?

Problems arising out of the use of political marketing

Segmentation and the identification of target markets are beneficial to the Party's electoral strategy. They present a challenge, as each market can have its own distinctive views and demands which Sinn Féin then have to balance. It is vitally important to this balance for Sinn Féin to remain the party of all-Ireland. This in itself can be the source of the most contentious problems, as Republic of Ireland voters have long accepted the legitimacy of their own security forces. In contrast, Sinn Féin and the IRA have continually identified the security forces of the south as 'Free State' entities and, as such, ultimately the enemy of all 'republicans'. A degree of opacity in its stance is the present tactic of Sinn Féin. When Gerry Adams was quizzed on his condemnation of the RUC and whether that denunciation also applied to the Gardai, he declared that 'there's only one army in the State [Irish Republic] and there's only one police service' (quoted in Walsh 2002: 1). This is not exactly a direct rejection of the role and legitimacy of the IRA, but more a carefully worded response to present circumstances, one which leaves open the possibility that the one army and police force of a future all-Ireland will be the very same IRA Adams was being asked to reject.

It is equally difficult for Sinn Féin to appeal to the two very different Catholic social classes that have developed in Ireland: their distinct economic experiences and outlooks have aggravated the division between the Catholics of Northern Ireland and those of the Republic. Northern Catholics identify themselves as an oppressed and deprived working class, while many of the working and middle classes of the south have experienced a 'Celtic Tiger' economy and a record of rising prosperity. With a socialist agenda, Sinn Féin appeals to all the working classes by emphasising its role as the representative of the oppressed, excluded and deprived. The party has a history of tilting against the windmills of the politically powerful and are readily identified as the party of the working class. Sinn Féin takes every opportunity to claim to represent minorities across Ireland – the travellers, the refugees, the youth, the unemployed and the republican prisoners. Added to these there are the protesters against Sellafield, waste-disposal incinerators, social housing policies, religious discrimination, the Nice Treaty, NATO and insurance rip-offs. By contrast, opposition politicians blot their own copybooks, inviting accusations of corruption and dodgy deals, not to mention apathy. Another source of conflict is the packaging of the party's agenda to address a capitalist Irish-American audience: here again it is a practised opacity that enables Sinn Féin to appeal to Irish-Americans' allegiance to the 'cause' while concealing its 'socialist agenda'.

Democratic implications of political marketing

As Sinn Féin has become immersed in the political process and reaped the legitimate rewards of democratic representation, the links with terrorism have become tenuous and embarrassing. Political marketing, Sinn Féin style, means that the professional and methodical promotion of the party can be synthesised with an historical and essential ideological purity. The main concern is for this allegiance to the democratic process to survive any painful interludes of election failure and subsequent decline in representation. The peaceable reaction to this would be a re-doubling of efforts to improve and apply political marketing strategies to electioneering. In this case, political marketing has become a means to entice the terrorists away from political violence and embed them in the democratic process.

There is, however, a concern that once political marketing fails to produce the gains necessary to win overall power, Sinn Féin will resurrect its links with terrorism and attempt to dominate the political landscape through violence and intimidation. For unionists the distinction between Sinn Féin and the IRA is hard to make; they view the discipline and forcefulness of the Sinn Féin–IRA use of political marketing as merely a reflection of terrorist tactics being employed to hijack and distort the democratic process. Either political marketing is being used cynically as another weapon in the arsenal of a group intent on political terrorism, or it is a tool to entice the terrorist away from violence and into the democratic process of resolving conflicts through the ballot box.

The democratic possibilities of a successful strategy of political marketing by Sinn Féin can be determined as proof that any political party can achieve significant representation through peaceful means. The indications in this case are that successful political marketing has drawn Sinn Féin increasingly away from links with the IRA, and that the party is required to encourage and even pressure the republican movement to disarm and to put its trust in elections and the right of people to choose through the ballot box who holds political power in the province.

Conclusions

Sinn Féin has moved away from links with terrorist groups and towards the democratic process of winning power and influence through elections, and while it has left behind the violence of military resistance, it has incorporated the discipline, innovation and dedication of those former times into its election strategies. The modern political arena and the vast majority of the electorate demand a far more market-oriented flavour to political representation. Local issues, low taxes, good services and policies that address individuals as well as groups have more credibility for the voter than the collectivist patriotism of Irish republicanism. Despite this, Sinn Féin cannot discard the essential elements of that republicanism without losing all sense of identity and ideological purity. Nevertheless, the party is attempting to change its election strategies to suit a volatile and diverse marketplace, while trying to retain an influence over the way that market sustains its support of and belief in an historical creed of republicanism. Sinn Féin has developed ways to merge market- and sales-oriented strategies with a product-based essentialism. Whatever the analysis, it is efficient political marketing that has enabled Sinn Féin to gain further successes in democratic politics.

Bibliography

Coakley, J. and Gallagher, M. (1999), *Politics in the Republic of Ireland*, London: Routledge.

Cowan, R. (2002), 'Sinn Fein builds on success while SDLP licks wounds', *Guardian*, 13 June.

Garvin, T. (1999), 'Democratic politics in independent Ireland', in J. Coakley and M. Gallagher (eds), *Politics in the Republic of Ireland*, London: Routledge: 350–63.

Hennessy, M. (2002), 'SF TD declines to urge people to inform on murder of Gardai', *Irish Times*, 26 February.

Holmes, M. (1999), 'Organisational preparation and political marketing', in M. Marsh and P. Mitchell (eds), *How Ireland Voted – 1997*, Boulder, CO: Westview Press: 29–56.

Judge, T. (2002), 'Adams predicts big gains for Sinn Fein', *Irish Times*, 8 February.

Kotler, N. and Kotler, P. (1999), 'Generating effective candidates, campaigns and causes', in B. Newman (ed.), *Handbook of Political Marketing*, Thousand Oaks, CA: Sage: 3–18.

Lees-Marshment, J. (2001a), 'The product-, sales- and market-oriented party and how Labour learnt to market the product, not just the presentation', *European Journal of Marketing*, special issue, 'Political marketing', 35(9–10): 1074–84.

Lees-Marshment, J. (2001b), 'The marriage of politics and marketing', *Political Studies*, 49(4): 692–713.

Lees-Marshment, J. and Lilleker, D. G. (2001) 'Political marketing and traditional values: "Old Labour" for "new times"?', *Contemporary Politics*, 7(3): 205–16.

Little, J. (2002), 'Sinn Fein attracting youth, Adams is told', *Drogheda Independent*, 1 March.

Lyons, F. S. (1985), *Ireland since the Famine*, London: Fontana Press.

Molony, J. (2002), 'Support of rookie voters key to SF triumph', *Sunday Independent*, 3 March.

O'Hanlon, R. (2002), 'McGuinness supports call by Adams for consent', *Irish Times*, 8 February.

O'Leary, C. (1979), *Irish Elections 1918–27: Parties, Voters and Proportional Representation*, London: Gill & Macmillan.

O'Shaughnessy, N. (1999), 'Political marketing and political propaganda', in B. Newman (ed.), *Handbook of Political Marketing*, Thousand Oaks, CA: Sage: 725–40.

Patterson, H. (1989), *The Politics of Illusion*, London: Hutchinson Radius.

Sinnott, R. (1995), *Irish Voters Decide: Voting Behaviour in Elections and Referendums since 1918*, Manchester: Manchester United Press.

Walsh, L. (2002), 'Adams calls on AG to withdraw SF comments', *Irish Independent*, 25 February.

Interviews

Doolan, D., Sinn Féin candidate (2002), interviewed by the author, Dublin, 16 March.

Lawlor, D., Ogra Sinn Fein activist (2002), interviewed by the author, Belfast, 15 March.

McNight, S., Sinn Féin director of elections (2002), interviewed by the author, Belfast, 15 March.

7

Political marketing in Germany: the case of the Social Democratic Party

Charles Lees

This chapter applies the comparative political marketing (CPM) model to the phenomenon of political marketing in Germany, and is divided into four segments. First the chapter discusses how to adapt the CPM model to political conditions in the Federal Republic. In doing so, it raises a number of epistemological and empirical issues that must be resolved but also points to data that support the underlying logic of the model. Second, the chapter applies the CPM model to a case study – namely the transformation of the marketing posture of the Social Democratic Party (SPD) over the period 1995–98. This case study involves a great deal of thick description and is the centrepiece of the chapter. Third, the chapter examines the impact of the SPD's 1998 Bundestag election campaign on the strategies adopted by the main political parties in the 2002 campaign, and in particular compares how the SPD's campaign compared with its groundbreaking campaign in the previous elections. Finally, in the conclusion to the chapter there is a discussion of the findings and arguments made – including an assessment of what they tell us about the utility of the CPM model in the German context – and their implications for democracy and participation.

Adapting the CPM model to conditions in the Federal Republic

The Lees-Marshment CPM model is a useful heuristic and its main strengths are its parsimony and its holistic approach to the two issues of organisational and programmatic development. It is a essentially a three-stage developmental model of political marketing in which political parties may or may not move from the status of a POP through that of a SOP to that of a MOP. As with all parsimonious models, however, difficulties arise when the model is applied to the warp and weft of practical politics in a given institutional setting. This section addresses those issues, and has three segments. First, there is a brief overview of the German electoral and party system. Second, there is an examination of the epistemic and empirical constraints on the use of the CPM model. Finally, I look at empirical evidence that nevertheless supports the application of the CPM model in the context of the Federal Republic.

Overview of the electoral and party system in the Federal Republic

Germany has an additional member system (AMS) of proportional representation, which was introduced in its present form in 1953. Under AMS each voter has two votes – one for the election of constituency members of the German Bundestag, the other being cast for a party list of his or her choice. Of the two votes, the latter is the more important because it is the second vote that determines the number of seats allocated to each party in the Bundestag. To qualify for representation a party must gain at least 5 per cent of the total national votes cast or secure the election of at least three of its candidates in the constituencies. With the exception of a brief period of majority government in the 1950s, over successive legislative periods the AMS system has produced a share of seats in the Bundestag that has made the formation of formal coalitions between the parties a necessity. AMS also encourages 'split-ticket' voting, whereby voters divide their allegiance between the first and second votes. This practice tends to favour small parties, which pick up a disproportionate share of second votes.

Since 1998, the Federal Republic has been governed by a so-called 'Red–Green' coalition, made up of the SPD and the environmentalist Green party, which was re-elected in 2002. Other parties in the Bundestag are:

- the CDU–CSU (a combined Christian Democratic party faction made up of the Christian Democratic Union and its Bavarian sister-party the Christian Social Union);
- the FDP (liberals); and
- the PDS (post-Communist successors to the ruling Socialist Unity Party of the former German Democratic Republic).

At present the division of the 603 seats in the Bundestag is as follows: SPD 251 (previously 298); CDU–CSU 248 (245); Greens 55 (47); FDP 47 (43); and PDS 2 (36).

Constraints on the application of the CPM model

In the CPM model the first two categories of POP and SOP implicitly preserve the divide between political parties' programmes (their product) and their promotion. By contrast, the MOP – as typified by New Labour in 1997 – does not just adjust its message to reflect the preferences of the electorate but actually transforms all aspects of its behaviour, including institutional structures and party programmes, in pursuit of enhanced market share/electoral success (Lees-Marshment 2001). Thus, product and promotion are blurred, the party 'brand' is progressively decoupled from any underlying content,[1] and party organisation becomes increasingly driven by marketing activities.

At the same time there are problems associated with this blurring of product and promotion. The argument is epistemological and empirical, and has two elements. First, this blurring of product and promotion makes the CPM model somewhat ahistorical and ignores the constraints imposed by national laws, standard operating procedures, ideology and internal politics on political parties' programmatic and institutional development. Second, and tangential to the last point, by making political parties' marketing posture the main causal variable, the CPM model also ascribes a central *will* to the political party as an institution. But, as Kenneth Arrow (1951) pointed out half a century ago, it is irrational to assume that complex organisations behave as unitary actors with a single set of preferences. We do make this assumption in many circumstances when it is heuristically useful to do so, but when one is trying to strike a culturally sensitive balance between specific historical context and a parsimonious model designed to capture the essence – rather than the detail – of generalisable trends across cases, it can be problematic. In order to demonstrate these points I look at four specific constraints imposed by conditions in the Federal Republic.

The first constraint that forces us to adapt the CPM model to local conditions is the Federal Republic's Basic Law, which strongly codifies the principles that determine not only a party's programmatic stance but its organisational structure and mode of governance. For instance Article 21 paragraph 3 of the Basic Law sets out clear parameters for party organisation, with an emphasis on the internal political processes by which parties formulate their 'political line'. These parameters were firmed up in the German Party Law of 1967 and cover such areas as:

- the regulation of the grass roots level of organisation;
- admission to and resignation from political parties;
- elections and votes within political parties;
- ballots in the case of the dissolution of political parties or their consolidation;
- ex officio members in party institutions;
- arbitration and internal party discipline; and
- protection of minorities with party organisations.

A detailed discussion of these constitutional and legal provisions are beyond the scope of this chapter,[2] but it is important to remember that such constraints on their internal structure and practices must limit political parties' ability to transform those structures and practices in the way that the CPM model suggests. At the very least, such provisions are a resource available to grass-roots members and others who might be resistant to the kinds of changes inherent in the move towards the ideal type of the MOP.

A second constraint on the ability of political parties in the Federal Republic to transform themselves in this manner stems from the nature of German federalism. Alfred Stepan's comparative analysis of federal systems (2001) works from the assumption that all federations, *qua* federations, are centre-constraining institutions. There are two elements of this phenomenon that are relevant to this chapter. First, the constitutional checks and balances common to federations are designed to protect the powers of the constituent units against the centre, in effect placing some policy areas beyond the centre's jurisdiction. This limits the scope available to political parties to construct electoral programmes that are both realistic programmes of government and at the same time respond to voters' preferences in the manner laid out in the MOP ideal type. In short, parties may not be in a position to make the kinds of commitments that would satisfy voters' preferences. Second, constitutionally protected sub-national tiers of government diffuse the *demos* into multiple *demoi*, divided into multiple authority structures. Again, this constrains the ability of parties at the national level to behave as unitary actors and creates veto players at the sub-national level. Stepan does argue that, compared to some other federal systems, such as Brazil, India and the USA, Germany's party system displays strong centralising tendencies and political parties are able to exert a high degree of party discipline over their members. But these centralising tendencies are offset by the presence of alternative power and resource bases in the *Länder* parties.

Third, as already noted, Germany's AMS system of electoral representation has generated a multiparty system in which coalition government is the norm. This has two important consequences. First, the incentive structure within which political parties operate is different from that found in the kind of two-party systems generated by plurality systems of electoral representation. In particular, for smaller parties there is less incentive to respond to voters' preferences in the way envisaged by the MOP ideal type. As long as such parties are confident of scaling the Federal Republic's 5 per cent hurdle to representation in the legislature it makes sense for them to remain product oriented in posture and to adopt flanking or niche positions along the dominant Downsian left–right axis. The second, and related, consequence of the focus on coalition government is that party programmes must not only be shaped to reflect voters' preferences but must appeal to potential coalition partners. This applies mainly to the two big catch-all parties, the SPD and the CDU–CSU, both of which must construct programmes and marketing strategies of appeal both to the median voter (Downs 1957) and to potential junior coalition partners whose own positions are further from the median point. This has been a particular problem for the SPD, which up until 1997 struggled to construct a successful marketing strategy that appealed to the political centre-ground from a position on the Centre-Left of the 'old politics' left–right axis, while at the same time being able to market itself along the 'post-materialist' dimension in order to appeal to 'new politics' voters and provide sufficient programmatical congruence with its junior coalition partner of choice, the Greens (see Lees, 1998, 2000, 2004). The difficulty in reconciling the preferences of voters and fellow party elites has meant that German political parties have retained a sales-oriented mode, albeit with increasingly sophisticated sales techniques, rather than make the more profound transformation to a market-oriented posture. This argument will be returned to later in the chapter.

Finally, the ability of political parties in Germany to construct programmes that are truly responsive to voters' preferences is constrained by the great emphasis placed by political parties in the Federal Republic on the formulation of their 'basic programmes'. Parties' basic programmes differ from electoral programmes in that they are designed to frame fundamental ideological underpinnings in a coherent and communicable manner. Moreover, such basic programmes cannot be imposed on a party by its leadership but must be voted on by the party membership. Thus basic programmes are not only hard to change but set clear limits on the level of responsiveness to voters' preferences that is possible in the election programme. Moreover, it is accepted by German political scientists that party programmes

should perform distinct *external* and *internal* functions. The list of external functions is consistent with the CPM model and includes:

*   PR within the populace, recruiting new members and winning political support;
*   profiling the party against competitors;
*   agitation and preparing the ground for confrontation with competitors; and
*   establishing the operational parameters within which political parties can frame
    their political demands both *vis-à-vis* other political parties and in the context
    of public opinion.

We must also take into account five internal functions:

*   a core integration function, which binds all members to a common set of
    principles;
*   to foster identification on the behalf of members, so that support becomes
    instinctive and routinised;
*   to stimulate political activism on the basis of that identification;
*   to allow the leadership to exert control over the political organisation and the
    membership; and
*   to legitimate political action in the eyes of agents and observers alike (see, for
    instance, Kaack 1995: 318–19).

Although these are empirical assertions, they also carry a strong normative charge
that further constrains the ability of political parties to adjust their programmatic
profiles to voters' preferences.

Empirical evidence in support of the application of the CPM model
The arguments and observations made above suggest that any application of the
CPM model in analysis of party politics in the Federal Republic must be accompanied by a degree of caution. On the other hand, data are available that support
the underlying rationale of the model, drawn from research into electoral preferences and the changing status and role of political parties.

In terms of electoral preferences there is plenty of evidence that German voters
are increasingly volatile in their allegiances and that electoral choice, when voters
bother to vote at all, is both increasingly instrumental and candidate centred (see,
for example, Forschungsgruppe Wahlen 2002; Maier and Rattinger 1999 and 2004;
Schmitt-Beck 2003). This has three consequences. First, political parties can no
longer rely on the support of *their* voters, and many votes are effectively up for grabs,
which increases the incentive to construct a marketing strategy that is responsive to
voters' preferences. Second, by its very nature voters' increasing focus on candidates
when making their electoral choice tends to both favour the leadership over the
membership and the needs of presentation over those of ideological substance.
Finally, having to appeal to a volatile, instrumental and candidate-centred electorate
forces political parties to concentrate resources in highly centralised and professionalised campaign machines. Taken together, these considerations provide a
strong *pull* factor in terms of the move towards a market-oriented posture.

Having established why political parties might *wish* to move towards a market-oriented posture, we must also ascertain whether they are *able* to do so. In other words, are there the necessary internal *push* factors to match the *pull* factors noted above? In order to make the move towards a market-oriented posture, political parties must have moved away from the 'mass party' model, with its reliance on an active and ideologically committed membership able to perform organisational and campaigning tasks. And in the Federal Republic there is evidence that this process has to some extent taken place. Over the period 1980–99 the absolute number of citizens who were members of political parties in Germany declined from 1,955,140 to 1,780,173. On the face of it, this does not seem like a huge fall; but what must be taken into account is the sizeable increase in the total electorate (from 43,231,741 to 60,762,751) over the period as a result of German unification. Thus membership as a percentage of the total electorate, known as the M/E ratio (Katz and Mair 1992), has declined dramatically, having almost halved over the period (from 4.52 per cent of the electorate in 1980 to 2.93 in 1999). This puts the rate of membership of political parties in Germany at the lower end of the scale compared to other European countries. Across a basket of 20 European democracies in the late 1990s the mean M/E ratio is almost 5 per cent, with a high of 17.7 per cent in neighbouring Austria. By contrast, only the Netherlands (2.51.), Hungary (2.15), the UK (1.92), France (1.57) and Poland (1.15) have lower M/E ratios.

Interestingly the decline in the M/E ratio varies across political parties. For instance, the Greens increased its membership from 18,320 in 1980 to 50,897 in 1999, although it remains the smallest political party in membership terms, and the Bavarian CSU increased its level of membership from 172,420 in 1980 to 184,765 in 1999. Elsewhere, however, the picture is one of decline in the absolute numbers of party members and, by definition, the M/E ratio as well. Both the SPD and the FDP suffered a 23.5 per cent drop in party membership over the period, with the SPD's membership dropping from 986,872 members in 1980 to 755,244 and the FDP's falling from 84,208 to 64,407. By contrast the CDU faired a little better, suffering a drop of 9.1 per cent from 693,320 in 1980 to 630,413 in 1999. And if we take the CDU–CSU as effectively a single unit the drop is a more modest 5.9 per cent from a combined membership of 865,740 members in 1980 to 815,178 in 1999 (Mair and van Biezen 2001).

In addition, recent research by Karsten Grabow (2001) demonstrates that the organisational structures of *Land*-level SPD and CDU parties in the new federal states of the former East Germany are much thinner than those found in the old federal states of what was West Germany. This leads Grabow to conclude that while *Land* parties in the 'old' Federal Republic still recognisably conform to the catch-all party model, those in the new federal states are closer to the ideal type of the cadre party. It will be recalled that cadre parties are characterised by thin organisational structures, weak inner-party democratic culture, top–down political processes, and a powerful and relatively autonomous leadership. These characteristics are consistent with the kind of organisational arrangements required for the transition to a market-oriented posture.

Taken in the round, it is apparent that the decline in the M/E ratio has affected the SPD and the FDP more than it has other political parties. In addition, the Green Party continues to have the lowest M/E ratio, despite increasing its membership over the last twenty years. It is therefore likely that if we are to discern movement towards the market-oriented ideal type this will be found within one of those three parties. Indeed, it is true that the most dramatic change in a German political party's campaign posture in recent years is that which took place within the SPD in the mid to late 1990s. The section which follows is a case study of this change, over the period from 1995 to the Bundestag elections in 1998. The third section examines the impact of the SPD's changed posture on other political parties' campaign postures in the subsequent 2002 Bundestag elections.

Case study: the SPD's 1998 Bundestag election campaign

Up until the 1990s the attitudes of political parties in Germany to political campaigning were relatively conservative. Parties' marketing techniques were fairly unsophisticated, relying on television spots and leadership debates, and at the local level providing citizens with free beer from the ubiquitous campaign stalls that sprang up in German town- and city-centres just before election day. The success of the sophisticated political marketing techniques associated with the Clinton presidential campaign of 1992 had a huge influence on left-of-centre parties in Western Europe, and similar techniques were used in a number of campaigns, including that of New Labour in the period 1994–97, and that of the SPD in the period 1995–98.

From 1995 onwards the SPD underwent a major overhaul of its approach. This process can be traced back to November 1995, when Rudolf Scharping, the SPD leader at the time, was ousted by the left-winger Oskar Lafontaine at the party's annual conference. Scharping's leadership had never been noted for its charisma and drive, but his failure to unseat the incumbent chancellor, Helmut Kohl, in the 1994 elections, combined with a run of disappointing *Land* elections in Hessen, North-Rhine Westphalia, Bremen and Berlin, made his position untenable. State elections in Berlin in October 1995 in particular were to prove the catalyst for Lafontaine's move against Scharping. In what had traditionally been an SPD heartland, the SPD lost 6.6 per cent of the vote across the city, with its vote share dropping by 4 per cent in the western half and 12.1 per cent in the east. As a result, the SPD was no longer the strongest party in any district of Berlin and, in the eastern half of the city, it lagged behind both the PDS and the CDU (see Lees 1996: 63–72).

Although on a smaller scale, the Berlin result was analogous to the Labour Party's disastrous 1983 general election defeat and prompted a similar degree of soul-searching. Here, the SPD made use of marketing tools such as market intelligence, use of professional consultants, direct marketing and target marketing. In terms of market intelligence, Lafontaine gave permission in 1996 for the commissioning of a study into how the SPD was perceived by ordinary voters. That report did not make for comfortable reading. The core of the problem was reduced to three points:

- Voters saw the SPD as fundamentally an opposition party rather than a potential party of government.
- The party did not project a clear image to the electorate as a whole, and in those areas in which it did the image was not attractive to voters.
- Voters did associate the SPD with the theme of 'social justice', but by and large the electorate had more confidence in the CDU–CSU when it came to policy areas that were of relevance to the future prosperity of the Federal Republic.

Taken in the round, the report said that voters saw the SPD as old-fashioned and irrelevant to the needs of modern Germany (Machnig 1999). The SPD's report did point the way forward for the party, though the route was less than easy. The changes advocated were to take place along three dimensions: technical and organisational (communication); resourcing; and product themes.

Technical and organisational changes in communication
In terms of technical changes, it was decided that the party had to rethink both its use of the media and its organisational preparations for the upcoming campaign. Regarding the former, there was to be a shift towards a more 'direct' form of marketing, with a strong emphasis on a powerful poster campaign aimed at target markets, backed up by the use of direct mail and, to a lesser extent, the internet. These methods were designed to appeal to young voters to whom the SPD had in recent years ceased to appeal. Moreover, as was demonstrated by the so-called 'two heads' campaign (discussed below), the marketing campaign swung into action much earlier in the pre-election period than had previously been the case. As for the organisational preparation for the campaign, it was decided that the party should move towards a continuous campaign model, with the formation of a new and permanent campaign apparatus in what became known as the *Kampa*, which was not only autonomous in respect of the mainstream party organisation but was even housed in a separate building in the centre of Bonn.[3] An 'organigram' of the *Kampa* organisation is provided in figure 7.1.

It is clear that the *Kampa*'s organisational structure drew heavily on that established by the UK Labour Party's operation at Millbank in central London. Campaign organisation stressed the idea of co-ordination and lines of command between project teams, the more important of which were, first, agency polling, second, opposition monitoring and rebuttal (*Gegner Beobachtung*), and finally, a special working group for the eastern states (*Arbeitsgruppe Ost*). The agency polling team concentrated on monitoring the work of the SPD's partner agencies with focus groups and reported back to party headquarters. It was the polling team's job to make sure that the campaign used only 'positives' and that the SPD used nothing in the campaign that would prove offensive to voters. The rapid rebuttal unit complemented this by making sure that any 'negatives' about the SPD did not become entrenched within the news' cycle. This normally involved

Figure 7.1 *Organisational structure of the SPD's* Kampa *election headquarters, 1998*

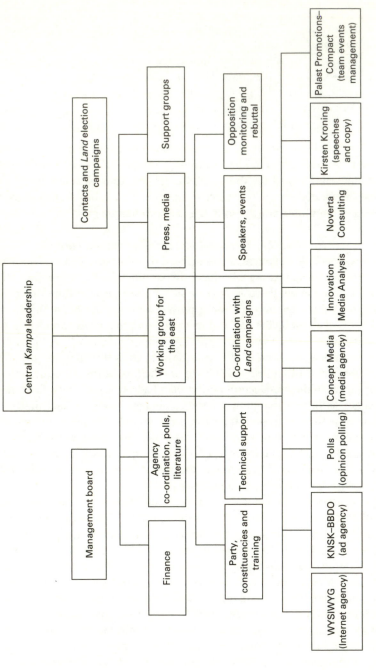

Source: Briefing at *Kampa* by Matthias Machnig, September 1998.

the countering of stories put forward by the other parties, though occasionally some spinning against members of its own campaign was required if they went 'off-message'.[4] Finally, the eastern working group was tasked with tailoring the SPD's overall message to voters in the new federal states: its previously dismal performance in those states had brought it home to the party that its understanding of the eastern German voters' thinking was tenuous. As already noted, party membership in the new states was very low both in absolute terms and in terms of organisational density. As a result the SPD lacked local intelligence and was worried that elements of the campaign that worked well in the west might be counter-productive in the east. So the eastern working group consisted of members who had grown up in and been socialised into eastern German political culture, and their job was, in effect, to weed out anything that easterners might consider irrelevant to the needs and perceptions of voters in the new federal states.

All three teams worked with the SPD's partner agencies, dealing with communications and advertising. There were eight of these in all, looking after different elements of the campaign. There were two 'creative' agencies, which were responsible for the broad ideas that underpinned the campaign, and a third agency was responsible for the dissemination of the campaign to the media. As the permanent campaign moved into the 'hot stage' in the run-up to the actual elections, the SPD employed another agency to poll target voters and assess the campaign's impact on them. The results of these private polls were then given to a team of media analysts which monitored and refined the campaign in the light of those data. The SPD also employed a number of consultants to ensure that the party machine operated smoothly at both national and *Land* levels. One company was responsible for training of party personnel; another had overall control of the organisation and marketing of party events; and all speeches were prepared and disseminated by yet another agency. Finally, the entire operation was co-ordinated through a secure 'intra-net' network of over 2,000 users, a task outsourced to yet another specialist agency.

Resource changes

These changes had profound consequences for the distribution and use of resources within the party organisation. In terms of campaign organisation, the separate *Kampa* building was very much a decentralised operation, while at the same time the central *Kampa* leadership remained under the close scrutiny of party headquarters (in the case of the 1998 campaign, *Kampa* operations chief Matthias Machnig reported directly to senior SPD politician Franz Münterfering). In terms of staffing, there was a significant use of consultants and outside expertise, the former assuming a much higher profile than had been the case. In addition the campaign had strong international links, and made some use of specialists who had taken part in the earlier Clinton and Blair campaigns. And as noted above, the *Kampa* operation relied heavily on a wide range of polling techniques, including focus groups, to monitor the success of the campaign and fine-tune it if necessary.

Product themes

Finally, the SPD made changes in terms of leadership and policy, at least on an overall thematic level, even if it fell short of a substantial re-design of the entire product. In terms of the themes used in the campaign, the SPD and its outside consultants devised a strategy with two distinct but inter-related goals. On the one hand, the campaign was designed to reconfigure the image of the party itself, while, on the other, the campaign would focus strongly on promoting voters' perceptions of competence and leadership in the party's choice of the chancellorship candidate, as and when the selection was made.

In developing such themes, the SPD appears to have understood the need for product adjustment, as contained within the MOP model. There was a realisation that the product had to be achievable: the SPD had to project a message that would serve to restore its credibility as a party of government and stake a claim to competence in new policy areas. It took account of the competition, nevertheless, aiming to be realistic while retaining its comparative advantage over the CDU–CSU in the field of social justice. There were similarities here with the objectives the New Labour leadership had set itself in the UK a couple of years earlier.

The campaign strategy responded also to market intelligence. It was based on four 'positives' associated with the SPD that had become apparent in the party's private research:

- the idea of 'political change';
- 'leadership';
- 'innovation'; and
- 'justice'.

Bundled together, these four positives were meant to constitute what marketing experts called an aura of 'future competence'; again noting the need for achievability. In practice, it meant concentrating on policy areas in which the SPD was perceived to be strong, such as labour market regulation, social and health provision, family life and youth. It also meant winning back a reputation for economic competence that had been lost in the late 1970s and early 1980s. The SPD managed to do this, pulling ahead of the CDU–CSU also on economic competence for most of the period running up to the election.

The most interesting aspect of the SPD's campaign was its use of the term 'innovation' and the thinking that underpinned it. The use of 'innovation' dates back to 1996, when the party first embarked on its re-think, and was a response to the popular perception of the SPD as an old-fashioned party in thrall to vested producer interests. The problem for the party was that its research indicated that simply stressing the SPD's reformist credentials would not dissipate that perception, because 'reform' also had considerable negative resonance with voters, being associated with cuts in social provision (and thus undermining the SPD's association with social justice). How voters reacted to the SPD's use of 'reform' depended on how they were questioned. When asked a general question about the need for change in the Federal Republic, voters answered in a socio-tropic manner, claiming that Germany needed to make big changes and that they were willing to vote for a party that would make such changes. When questioned more closely about their own personal circumstances, however, voters' declared willingness to change was less forthrightly expressed and self-interested responses came to the fore. In short, researchers had uncovered a classic free-rider problem, in which voters recognised that the future prosperity of the country depended on reform but were at the same time unwilling individually to make the necessary personal sacrifices. Therefore, the trick for the SPD's campaign strategists was to pick up the positives associated with the idea of reform and change while avoiding the negatives. Polling indicated that 'innovation' was the term that best fitted the bill, and it was to play a central role in the party-oriented strand of the campaign for the two years prior to polling day.

The SPD also made changes to the leadership aspect of its product – the candidate-oriented strand of the campaign. This was initially hampered by the failure of the SPD to nominate a chancellorship candidate until March 1998, when Lafontaine finally conceded the role to Schröder following the latter's triumph in the Lower Saxony *Land* election, where he was the incumbent minister–president. Up until that point, the party promoted the two politicians as a leadership duo in the so-called 'two-heads' campaign. On the one hand, the 'two-heads' campaign awakened unhappy memories of the 1994 Bundestag election, when the lacklustre performance of chancellorship candidate Scharping led to the promotion of the so-called *Troika*, in which Scharping's public profile was increasingly augmented by images of Lafontaine and Schröder. On the other, however, the 'two-heads' campaign appeared to turn necessity into a virtue and the image of Lafontaine served to reassure the SPD's members and electoral core as the party underwent a process in which the old Social Democratic certainties were reconfigured as the political campaign developed.

In contrast to Lafontaine, Schröder made a point of associating himself with this process of reconfiguration and, in particular, with the development of the SPD's own version of Tony Blair's 'Third Way', known as the 'New Centre' (*Neue Mitte*). The New Centre was a variation on the New Democrat/New Labour strategy of 'big-tent' politics and served a dual purpose in that it provided the means by which to build an electoral coalition that would occupy the centre ground while allowing the SPD to leave open the possibility of coalition with the Green Party. However, just like Blair's Third Way, the New Centre was defined more easily by what it wasn't than by what it was, and it is interesting to note that the publication (June 1999) of the British–German joint policy document on the 'Third Way'–'New Centre' – designed to flesh out the idea of a new progressive politics – was greeted with some derision and, in Germany at least, significant hostility (Lees 2000). Essentially, the idea of the New Centre worked best as a discursive tool, both in the SPD's electoral struggle with the CDU–CSU and also in Schröder's more personal political struggle with the somewhat traditional Lafontaine.

Finally, after almost three years of permanent communication, the SPD faced the German electorate on the 27 September 1998. When the results of the election came through in the early evening of that day, it was clear that the changes the SPD had made, alongside improvements in its electioneering techniques, had paid off. Overall, the SPD won 40.9 per cent of the party list vote, giving it 298 seats, while the CDU–CSU polled 35.1 per cent (245 seats). In addition, the SPD's preferred coalition partner did reasonably well: polling 6.7 per cent (47 seats), compared with the FDP's 2 per cent (44 seats), and the PDS' 5.1 per cent (35 seats, including 4 directly elected constituency seats in the East) (Statistiches Bundesamt 1998). Thus the SPD enjoyed a reasonable majority of 53 seats over the CDU–CSU, in a legislature of 669 seats. It fell 37 seats short of the minimum winning majority of 335 seats, but very quickly struck a coalition deal with the Green Party in order to scale that hurdle.

What made the 1998 campaign so momentous was that it was the first instance in the history of the Federal Republic of an incumbent governing coalition being voted out of office at a Bundestag election. It was generally accepted that the SPD's strategy had played a central role in this achievement. After such a sea-change in German politics it was clear that the SPD's political competitors would attempt to emulate the party's approach.

The impact of the SPD's 1998 campaign

In retrospect, the 1998 SPD campaign was a watershed in political campaigning in the Federal Republic and the *Kampa* model in particular was adopted by the CDU–CSU in the 2002 campaign, in which it was called 'Arena'.[5] As it turned out, the Arena organisation produced a forceful CDU–CSU campaign that, although ultimately unsuccessful, demonstrated that the CDU–CSU had learned the lessons of defeat in 1998.

For its part, the incumbent SPD–Green Party coalition attempted to deflect attention from an indifferent policy record by stressing the relative popularity of Chancellor Schröder and the Greens' high-profile politician Joschka Fischer. The Greens' emphasis on personalities over issues in the 2002 campaign was particularly noteworthy, given the party's roots in the new social movements of the 1970s, and the party's slogan, 'The second vote is a Joschka vote' (*Zweitstimme ist Joschkastimme*), was evidence, if it was needed, of the distance the party has put between itself and its roots. At the same time, Gerhard Schröder sought to exploit his own popularity by portraying the election as a straight fight between him and the CDU–CSU's chancellorship candidate Edmund Stoiber. As table 7.1. demonstrates, this was a shrewd move by Schröder, who – despite the relative unpopularity of the SPD compared with the 1998 elections – enjoyed a clear lead over Stoiber in terms of general candidate preferences and most specific evaluations of competence.

Interestingly, table 7.1 demonstrates that in the run-up to the 2002 election Stoiber was ahead of Schröder on the key issues of unemployment (33 per cent to 18 per cent) and the economy (33 to 24 per cent). Crucially on both these issues, however, the largest single group of respondents saw no difference between the two candidates. By contrast, Schröder led Stoiber in terms of the public's perceptions of

Table 7.1 *2002 Bundestag elections: public perceptions of candidates and their competences (%)*

		Schröder	Stoiber	No difference
Who can best . . .	create jobs?	18	33	43
	solve economic problems?	24	33	37
	solve future problems?	34	26	33
	represent german interests?	52	21	21
	lead the government?	42	22	27
Who is . . .	the more trustworthy?	40	20	38
	the more 'sympathetic' character?	63	17	18
	a 'winner'?	61	13	23

Source: Forschungsgruppe Wahlen 2002.

their respective abilities to 'solve future problems' (34 to 26 per cent), 'represent German interests' (52 to 21 per cent) and 'lead the government' (40 to 20 per cent). The most striking figures relate to the public's general perceptions of the candidates as personalities. Here Schröder beat Stoiber convincingly, enjoying massive leads over Stoiber with regard to trustworthiness (40 to 20 per cent), 'sympathetic' qualities (63 to 17 per cent), and being a 'winner' (61 to 13 per cent) (Forschungsgruppe Wahlen 2002: 35–7).

Schröder's lead over Stoiber contrasted with the SPD's generally poor showing in terms of party competence. Table 7.2 sets out the public's perceptions of the relative competence of the SPD and CDU–CSU in the six issue areas of jobs, the economy, the future, education and training, the family and foreigners. Although the SPD enjoyed leads over the CDU–CSU in the three areas of the future (35 to 32 per cent), the family (43 to 30 per cent) and foreigners (35 to 34 per cent), it lagged behind the CDU–CSU in the key issue areas of jobs (29 to 38 per cent), the economy (31 to 36 per cent), and education and training (30 to 35 per cent) (*ibid.* 2002: 42–4). Given this disparity between popular perceptions of Schröder as a candidate and the competence of his party, the strategy of fighting a highly personalised campaign in the 2002 Bundestag elections was a rational one. Nevertheless, perhaps because of the ruling coalition's record in government, it was clear the SPD's campaign had failed to make the impact on perceptions of candidate *and* party that had

Table 7.2 *2002 Bundestag elections: public perceptions of party competence (%)*

Issue	SPD	CDU–CSU	Undecided
Jobs	29	38	29
Economy	31	36	29
The future	35	32	28
Education and training	30	35	23
The family	43	30	18
Foreigners	35	34	17

Source: Forschungsgruppe Wahlen 2002.

been achieved in 1998. Political marketing had been used, but the SPD did not adopt a comprehensive market orientation with regard to its policies, delivery and the party as a whole; it was more reliant on the popularity of the leader, a point to which I return in the conclusion to the chapter.

Finally, a point that is worthy of note is the extent to which older campaign techniques remained in place during the 2002 elections, reflecting the impact of path dependence and standard operating procedures on German politics. For instance, political parties remained highly reliant on the old indirect form of marketing through press and television coverage, and in this respect research indicates that the SPD and the Green Party as political incumbents won that particular battle (Eilders *et al.* 2004). In addition, the traditional format of television debates between the chancellorship candidates also had a high-profile role, at least in reinforcing the overall message and mobilising those voters already well disposed towards a particular candidate (Faas and Maier 2004). Ironically, given the relative popularity of Schröder *vis-à-vis* his party after four years in government, the SPD was more reliant on these relatively old modes of campaigning in the 2002 Bundestag election than it was in the 1998 campaign.

Conclusion

In the context of political marketing in the Federal Republic of Germany, the Lees-Marshment CPM model does allow one to frame an analysis of parties' marketing strategies in comparative context. In particular, the model works well as a means by which to order the thick description of the chapter's case study, in which the ideal types of the POP, the SOP and the MOP serve as useful analytical reference points to describe the transformation of the SPD's marketing strategy over the period 1995–98.

At this point, however, four observations have to be made. First, the CPM model must be seen as a set of three ideal types against which we can assess the more untidy reality of practical politics, rather than as a more empirically driven three-stage typology. If, on the other hand, the CPM model is assumed to be a typology of real-world political phenomena, the model will inevitably fall foul of the kind of caveats outlined at the start of chapter. The precise nature of those caveats will vary from case to case, but it can be taken as a given that single-country or area-studies specialists can and will be tempted to use thick description to unpick the underlying rationale of the model. Thus, as a typology, the model's parsimony and holism become a weakness rather than strength.

The second observation is empirical in nature. It will be recalled that in the 2002 Bundestag election the SPD failed to conform as closely to the MOP ideal type as it had managed to do in 1998. This was because, unlike 1998, the 2002 campaign was constrained by the SPD's record in government over the previous four years. In 1998 the party's campaign strategists were able to transform the SPD's image on the basis of private polling, focus-group research, and so on. In particular, 'innovation' was used to harness the positive resonance of the party's reformist credentials while avoiding the negative connotations of 'reform'. Yet it was precisely because the party had been in opposition for the previous sixteen years that this transformation was possible. In a sense, the SPD's marketing strategists were working from the *tabula rasa* of a party unencumbered by the compromises and disappointments of government. By contrast, the 2002 campaign had to be more limited in scope. Any attempt to construct the kind of 'future competence' narrative used in 1998 would have been greeted with incredulity by the voters. That the SPD's record in government was indifferent only aggravated this problem. As a result, the party was forced to downplay its record in government and stress the more amorphous leadership qualities of Chancellor Schröder. To sum up, the evidence of the 2002 campaign suggests that the SPD remains best described as an SOP. The implications of this are twofold. First, the ideal type of the MOP seems to be more appropriate to opposition parties than it is to parties of government. Opposition parties have more scope to construct party programmes that are responsive to voters' preferences, while governing parties must fight on their records. By definition those records will be flawed and less attractive to voters than the promises of opposition parties, especially opposition parties whose time has come (such as New Labour in 1997 or the SPD in 1998). Second, it means that there is no 'ratchet-effect' in the CPM model. In other words, it is not a one-way process from a product-oriented, through a sales-oriented to a market-oriented posture. Thus, in the case of the SPD, the organisational characteristics of the market-oriented ideal type remained in place in the 2004 campaign, but the need to defend a flawed record in government meant that the party's posture moved 'backwards' somewhat towards that of the sales-oriented ideal type.

This leads to the third, theoretical, observation. At present, the conventional understanding of the dynamic of the market-oriented ideal type is that of the 'one-play game', in which political parties subordinate internal organisation, ideological baggage and external profile to satisfying voters' preferences and the business of winning elections. Although, as this book has noted, the MOP model is more complex than that, there is a general concern that political reality is more complex and less classifiable than we might desire. The observations made above demonstrate that political competition is really an 'iterated game', with multiple plays, characterised by an increase in information flows over time. For incumbent parties, the more this game is played the more constrained they become, and that is why, despite the advantages of incumbency, such parties will eventually lose the game and be thrown out of office. It is also why it still holds true that all political careers inevitably end in failure.

Finally, the failure of political parties in Germany to conform to the MOP ideal type reveals the limits of political parties' ability to be responsive to voters' preferences. In Germany, as in other countries, there has been much debate over the previous decade about the extent and the implications of public disenchantment with the political process – particularly in the new federal states (see, for instance, Jeffery and Lees 1998). In theory, at least, the emergence of market orientations among established and newer political parties might do much to alleviate this disenchantment and introduce new dynamism into the political process by presenting voters with genuine electoral choices more attuned to their preferences. But it could also be argued that in complex and increasingly diverse societies such as Germany's it is impossible to aggregate preferences in this manner and that – given voters' increasing volatility and inchoate, contradictory and often illiberal preferences – it is anyway unwise to try to do so. It is beyond the scope of this chapter to discuss these issues any further, but if it is not possible for political parties to become more responsive to voters' preferences then the political sleight of hand and dissembling inherent in the sales-oriented marketing posture will remain the norm in party politics in the Federal Republic for the foreseeable future.

Notes

1 The increasingly free-floating nature of what is called 'brand meaning' over the period since the early 1990s is a phenomenon much commented on in the mainstream marketing literature (see Doyle 2003: 79–80). Although there are clearly differences between marketing training-shoes or coffee and performing an analogous function for political parties, there would appear to be no empirical reason why political parties and the political marketplace should be wholly immune to the process noted above.
2 For more on this subject see for instance, Mintzel (1984).
3 I wish to thank Matthias Machnig and staff at *Kampa* in Bonn for the briefing that informs this passage.
4 The most notable victim of this aspect of their work was Jost Stollmann (Schröder's economics advisor at the time, but not an SPD member) when he began to talk too explicitly about the need for supply-side reforms of the labour market in the last week of the 'hot stage' of the campaign.
5 The author wishes to thank the staff at CDU–CSU headquarters in Berlin for their briefing on campaign strategy and techniques in September 2002.

Bibliography

Arrow, K. J. (1951), *Social Choice and Individual Values*, New York: John Wiley & Sons.
Downs, A. (1957), *An Economic Theory of Democracy*, New York: Harper & Row.
Doyle, C. (2003), *Collins Dictionary of Marketing*, Glasgow: HarperCollins.
Eilders, C., Defenhardt, K., Herrmann, P. and von Der Lippe, M. (2004), 'Surfing the tide: Social Democrats and Greens stayed on top – casualties among other parties. An analysis of party- and issue-coverage in the national election campaign 2002', in T. Saalfeld and C. Lees (eds), *Bundestagwahl 2002: The Battle of the Candidates*, London: Frank Cass.
Faas, T. and Maier, J. (2004), 'Chancellor-candidates in the 2002 televised debates', in T. Saalfeld and C. Lees (eds), *Bundestagwahl 2002: The Battle of the Candidates*, London: Frank Cass.
Forschungsgruppe Wahlen (2002), 'Bundestagswahl: Eine Analyse der Wahl vom 22 September 2002', FGW Nr. 108, Mannheim.
Grabow, K. (2001), 'The re-emergence of the Cadre party? Organisational patterns of Christian and Social Democrats in unified Germany', *Party Politics*, 7(1): 23–43.
Jeffery, C. and Lees, C. (1998), 'Whither the Old Order? The role of West German parties in the last days of the German Democratic Republic', in P. Davies and J. White (eds), *Political Parties and the Collapse of Old Orders*, New York: SUNY Press.

Kaack, H. (1995), 'Functions of party programmes', in J. Thesing and W. Hofmeister (eds), *Political Parties in Democracy*, Sankt Augustin: Konrad Adenauer Stiftung.

Katz, R. and Mair, P. (1992), 'The membership of political parties in European democracies, 1960–1990', *European Journal of Political Research*, 22(3): 329–45.

Lees, C. (1996), 'A watershed election: the Berlin state and city elections of 22 October 1995', *Regional and Federal Studies*, 6(1): 63–72.

Lees, C. (1998), 'Red–Green coalitions in the Federal Republic of Germany: models of coalition formation and maintenance', unpublished thesis, Birmingham University.

Lees, C. (2000), *The Red–Green Coalition in Germany: Politics, Personalities and Power*, Manchester: Manchester University Press.

Lees, C. (2004), *Party Politics in Germany: A Comparative Politics Perspective*, Manchester: Manchester University Press.

Lees-Marshment, J. (2001), 'The product, sales and market-oriented party: how Labour learnt to market the product, not just the presentation', *European Journal of Marketing* 35(9–10): 1074–84.

Machnig, M. (1999), 'Die Kampa als SPD-Wahlkampfzentrale der Bundestagswahl '98: Organisation, Kampagnenformen und Erforlgsfaktoren', *Forschungsjournal NSB*, 12(3): 20–39.

Maier, J. and Rattinger, H. (1999), 'Economic conditions and the 1994 and 1998 federal elections', *German Politics* 8(2): 33–47.

Maier, J. and Rattinger, H. (2004), 'Economic conditions and voting behaviour in German federal elections, 1994–2002', in T. Saalfeld and C. Lees (eds), *Bundestagwahl 2002: The Battle of the Candidates*, London: Frank Cass.

Mair, P. and van Biezen, I. (2001), 'Party membership in twenty European democracies, 1980–2000', *Party Politics*, 7(1): 5–21.

Mintzel, A. (1983), *Die Volkspartei. Typus und Wirklichkeit*, Opladen: Leske & Budrich.

Schmitt-Beck, R. (2003), 'Mass communication, personal communication and vote choice: the filter hypothesis of media influence in comparative perspective', *British Journal of Political Science* 33(2): 233–59.

Statistiches Bundesamt (1998), available: www.destatis.de/d_home.htm.

Stepan, A. (2001), *Arguing Comparative Politics*, Oxford: Oxford University Press.

8

The rise and fall of populism in Austria: a political marketing perspective

Andreas Lederer, Fritz Plasser and Christian Scheucher

This chapter discusses the transformation of the populist Freedom Party (Freiheitliche Partei Österreichs; FPÖ) in Austria between 1986 and 2002. It is argued that this party has adopted aspects of all three political marketing orientations during this period with varying electoral success. The case study focuses on the time under the chairmanship of Jörg Haider from 1986 to 2000, together with a brief analysis of the party's involvement in government from 2000. Under Haider's leadership, the FPÖ's electoral fortunes were transformed from only 4.98 per cent of the vote and 12 of 182 seats in Parliament in 1986 to becoming the second strongest party in Austria 13 years later with 26.9 per cent of the vote (52 seats) and entered government with the conservative People's Party (Österreichische Volkspartei; ÖVP). It therefore appeared in 1999 to be a very successful populist party. In 2002, however, the party lost almost 65 per cent of its former voters and were reduced to eighteen seats. We examine the reasons behind such a dramatic rise and fall in electoral fortune, analysing the phenomenon of apparent populism from a political marketing perspective.

The Austrian political context

Austria appears to be somewhat resistant to the influx of political marketing practices, use of which is observable in many Western European democracies. Institutional features like a party-centered system of political competition, a proportional election system, coalitional governments, a generous public campaign finance system, very limited access to free or paid television advertising and a highly concentrated media market dominated by one public radio and television corporation seem to foster traditional party- and organisation-centered campaign practices.

The nature of the Austrian system, therefore, has a couple of implications for the marketing of political parties:

- Due to its proportional election system, parties usually are forced to enter coalition governments, which affects their ability to deliver, since coalitions are ruled by policy compromise.

• Furthermore, government policy, especially economic policy, is commonly the result of a system of reconciliation of interests between labour and employee organisations, rather than parties, members or the voters at large, a process called *Sozialpartnerschaft*,[1] which constrains the ability of government to shape policies.

Nevertheless, this system and the obvious lack of public transparency became unpopular in the mid 1980s, which provided a window of opportunity for the populist FPÖ and potentially for political marketing.

The Austrian system has several political parties. There are two major parties, the Social Democratic Party (Sozialdemokratische Partei Österreichs; SPÖ) and the conservative ÖVP, as well as the FPÖ. These three parties have been represented in Parliament since the beginning of the second republic, but since 1986 a fourth party, the Green Party (*Die Grünen*), began to win public and electoral support. Between 1993 and 1999 the Liberal Party (Liberales Forum; LIF), a spin-off from the FPÖ, has also won seats in Parliament. Party competition changed in the last quarter of the twentieth century, with increasing fragmentation of the vote, as support for the FPÖ grew from 5 per cent to 27 per cent in the 1980s under the leadership of Jörg Haider, and new parties such as the Greens and the LIF entered the system.

The SPÖ and the ÖVP, the two major traditional parties, have been and still are characterised by very strong organisation. Up to 25 per cent of the population were members of one of these two parties in 1969, in the late 1990s it was still 15 per cent, an unusually high percentage in terms of international comparison (Plasser and Ulram 2002: 97). More than 30 per cent of those who vote for the SPÖ and the ÖVP are party members. Such strong organisation encourages these parties to remain heavily committed to representing the interests of certain groups, whereas the FPÖ, which at its peak had only about 40,000 members, was able to be more flexible in its product design and was therefore more competitive.

Overall, the context of political competition in Austria therefore differs substantially from that in the UK, France or Italy (Plasser 2002: 78–80). The main parties are in a very different situation to that in the UK, potentially limiting the use of a market-oriented approach. For example, a degree of consensus entered the system in the 1980s as the main parties became more co-operative in an attempt to limit Haider's influence and keep his party out of government. The Austrian political system has commonly been regarded as a 'special case' among the family of Western European democracies which suggests it will exhibit a distinctive use of political marketing.

In the last decade, however, a definite shift has taken place both in the voter market and in the way parties have waged their campaigns and communicated with potential voters (Plasser and Ulram 1999: 31). Until the early 1970s Austrian voting patterns could be described using the notions of *Lager* culture and *Lager* affiliation (Pelinka and Plasser 1989): embedded in specific sub-cultural milieus – characterised by the relative stability of distinct structural features such as socio-cultural orientation – emotional attachment and disciplined partisanship shaped the political behaviour of electors and the parties' base vote. Accordingly, electoral volatility – with exception of the parliamentary elections of 1970 – was, by international standards, quite low (Plasser, Ulram and Grausgruber 1992).

Over time, however, the static and politically segmented electoral market was challenged as society changed. The traditional parties' core social groups declined, breaking up traditional social networks that once guaranteed the social accord of political attitudes (Plasser Ulram and Grausgruber 1992). The two major traditional parties, the ÖVP and the SPÖ, have lost some of their sub-cultural base, and with it a generation of loyal voters. There has been an organisational destructuring of the electorate. This process has been accelerated by rise of mass media as key players in the political communication process, which almost vanquished the party press and increased the importance of independent media in general and of television in particular. Summing up, this has resulted in a fundamental change in the traditional parameters of party competition (Luther 1998).

History of political marketing in Austria

Political marketing has existed for some time in Austria, but mainly in terms of the use of marketing techniques rather than its concepts. For example, the first political poll was taken in 1954, commissioned by the occupying powers after the Second World War to gain a picture of Austrian public opinion. At the end of the 1950s the ÖVP started to commission regular professional surveys examining party preferences and approval ratings for several politicians. However, polls at that time had a very limited effect on party behaviour. Until the end of the 1960s, political products and campaigns consisted primarily of appeals to a party's own supporters, mobilising them through party slogans and appeals to ideology and loyalty, with the major parties adopting *product-oriented* strategies to mobilise their base vote.

The use of marketing communications increased in the 1970s. At the end of the 1960s, the SPÖ started a professionalisation initiative and utilised a new polling institute created by one of their own political figures (Meinhart and Schmid, 2000: 52–5). Parties were increasingly attempting to meet the political expectations, desires and moods of a more mobile electorate, in terms, at least, of utilising commercial advertising methods to strengthen their profiles or to establish a candidate's image. The planning and development of Austrian electoral campaigns has become more professional and increasingly oriented towards international and, in particular, US models (Müller and Plasser 1992: 27–8).

The sales-oriented approach has dominated major party behaviour. The two major Austrian political parties, the SPÖ and the ÖVP, have transformed themselves from POPs to SOPs. Contrary to the situation in the UK where Labour and the Conservatives 'are competing to be the most market-oriented' party (Lees-Marshment 2001: 212), the SPÖ and the ÖVP as the two major parties use market intelligence primarily for presentation and for appropriate media designs rather than for the design of policy and behaviour. As we have already noted, Austrian parties are restricted regarding product design and adjustment by the interests of the particular groups affiliated to them and by the traditional issue agenda. Demonstrating issue ownership and a relentless struggle to shape the news cycle in the dominant Austrian media seem to get far more attention than does listening receptively to the concerns and demands of key swing voters. Therefore, available market intelligence is perceived as a guide to be used to improve communication activities rather than as a device for redesigning their products.

With regard to the FPÖ prior to 1986 it was a classic POP. It mobilised a small group of core voters and did not attempt to appeal to other voter groups, because it was anchored in society as the third national *Lager* after the SPÖ and the ÖVP. The FPÖ had loyal voters with around 5–6 per cent of the popular vote. In 1983, having had the poorest election result in its history with 4.98 per cent, the party entered government for the first time in coalition with the SPÖ. However, when the polls indicated that the FPÖ would fail to get into Parliament at the next election Jörg Haider in a coup took over the chairmanship in 1986. Shortly after that the SPÖ terminated the coalition, not wishing to have Haider as the chairman of its coalition partner. It was only then that the FPÖ started to move towards a sales or market orientation, responding both to the coalition's termination and the party's decline in popularity that was threatening its existence.

Political marketing has therefore been utilised in Austria for some years, albeit in a less developed way than in such countries as the USA and the UK, arguably due to Austria's distinctive political system. As a general rule parties have increased their use of marketing only when factors such as election defeats, moves by main competitors to modernise or professionalise or the change from government responsibility to the oppositional role offer the incentive or the necessity to do so.

Case study: populism as a selling and marketing approach – Jörg Haider's FPÖ

Discussion of Jörg Haider's FPÖ's political marketing orientation in 1986–2002 is in two parts. The first part describes the opposition era under the chairmanship of Jörg Haider from 1986, when he took over the party, until 2000, when the party entered government and Haider resigned as chairman. This phase led to an all-time high in electoral success, with the party gaining 26.9 per cent of the votes in the 1999 national election. The second part looks briefly at the FPÖs performance in government, especially its, election campaign in 2002, when the party won only 10 per cent of the votes.

Methodologically the case study draws on selected media coverage during that period, as well as official data and documents about the FPÖ, such as party history, voter analysis and analysis of FPÖ communications. It makes use also of primary data in the form of explorative interviews with senior FPÖ officials about the party's marketing efforts in its 2002 election campaign, as well as with officials of Austria's other three parties. The interviews were conducted in July 2003, the interviewees being the campaign managers of ÖVP, SPÖ, FPÖ and the Greens, plus the parties' officials responsible for strategic communications and opinion research

activities during the election campaign of 2002. The interviews were in part conducted face-to-face, in part via questionnaires.

The FPÖ was selected to enable the application of political marketing theory to
the phenomenon of populism, an undertaking that has not previously been
attempted. Moreover, the development of the FPÖ from a minor party, with 5 per
cent of the vote in 1986, to a one that equalled the share of the vote of one of the
two major parties (in 1999 the FPÖ and the ÖVP both achieved 26.9 per cent),
changed Austria's party competition and challenged the traditions of its political
system. The FPÖs development requires an explanation, and this case study offers
a new approach to that end by utilising the political marketing framework.

We contend that the FPÖ in the last sixteen years has moved through all three
orientations of the model. From 1986, when he took over as chairman, Haider
modernised the party in a way that blurred the distinction between the selling and
market orientations. We argue that in 2002 the party regressed towards a product
orientation and that this was at least part of the reason for its almost catastrophic
electoral defeat.

The development of a market for the FPÖ

In order to understand the party's development it is necessary to explore how
the market changed. From the early 1980s, Austrian society became more diverse
and complex, providing an opening for a populist party. Dissolution of 'cultural
matters of course', emphasis on individualism, fragmentation of social structures,
pluralism of lifestyles – all increased insecurity, alongside an intensification of
de-alignment. Overall trust in the political process and parties also declined after
several political scandals (Plasser and Ulram, 1995: 471–4). The building of a great
coalition in 1986 between the SPÖ and the ÖVP, which together held 85 per cent
of the vote, only reinforced the feeling that Austria was being run by a bureaucratic
elite, unchecked by an effective opposition, which was criticised for its inability to
reform the country. The public also increasingly saw the two major parties as
uniform. The Austrian tradition of *Sozialpartnerschaft* and the lack of discussion,
in public or in Parliament, about party policy development intensified the idea that
politics in Austria was made by elites in smoke-filled backrooms: hence the gap in
the market for a new and *real* opposition.

The FPÖ's history, goals and product

Traditionally a minor, or third, party, the FPÖ was founded to integrate former
National Socialist voters into the party system of the second republic with the goal
of providing an effective opposition. However, from the mid-1960s it tried to
move in a more ideologically liberal direction that would be acceptable for the
other two parties (Luther 1997: 267). The FPÖ supported the minority government of the SPÖ for the year of 1970 and from 1983 to 1986 the party formed a
coalition government with the SPÖ under a liberal FPÖ chairman. In 1986, when
Haider took over the party, the FPÖ became more critical of the two major parties,
and Jörg Haider asserted that his new goal was to become chancellor of Austria by

attracting so many votes that the other parties would have to take notice of the FPÖ. Under Haider's leadership the party also achieved its goal of influencing the national agenda by setting issues and topics for public discourse.

The political product of the FPÖ included the representational party personnel (young officials, with a dynamic and *a* political style of presentation the contrasted with the traditional style of other politicians), the policy programme (populist), the party organisation (for a time the party transformed itself into a 'social movement' to attract voters who were motivated by concerns other than overtly political ones) and communication (emotional, negative, aggressive, appealing to patriotism). Although the party had a membership, those members were given little say: power was concentrated in the hands of Jörg Haider and close associates. Attempts to hold public primaries and to open the party organisation to a broader audience by transforming it into a 'social movement' failed due to the authoritative structure and leadership style.

The rise of populism – the FPÖ between 1986 and 1999

The analysis of the FPÖ behaviour in this first period is undertaken against the MOP model to gauge the extent to which the party fits this framework.[2]

Stage 1 Market intelligence   Market research was organised informally. The FPÖ itself always denied having commissioned research, but there are indications that it eventually did (Meinhart and Schmid, 2000: 132) or, from time to time, at least had access to opinion research data. Most of the market research was gathered informally, such as via feedback at party rallies. Issues at those rallies that attracted public attention were taken up at the state level and, if still relevant were carried to the national level. This was almost a form of test marketing the party's messages, issues and candidates.

The FPÖ also conducted research on opposition parties, although it lacked technical sophistication. Substantial intelligence about allegedly scandalous behaviour among politicians, civil servants and journalists was gathered from private contacts in institutions. The party's competence in conducting opposition research was an important factor in its electoral success, enabling a communication strategy of 'scandalization'. For example, during a televised debate in 1995, Haider was criticised by the editor of one of Austria's biggest magazines. Haider responded by attacking the editor's credibility in a highly personal manner: he produced the contract of a National Bank of Austria employee, referred to his scandalously high wages and other privileges, and asked the editor whether he was acquainted with this individual. When his inquiry was met with silence, Haider revealed that this employee was, in fact, the editor's father-in-law. (Meinhard and Schmid 2000: 117). This anecdote demonstrates the FPÖ's style of communication as well as its competence in opposition research.

Stage 2 Product design   Haider reacted to the market situation as described above in two ways, one market oriented, the other sales-oriented: he changed the

FPÖ's position to market demands by focusing on popular issues, creating an attractive personal offer (mainly himself), and, on the other hand, be actively created demand for his policy by setting and reinforcing issues, something he did very effectively. In terms of the market-oriented aspect, Haider changed the party's image to that of a young, modern and 'stylish' organisation. The party's main officials at that time were usually around 25 years of age and differed in age from the personnel of the literally 'old' main parties. Haider also started to present himself in non-political situations and in doing so conveyed an image of something of an 'anti politician'. He changed the party's orientation on two major issues on which it had a long, ideologically rooted, tradition: the FPÖ changed from a pro-European Union orientation and became anti-EU and its ideological and jingoistic Germanic emphasis shifted to a focus on Austrian patriotism.

In 1986 Haider started to present the FPÖ as a new and dynamic party, and appealed, above all, to people's negative perceptions of politics and its practitioners, and the wasting of tax payers' money. However, from the late 1980s he adopted populist strategies, and constantly played on three topics:

- *Anti–establishment orientation*: traditional political institutions were portrayed as the enemy of the people, acting in their own interests, not the voters', enabling an FPÖ attack on the (traditional) parties, Parliament and the Government ('All politicians have privileges'; 'They are unable to solve the "real" problems, only pursue their own interests, and don't care and/or listen to the people'). He attacked the administration in Brussels in a similar way ('They take away our money'; 'They try to control us', etc.) and opposed the introduction of the Euro, appealing to the Austrian people's emotional attachment to its own currency.
- *Xenophobia*: the highly emotional issue of immigration was one of Haider's strongest suits and one that be used most effectively. He also campaigned against the EU's enlargement and forged a 'Temelin' petition for a referendum, demanding an Austrian veto to the Czech accession to the EU, fearing the Czech's would refuse to shut down the 'Temelin' nuclear power plant. The referendum appealed to fear of a nuclear catastrophe, on the one hand, and to a xenophobic element, on the other.
- *Law and order*: this issue often was connected with that of immigration, and the FPÖ often reinforced stereotypes like black drug-dealers or immigrants being inevitably drawn to criminal activities. Haider exploited emotional issues and constructed a clear 'enemy' to provide an orientation for popular anxieties in times of a more complex reality.

This transformation of the programmatic aspect of the FPÖ´s political product into a populist form is demonstrated by table 8.1, which shows the prime motivations of people voting for Haider in 1986, just after he took over the party, in 1994 after his populist turn, in 1999 at the height of his electoral success just before the party entered government and in 2002 after the FPÖ had lost about 65 per cent of its voters.

Table 8.1   *Transformation of reasons for voting for the FPÖ, 1986–2002*

1986	(%)	1994	(%)	1999	(%)	2002	(%)
Person/image of Jörg Haider	54	Fight against scandals and privileges	22	Rejection of great coalition/ change	22	Anti-immigration and anti-EU enlargement orientation	18
Change	10	Person/image of Jörg Haider	17	Immigration policy	14	Traditional FPÖ Voters	11
Fight against scandals and privileges	9	Immigration	12	Person/image of Jörg Haider	12	Party programme	8
Ideology	8	Effective opposition/ control	11	Concepts of politics	11	Lesser evil or satisfaction with political performance	7
Protest, dissatis-faction with politics	7	Lesson for the coalition parties	10	Lesson for coalition parties	7	To prevent a coalition between SPD and the Green Party	6

Source: Plasser and Ulram, 2000: 229f. and Plasser, Ulram and Seeber 2003: 142.

The table shows the change from motives based on the somewhat vague hope for a new and fresh approach to politics, embodied by Jörg Haider himself in 1986, to motives that were much more emotional and populist in 1994 and 1999 such as the anti-establishment issues of combatting privilege, the need for an effective opposition and lesson for the coalition parties, allied to demands for a restrictive immigration policy and an emphasis law on and order.

The party organisation aspect of the product was also changed, but not in a market-oriented manner. The party was structured around Haider's authoritative leadership, which minimised internal as well as external opinion but proved very efficient in implementing decisions. The FPÖ was a *charismatic* party in which there was a total symbiosis between the leader and organisational identity (Müller, Plasser and Ulram 2004). The success of the FPÖ was inseparable from the party's political communication performance, and the populist self-promotion and rhetorical ability of Haider.[3]

Stage 3 Product adjustment   As a long-term opposition party the FPÖ's policy proposals were often neither readily achievable nor realistic. A good example was the 1999 proposal of a flat tax, by which was meant a single level of taxation for all.

One of its main issues in the campaign prior to entering government, the Flat Tax proposal proved to be an effective campaign vehicle, since the idea was very simple and easily demonstrated. However, the party itself started to doubt its achievability shortly after the election when the FPÖ initiated coalition talks with the ÖVP. The flat tax proposal was not even mentioned in these talks.

Because the FPÖ was until 2000 very centralised in its structure, in the very few cases where there was resistance within the party the officials responsible were either excluded from the party or forced to change their behaviour, indicating a significant neglect of product adjustment.

Nevertheless, the product was positioned far from those of the other traditional parties and was clearly distinctive. The anti-establishment emphasis allowed the party to present itself as a distinct alternative, an 'anti party'. For a short time, the party even transformed itself into a *movement* to demonstrate its differentiation. This initiative was, however, short lived because it failed to generate additional support, arguably because the bottom–up concept of a movement was incompatible with the way in which the party was structured around Haider. Overall the FPÖ did not carry out comprehensive product adjustment.

Stage 4 Implementation   Implementation tended to be undemocratic: Haider set a direction and the party followed. Alternative ideas resulted in the exclusion from the party of the proposers or a forced change in their behaviour. An example of this was the disagreement over the appointment of the executive manager in a state-level party organisation in April 1998. The organisation's chairman severely criticised Haider in public over the appointment, and Haider's reaction was to force him to resign, taking the organisation into his own care, and even dismissing all 700 officials who had defended their chairman. The crisis was resolved a week later when, having made a public apology, the former chairman was reinstated.

There were plenty of signs of internal dissatisfaction with Haider's leadership. In February 1993 five FPÖ members of parliament left to found their own left-liberal party (LIF), which positioned itself as the firmest opposition to Jörg Haider, although it won no parliamentary seats until 1999. Haider's authoritative behaviour is perhaps best described as product oriented, since he designed the product to address voters' needs but did not adjust it to take account of the members' and officials' beliefs and needs, and its implementation was forced.

Stage 5 Communication   The electoral success of Haider depended on the FPÖ's media presence and performance to a significant extent. This was due to its deficient organisation, its weak anchoring in the social structure and its extreme dependence on public moods and emotions. The FPÖ had to try to influence the media agenda and to actively manage political and social issues, so directing public attention to its own framing of problems (Plasser and Ulram 2003a). The party organisation was largely a forum for events staged to attract media attention. Although this applies to some extent to the other parties, the FPÖ surpassed them all in this respect (Müller, Plasser and Ulram 2004).

Haider was adept in manipulating television appearances to best effect. His televised debates with political opponents became the main basis for the image of the FPÖ as an effective opposition party. He presented himself as the aggressively truthful 'anti-politician'. Haider's style of communication was characterised by emotionalism and scandal-mongering. He presented issues in a dramatic and emotional manner, engaged in both impression management and affect management, appealing to people's fears and anti-establishment attitudes and addressing himself to marginalised groups in society.

Haider used the disclosure of (alleged) political scandals as a marketing tool. This made him very attractive to the Austrian boulevard paper *Krone*, which has a reach of about 42 per cent of the country's newspaper readers, and is therefore very influential and his 'partnership' with the Austrian boulevard was another factor in his success. One problem for him and his party, however, was that this radical style of communication and its reliance on scandals and the taboo necessitated ever-increasing doses, and he had to keep meeting this demand in order to stay attractive for the boulevard and the voters. Such sensationalism was possible only for a limited time.

Communication centred around the specific issues which made up the product's policy programme: anti-establishment protest, immigration and law-and-order. These issues enabled him to engage in a 'hard selling' of politics, such was their emotional charge and their appeal to popular fear, anger or Austrian patriotism and national pride.

Jörg Haider fashioned a new campaigning instrument in the Austrian context, using petitions for a referendum as a mobilising and agenda-setting mechanism. Although originally used as a means of citizen participation, Haider used petitions to campaign for his own cause, seeing them as 'campaigns between elections'. Two major examples were the 1993 petition for a more restrictive immigration policy entitled 'Austria first!' and the above-mentioned 2002 'Temelin' petition. The issues selected were always highly emotive and polarising.

Jörg Haider also engaged in sophisticated targeting. He changed his clothes as many as ten times a day in adapting his appearance to his audience: varied leather jackets, regular leisure suits, Carinthian traditional clothing, polo-shirts and Armani suits were among the items he selected, with the help of a design agency, to appeal to the public. Whether addressing managers of big companies or a gathering in a beer tent, he always adapted both his 'look' and his performance, sometimes adopting a regional accent to really *speak* to *his* audience. Haider also dressed in a fashionable, non-official style, participated in a 'culture of the body', including bungee-jumping, and wore 'sexy' outfits at staged media events often with a non-political theme.

Haider brought the 'permanent campaign' – i.e. long-term communication before any official short campaign – to Austria. The FPÖ engaged in national poster campaigns as many as four times per year. This allowed the party to convey messages unsuited to mass-media delivery, making use of the best bill-boards which reached the highest frequency of target voters. This was strategically important

because posters in Austria are still the most important paid media channel of political communication. The FPÖ relied heavily on paid communications, more than
did the other parties. Recently it was estimated that the 'Jörg Haider' brand had cost
about 70 million Euros since 1979 in paid communication, an unprecedentedly
large sum of money for Austrian politics (Kuch and Galley 2003: 15).

Reflecting the emphasis placed on the leader within the product, Haider himself
was always highly involved in designing the party's communications. Advertising
and campaigning were concentrated on a single advertising agency, founded (and
owned until 2001) by the party, though Haider himself wrote the slogans for many
campaigns and was also involved in designing the posters: indeed, he once said:
'that's the thing I am really good at. Perhaps after my political career I will change
to the advertising business' (quoted in Dutzler 1999: 28). This is just one indication of Haider's focus on selling.

Overall, under Haider's leadership the FPÖ was an extremely candidate-centered
party with a new 'non-political' style. The party presented itself as a television or
media party, a symbolic mobilisation agency that tried to focus latent protest attitudes, resentments and deeply rooted frustrations on the figure of a leader who is also
a media 'star'. On the whole, this kind of communication is viewed as manipulative
because of its highly emotional nature. Its scandal-mongering and emotionalisation
are clearly sales-oriented tactics, while the selection of issues can be seen as market
oriented.

Stage 6 Campaign   The party's populism was undergirded by permanent campaigning. The FPÖ campaigned more intensively at election time, its campaign was
on-going between elections, as can be seen from its petitions for referenda and the
fact that it conducted up to four nationwide poster campaigns each year.

Stage 7 Election   The FPÖ's voting share on the national level rose from 4.98 per cent
in 1983 before Haider became chairman to 26.9 per cent in 1999 before the party
entered government. In the 1995 national election the party lost 0.6 percentage points
but at the same time gained votes in absolute terms. In that whole period it increased
its share of the vote in every state election – without exception.

Over time, Haider definitely followed a strategy of maximising his party's voter
share even by scaring off former target groups. This is a strong pointer to a market
orientation. Under Haider the party set aside it's ideological constraints and
affiliation with specific groups in the population as no other party in Austria had
done, and designed its product to gain the biggest possible share of votes. One
reason why this was possible for the FPÖ and not for other parties is probably the
fact that it had never gained more than 6 per cent prior to Haider´s leadership, and
so had little to lose by changing its orientation.

As a consequence of this change in orientation there was a considerable change in
the FPÖ's electorate. Prior to 1986 the core voters of the party consisted of employers, freelancers and senior civil servants. The average age of the party's electorate was
relatively high. In the first years of Haider's chairmanship the electorate changed,

becoming significantly younger on average and consisting of employees and civil servants. On the whole it can be described as a young white-collar party. After Haider's populist turn in the early 1990s the workers became the largest part of the FPÖ's electorate. In 1999 the FPÖ became the strongest party within the voter group of blue-collar workers and displaced the SPÖ, which had relied heavily on the support of blue-collar workers. At the end of the 1990s, the FPÖ also became the first-choice party of the 18–30 year-old voter group.

Between 1983 and 1999 the FPÖ changed from a traditional liberal party to a *young* workers' party, but also targeted, especially in the early 1990s, employees and civil servants. (Plasser and Ulram 1995: 482–6) This indicates that the party did not stick with certain voter groups, but kept changing its strategy to target new and bigger groups, even if that meant losing former ones. This also strongly indicates a market orientation. The FPÖ adopted a hybrid selling *and* marketing orientation, although the more populist the party became the more successful it was at elections.

Populism: blurring the line between the selling and market orientations
The FPÖ, in it's unorthodox way, was very effective in test-marketing its messages informally. In order to meet the mood (not necessarily the needs) of the market, the party also changed its general focus on deeply rooted issues, such as accession to the EU and how that related to an autonomous Austrian nation, to an orientation that was appealing to the market rather than to their former core voters, many of whom the party lost. As our analysis of the transformation of the FPÖ between 1983 and 1999 showed, the party adopted a strategy of maximising its share of the electorate, even at the cost of scaring off certain former voting groups.

While the case study revealed that there are indeed signs of a market orientation, there was, for example, certainly little product adjustment. The strong emphasis on the highly emotive anti-establishment and immigration issues, which were communicated in a very aggressive way using simple stereotypes leaves no doubt that the FPÖ had also adopted a sales-oriented approach. Communications were often designed to appeal to populist fears, national pride or simply to a general protest attitude against the establishment and politics, which emerged from the early 1980s on in Austria. This has to be seen as 'hard-sell' politics, and proved highly persuasive. Therefore, although there are some indications of a marketing orientation, the party's populism seems to be more sales-oriented, though this blurs the distinction between the SOP and the MOP in the Lees-Marshment framework.

The FPÖ in government: 2000–2

The FPÖ's time in government was one of mixed directions, pursued by the populist faction and the pragmatic faction. Officials closest to Chairperson and Vice-Chancellor Susanne Riess-Passer pursued a pragmatic policy programme, while Jörg Haider, then formally only an ordinary member of the party, but governor of the state of Carinthia and, indeed, still the most powerful person in the party, pursued an oppositional programme. This divergence in direction was exacerbated by the fact that the party lost a series of state and local elections – for the first time since 1986 – after they had entered government. At the 2002 national elections, the party lost 17 percentage points, more than 60 per cent of their voters, and gained only 10 per cent of the votes. In what follows we briefly present a few reasons for the catastrophic defeat of the FPÖ from a marketing viewpoint.

The fall of populism

The party did not have a clear product. The struggle over the general direction of the FPÖ made it impossible for the party to design, implement or communicate a clear and cohesive product. Organisationally, after Haider stepped down as chairman, they lacked a central authority for development or implementation. Haider, as the long-term main communicator of the party, was replaced by a 'choir of many voices'. By the time of the 2002 elections, with Haider badly damaged by his visit to Iraq to meet Saddam Hussein on the eve of the bombings, the FPÖ had no personnel with whom to attract voters.

By entering government the FPÖ had brought itself into a situation where its scope to design its own product was considerably limited. Prior to 2000 the competitive strategy of the other parties was to keep the FPÖ out of government, and this had provided the FPÖ with a very distinct position in the party marketplace; but once the ÖVP agreed to form a coalition with the FPÖ, the latter lost that strategic advantage.

By the 2002 elections, as can be seen in table 8.1, the FPÖ had lost credibility on all its core competences except the immigration and EU issues. The party lost credibility because it failed to deliver the promised product of a party without scandals and privileges. For example, FPÖ officials were supposed to donate any of their wages which exceeded 4,400 Euro per month, but this was never transparently shown to have taken place (though since 2000 several FPÖ ministers publicly do so).

The planning of the election campaign that followed the coup by the Haider faction within the FPÖ was rather amateurish and chaotic. The resignation of the FPÖ chairperson, Riess-Passer, which was preceded by weeks of internal conflicts about the party's direction, not only triggered the premature end of the coalition with the ÖVP, necessitating new elections, but created personal turmoil within the membership. Riess-Passer's hastily proclaimed successor resigned from office after only two weeks, just as the billboards were being pasted to display posters of his face. The FPÖ had to nominate a new leading candidate and party chair, Herbert Haupt, in a hurriedly summoned party convention. Due to the resignations of leading staff members who left alongside Riess-Passer, the FPÖ was forced to entrust comparatively inexperienced personnel with the planning and organisation of its campaign. The result was a campaign conducted in a chaotic, inconsistent and defensive manner.

As for policy delivery, the party's lack both of experience in government and of qualified personnel for its ministries made it difficult for the FPÖ to get its policies accepted by its coalition partner: there was a lack of policy consensus within the party. Moreover, and indicative of the neglect of product adjustment, many of the promises it made in opposition simply were not achievable and the party's delivery record was therefore very poor. To make matters even worse, credit for any policies that proved popular went to the ÖVP instead. Overall, there was a regression to a product orientation, with a lack of market intelligence, and the design of the product, rather than voters' interests and needs, was the dominant concern of the party's factions.

Difficulties translating UK practice to another country

Parties in countries with a proportional electoral system have problems with delivery due to the fact that they have to form party coalitions and make policy compromises. However, the FPÖ's extraordinary problems with delivery were due also to its total lack of experience of governance, which made it hard for the party to get its policies accepted by its coalition partner, as well as to the populist nature of its promises which are generally unlikely to be deliverable.

Another problem related to coalition government is the difficulty voters have in evaluating the relative contribution to any success of the parties concerned. Which one do they credit for successful initiatives? In coalition governments it sometimes is impossible to say which aspects of a policy was initiated by one or other party. In terms of the Lees-Marshment model, it is therefore possible that a party delivers but is not credited for doing so by the voters! Such problems make the evaluation of delivery difficult and uncertain where the party in question is a partner in government.

Another issue is the fact that the FPÖ resists classification in terms of a single orientation. Between 1986 and 1999 its behaviour can only be described as a hybrid, displaying aspects of both a sales and a marketing orientation. This hybrid was, however, highly successful with regard to election results. Indeed, its success contradicts the claims of the model that, of the three, it is the market orientation that is most likely to yield success in an election and that it would make persuasive communication obsolete.

Difficulties or issues arising from the use of political marketing generally

The introduction of marketing techniques into politics gives rise to the question of whether politics by its very nature can ever be market oriented; the FPÖ's blurring of the marketing and selling orientations, evident from this analysis, underscores that doubt. Although this case study is of a populist party and is not necessarily generalisable, it has to be asked whether politics and the principle of marketing to 'satisfy customers' needs' can be fully reconciled. Perhaps it is the case that politics is always persuasive to a certain extent; and, if so, there is a general problem with the market orientation's claim that an MOP would *inform* voters about its product instead of trying to *persuade* them to want it, and so bring about a change in people's attitudes. This is to question whether a *pure* market orientation can be said ever to exist.

Politics is always caught between leading and following the electorate. The practice of politics has to have a leadership function, and as an incentive to further discussion we ask, sceptically, to what extent this can be reconciled with the marketing doctrine *per se.*

Notes

1 *Sozialpartnerschaft* describes a neo-corporatist system of co-operation between the major organisations of employers and employees with regard to economic policy. The Austrian Government has implemented the policies developed by this institution for more than thirty years without questioning its advice.
2 Stages 1–7 of the model are applied; stage 8 – delivery – does not apply to the period under consideration: the FPÖ under Haider entered national government only in 2000, and until then the party was not called on to deliver.
3 After Haider resigned as party chair and withdrew from all federal functions, the escalating internal disputes resulted in a coalitional crisis and defeat at the parliamentary election 2002 (Luther 2003).

Bibliography

Dutzler, K. (1999), 'Haider einmal andersrum', *Format* (Vienna): 28–9.
Kuch, K. and Galley, J. (2003), 'Haider macht mobil', *NEWS* (Vienna), no. 35, 28 August: 15.
Lees-Marshment, J. (2001), *Political Marketing and British Political Parties*, Manchester: Manchester University Press.
Luther, K. R. (1997), 'Die freiheitlichen', in H. Dachs, P. Gerlich, H. Gottweis *et al.* (eds), *Handbuch des politischen Systems Österreichs: Die Zweite Republik*, Vienna: Manz: 286–304.
Luther, K. R. (1998), 'From accommodation to competition: the "normalization" of the second republic's party system?', in K. R. Luther and P. Pulzer (eds), *Austria 1945–95: Fifty Years of the Second Republic*, Aldershot: Ashgate: 121–60.
Luther, K. R. (2003), 'The self-destruction of right wing populism? Austria's election of 24th November 2002', *Working Paper 16*, Keele European Parties Research Unit, available at: www.keele.ac.uk/depts/spire/Working%20Papers/KEPRU/KEPRU%20Paper16.pdf (accessed 10 November 2003).
Meinhart, E. and Schmid, U. (2000), *Spin Doktoren: Die hohe Schule der politischen Manipulation*, Vienna: Czernin.
Müller, W. C. (2000), 'Wahlen und die dynamik des österreichischen parteiensystems seit 1986', in F. Plasser, P. A. Ulram and F. Sommer (eds), *Das österreichische Wahlverhalten*, Vienna: WUV: 13–54.
Müller, W. C. and Plasser, F. (1992), 'Austria: the 1990 campaign', in S. Bowler and D. M. Farrell (eds), *Electoral Strategies and Political Marketing*, London: St Martin's Press: 24–42.
Müller, W. C., Plasser, F. and Ulram, P. A. (2004), 'Weakness as an advantage and strength as a handicap: party responses to the erosion of voter loyalties in Austria', in P. Mair, W. C. Müller and F. Plasser (eds), *Parties in Electoral Markets*, Thousand Oaks, CA: Sage.

Pelinka, A. and Plasser, F. (1989), 'Compared to what? The Austrian party system in an international comparison', in A. Pelinka and F. Plasser (eds), *The Austrian Party System*, Boulder, CO and London: Praeger: 1–19.

Plasser, F. (2002), *Global Political Campaigning: A Worldwide Analysis of Campaign Professionals and Their Practices*, Westport, CT: Praeger.

Plasser, F. and Ulram, P. A. (1995), 'Wandel der politischen Konfliktdynamik: Radikaler Rechtspopulismus in Österreich', in W.C. Müller, F. Plasser and P. A. Ulram (eds), *Wählerverhalten und Parteienwettbewerb: Analysen zur Nationalratswahl 1994*, Vienna: Signum: 471–504.

Plasser, F. and Ulram, P. A. (1999), 'Trends and ruptures: stability and change in Austrian voting behavior 1986-1996', in G. Bischof, A. Pelinka and F. Karlhofer (eds), *The Vranitzky Era in Austria*, Boulder, CO: Westview: 31–55.

Plasser, F. and Ulram, P. A. (2000), 'Rechtspopulistische Resonanzen: Die Wählerschaft der FPÖ', in F. Plasser, P. A. Ulram and F. Sommer (eds), *Das Österreichische Wahlverhalten*, Vienna: Signum: 225–41.

Plasser, F. and Ulram, P.A. (2002), *Das österreichische Politikverständni: Von der Konsens – zur Konfliktkultur?* Vienna: WUV.

Plasser, F. and Ulram, P. A. (2003a), 'Striking a responsive chord: mass media and right wing populism in Austria', in G. Mazzoleni, B. Horsfield and J. Stewart (eds), *The Media and Neo-Populism: A Contemporary Analysis*, Westport CT: Praeger: 21–43.

Plasser, F. and Ulram, P. A. (eds) (2003b), *Wahlverhalten in Bewegung: Analysen zur Nationalratswahl 2002*, Vienna: WUV.

Plasser, F., Ulram, P. A. and A. Grausgruber (1992), 'The decline of *lager*-mentality and the new model of electoral competition', in K. R. Luther and W. C. Müller (eds), *Politics in Austria: Still a Case of Consociationalism?* London: Frank Cass: 16–44.

Plasser, F., Ulram, P.A. and G. Seeber (2003), 'Erdrutschwahlen: Momentum, Motive und neue Muster im Wahlverhalten', in F. Plasser and P. A. Ulram (eds), *Wahlverhalten in Bewegung*, Vienna: Signum: 97–159.

9

Change to win? The Brazilian Workers' Party's 2002 general election marketing strategy

Josiane Cotrim-Macieira

Brazil is a young Latin American democracy in which ideology and traditions are still in their adolescence since re-democratisation, in the 1980s, after more than twenty years of military dictatorship. Its lack of an established democracy could suggest that political marketing and the Lees-Marshment model has little relevance to Brazil, given the country's striking contrasts with most of the other nations studied in this book. Nevertheless, political marketing is already at work in Brazil, even in a market-oriented form. This chapter seeks to understand why, to what extent and with what consequences a UK–US-generated practice can be implemented in the very different political market environment that Brazil presents. To do so, it focuses on how the Brazilian left-wing Workers' Party – Partido dos Trabalhadores (PT) – led by Luiz Inácio Lula da Silva changed its behaviour in order to win the 2002 presidential election.

The PT is an interesting case for consideration from a political marketing viewpoint. It had exhibited the most ideologically driven behaviour of any Brazilian party since 1989, and as a result had lost three elections. To win in 2002 it had to attract more than the usual 30 per cent of the electorate which PT, in coalition with the Left, had always gained (Jacob and al. 2003: 287). Changes, too, were necessary, to the personal image of the party's leader and presidential candidate, and to its political strategy, by entering into coalition with the conservative Partido Liberal (PL) and moving the party towards the Centre. This was a major departure from the PT's previous avoidance of co-operation with any but left-wing parties. The strategy was very successful: Lula da Silva was made the PL's leader, and with José Alencar as vice-president the party almost won outright on the first election stage (with 46.44 per cent of the vote) in October 2002; at the second stage, in November, the PT achieved a spectacular victory with 61.27 per cent of the total valid votes.

The chapter explores the change in approach and the movement towards a more market-oriented form of politics in Brazil, as well as whether the victory was the result of a well-conducted political marketing exercise. Signates (Jury 2003) argues that it is incorrect to think that political marketing on its own can decide an election, though he recognises that the PT's candidate managed to win the presidential election only after adopting professional communication and campaigning techniques. However, political marketing influences the politics, not just the presentation, and it was only when PT promoted a re-articulation of its policies that it became possible to increase the party's 'captive' voters (see Jury 2003). The chapter also considers the utility of the Lees-Marshment model and its applicability to Brazil's political context.

Brazil's political system and market

Brazil's political system is in many ways distinctive, although similarities exist with other democracies examined in this collection. The first presidential election after twenty-one years of military dictatorship was held in 1989. The Brazilian political system, with its electorate of 115 million presents contrasts, inconsistencies and frequent advance-and-retreat movements. Its electoral rules and legislation are complex and inefficient, and while the aim is to prevent corruption they can make political stability extremely difficult and increase voters' disorientation, although these outcomes are not unknown in other, more established, liberal democracies; for example, the 2000 US presidential election produced an unclear and contested result, and there was considerable debate about the legitimacy of voter registration in Florida.

The introduction of a new constitution in 1988 means that Brazil has a presidential system[1] and an electoral system which allows two rounds of voting at both national and provincial elections. According to the new rules for presidential and provincial government elections, and for the election of mayors in towns with more than 200,000 inhabitants, a second voting round may take place if a candidate does not gather at least 50 per cent of the vote in the first turn; in that case the two candidates with the most votes in the first round dispute the second. There were two rounds held in 1989 when Fernando Collor de Mello won, but only one in 1994 and 1998 because Fernando Henrique Cardoso received 54.3 per cent and 53.1 per cent of the vote, respectively. Luiz Inácio Lula da Silva of the PT contested all three elections, but won only in 2002 with 61.27 per cent of the vote in the second round, a comfortable lead of 22.6 per cent on his opponent José Serra, the governing party's candidate (hereafter, the situation candidate), who got 38.73 per cent of the valid vote (Jacob *et al.* 2003: 295). Such a system can obviously have implications for political marketing strategy (see Nicolau 2001: 9).

Other complexities exist, such as the co-existence of compulsory voting (for those over 18) and facultative (for those aged 16–18 years and for those over 70). Most Brazilian citizens of voting age are compelled to participate in the electoral process, under the threat of legal punishment in the case of no-shows, yet it is possible for voters to formally justify their non-participation (thus avoiding sanction) if absent from their constituency by filling in a specific form.

Electronic voting was introduced in the 2002 presidential election, which makes possible a 'blank' vote (meaning a lost vote or a vote for no one) or even a deliberately incorrect vote (for example, by indicating a non-existent candidate or using the wrong candidate number). The opportunity for blank and incorrect votes in electronic elections was preserved to permit voters to express protest and non-conformance, thereby further destabilising the system.

Nevertheless, participation, arguably as a consequence of the rules, is high in Brazilian elections. Moreover, most voters avoided blank or intentionally incorrect voting in the 2002 elections when, of the 91 million voters (out of a total of around 115 million eligible voters) only 1.88 per cent cast blank votes and 4.12 per cent nulls (www.tse.gov.br [accessed June 2003]). Indeed, the percentage of valid votes in the 2002 election significantly increased in comparison to that in 1998, from 81.3 per cent to 89.6 per cent (Jacob *et al.* 2003: 288), as is evident from an analysis of the geographical voting map. The reasons for this were both the introduction of the electronic ballot and the strong competition between the four main candidates, as well as 'the role of the media, mainly television, that promoted a broad debate about the succession of Fernando Henrique Cardoso' (Jacob *et al.* 2003: 289).[2]

As presidential elections were re-introduced only about fifteen years ago, Brazilian political party organisation is relatively young and has its origin in dictatorship. It was re-organised in the late 1970s when the military dictatorship was still ruling the country, but the Political Party Reorganisation Act was implemented in October 1979 which permitted a party realignment. As Passador (1999: 23) states:

> Arena renamed as PDS, and MDB renamed as PMDB, emerged as the two biggest political parties, along with the organization of new parties linked to the labor movement: PDT, PTB and PT. To some extent, the real novelty – by its style and discourse – was PT, Partido dos Trabalhadores – Workers Party . . . Its origins were linked to the strikes held around by the end of the 70s and beginning of the 80s in the 'enlarged ABC', a region in São Paulo (a metallurgical area) and to the recognition of the strikers' leadership as representative of the workers' class sector. It sprang from the São Paulo trade union movement and pursued an organized and centralized form of political action.

Civilian and democratic rule in the 1980s led Brazil into a period of political transition, and individual political liberty was enlarged: amnesty was decreed for political crimes; political persecution ceased; permission was granted for social and political demonstrations and there was a return to direct voting and free balloting. However, this transition was marked by a deep social and economic crisis (in Sarney's Government), triggered by the failure of successive stabilisation plans, the inability to manage the country's social problems and the insolvency of government policies.

Such problems jeopardised the voters' belief in governmental and political structures, providing an ideal opportunity for a candidate such as Fernando Collor de Mello, who was independent and not linked to any party, to succeed. The ordinary voter saw Collor's isolation from the whole system of political parties as a virtue. His campaigners utilised the complete range of political marketing tools intensively and he won in the second voting round against Luiz Inácio Lula da Silva in 1989. As Sallum, Graeff and Gomes de Lima (1990: 15) observed:

> The novelty presented by Collor's campaign does not fall – it is important to stress – in the association with the organized schemes to access the media, the opinion polls, publicity and personal contact with voters. This can exist in any major electoral

campaign. The novelty is in the creation of a political–electoral enterprise virtually exempt of any political party framework, taking the PRN [candidate's party] as a mere label used to attend to the electoral legislation requirements.

Collor's period in power was, however, marked by a lack of delivery and he was impeached after only thirty months. Vice-president Itamar Franco assumed the presidency and launched a new economic plan.[3] Fernando Henrique Cardoso, the finance minister responsible for the plan, became a candidate for the presidency, winning in 1994 and again in 1998. Voters wanted not change, but rather 'the continuity of an economic policy that stabilized the currency' (Figueiredo 2003: 65).[4] This scenario only changed in 2002 when Lula beat the situation candidate José Serra in the second round of the election, as predicted by polls (*ibid.*).

The main points from this brief survey of recent Brazilian political history are that the system is young, not having been in place for many years; the national political scene is not stable and the dynamics of elections are influenced more by personal leadership than by a true and well-defined ideological competition among political parties. Most political parties lack tradition and consolidation and often resort to opportunistic strategic formulation. As Passador (1998: 32) commented: 'to some extent, the Brazilian political parties remained conspicuously underdeveloped . . . [and] the electoral system . . . reinforc[es] the politicians' individualistic electoral behavior as well as situations that tend to make parties fragile'. The leader is therefore the most important aspect of the product in Brazilian presidential elections.

This focus on the leader is intensified by the Brazilian media, and in 2002 the attention they paid to the leader increased further. Aldé (2003: 93) analysed the election coverage by the main Brazilian newspapers, and concluded that 'in the 2002 presidential election the media [were] more inclined to focus on the electoral subject as a "news fact" than the 1994 and 1998 presidential campaign'. In the 2002 election, the news and entertainment programmes also dedicated an extensive amount of time, outside of that allowed by the electoral rules, to the candidates. 'An endless series of individual interviews of the candidates along with debates between them became the campaign landmark' (Figueiredo and Coutinho 2003). For instance, during the campaign Globo Network, the leading television network in Brazil, broadcast a live interview with each of the candidates during its evening news programme, the first time this had ever been done. It attracted a significant audience: 'an average of 40 points in Ibope [the institute which measures audiences] which means that around 2.1 million spectators a minute in the whole country were on average assisting' (Figueiredo and Coutinho 2003) – parties had to focus significant energy on television appearances by their candidates.

Indeed, Mainwaring (1991) argued that no democracy in the world gives politicians as much autonomy in relation to political parties as the Brazilian democracy. Laws relating to the behaviour of political parties stimulate autonomy and work against compromise, solidarity, discipline and cohesion, providing party leaders with greater power and space to implement a new product design, unlike their UK counterparts, as is evident from Brazil's trend towards an increasing use of political marketing in recent years. Brazil's parties are also less ideological, facilitating the development and implementation of a market-orientation. In a study of the Brazilian political party system, Nicolau (2003: 18) noted that, with the exception of the PT, 'the main Brazilian political parties are pragmatic and only faintly ideological'. Once in power, a party is likely to focus on the political centre; furthermore, most other parties would co-operate with it.

Another systemic factor of significance is that Brazilian electoral legislation stipulates each party has free television time, during a period prior to and during elections, in which to broadcast its electoral programme.[5] In principle, the Brazilian legislation allows two types of political programme on radio and television: the party broadcast, in which political parties aired their policies during normal periods of governance, and the electoral broadcast, in which candidates would promote themselves and their policy proposals during the official campaign. The HPEG (*horário político eleitoral gratuito* – political electoral free time) was an important step towards equalising the political dispute bases (Miguel 2003).[6] The Brazilian electorate is huge (115.2 million) and significantly divided in terms of income, the majority being poorly educated and having insufficient income. Television as an inexpensive source of entertainment and information for the masses (87.7 per cent of residences have at least one TV set), covering 99.86 per cent of the national territory (see Figueiredo and Coutinho 2003: 9), so that television plays a crucial role during Brazilian elections.

Figueiredo (2003: 39) has observed that there is a difference between marketing and the exaggeration of marketing, which he calls *marquetismo*. For him, 'this distorted kind of political marketing will simply disappear as it proves to itself its own inefficiency'. An example of this distortion is the fact that 'many times, the media [give] much more space to a marketing expert than to a candidate with little electoral chances' (*ibid.*: 7). *Marquetismo* is on the one hand the result of the hyper-development of political marketing in Brazilian politics and on the other a consequence of its underdeveloped political parties. However, and in contrast to the parties' inefficiencies, he notes how Brazilian elections have demonstrated that the voters themselves display considerable responsibility, refusing to vote for candidates whose campaigns are marked by the use of 'tricks' to confuse or deceive them. He concludes that *marquetismo* has a double – and definitive – imperfection: it is neither constructive for the democracy that sustains it nor efficient for the candidates who adopt it. It should be noted that Lees-Marshment's comprehensive or marketing-oriented form is not the same as *marquetismo*.

The Brazilian political system is still in a process of maturation: modalities of participation and representation are constantly developing. That process has seen a number of leaders attempt to make government more efficient and honest. Corruption, and attacks on corruption, remain a strong part of Brazilian political life and a considerable number of cases have been 'tried and convicted', amid acrimonious and turbulent exchanges between political factions both in Parliament and in society in general. It is therefore difficult to make firm predictions about how the Brazilian political system and political marketing practices will impact on one another.

Political Marketing in Brazil: a brief history

Although it can be considered a relatively new activity in Latin America, political marketing has 'bloomed powerfully in Brazil' as Figueiredo (2003) states. In his book *Marketing Político e Persuasão Eleitoral (Political Marketing and Electoral Persuasion)*, this Brazilian academic writes that nowadays it is impossible to conceive of presidential, provincial or local election campaigns in Brazil without the use of modern political marketing techniques (2000: 18). Additionally, market intelligence is conducted, and Figueiredo notes that efficient public opinion polling agencies have developed in Brazil, alongside public relations agencies. Brazil also 'exports political marketing professionals' (p. 19) to service campaigns in Argentina, Paraguay, Bolivia, Angola and Mozambique. Indeed, the 2002 presidential election in Brazil produced more opinion polls than have been seen before in the country during an electoral process. Figueiredo and Coutinho (2003) list seventy opinion surveys results released between January and the beginning of October 2002: 23 from IBOPE, 15 from Datafolha, 12 from the Instituto Sensus and 20 from Vox Populi.[7] 'Evidently, each one was followed by analysis, forecasts and comments by journalists, sociologists, political scientists, economists, publicity professionals, politicians and, sometimes, even psychoanalysts' (Figueiredo and Coutinho 2003: 1).

Figueiredo's (2003) analysis tends to focus on the use of political marketing communication and campaigning, whereas this chapter and the Lees-Marshment model calls for consideration of the influence of marketing, and public opinion, on political behaviour or product design. Collor de Mello's 'anti-party' victory in 1989 reflected the politician's response to voter distrust of any established political organisation: he appealed to people's aspirations regarding, and demands for, a new form of government, thereby adopting an element of a market orientation. Nevertheless, other Brazilian political parties failed to mirror people's desires and needs very effectively: most of them, far from acting as people *fora*, preferred to act as instruments favouring specific clients. Furthermore, Collor's success was limited: his Government was plagued by inexperience and inefficiency, and fell into corruption. As Lees-Marshment (2001a: 700) writes 'the ultimate judgment is obviously the general election, but just because a party wins does not mean it will provide satisfaction'. Despite a successful electoral campaign, Collor was quickly seen to be failing to deliver his promises, and he resigned before he was impeached. Prior to 2002, then, there were elements of political marketing in Brazil but it had never been used comprehensively. In order to understand how PT broadened political marketing practice in Brazil we need to focus on the party's history.

PT: a POP by tradition
The history of the major Brazilian political party PT officially starts on February 1980, when it was launched in the Colégio Sion (Sion School), of São Paulo, with

1,200 people in attendance. Its original support base included a blend of leftist militants, religious activists, popular movements and union leaders remaining from the resistance movements that fought the military dictatorship. From the beginning, although being clearly positioned as a leftist party, it avoided commitment to any doctrine, including Marxism (Meneghelo 2003: 42), presenting itself as an ideologically pluralist party and soon took the 'socialism with democracy' approach as a fundamental reference. It is therefore quite different from established parties such as the UK Conservative Party which has decades of history and an ideological tradition that bind it and can present internal obstacles to any leader who wishes to change it.

Nevertheless, for the first three post-dictatorship elections in Brazil, PT embraced a rather vague socialist society project, defined mainly through its opposition to capitalism and its criticisms of social-democratic ideas: 'the PT project is to conquer power (not only government) in order to transform Brazil into a socialist society [...] PT is critical of the social-democratic proposals. The social-democratic trends do not present, today, any real perspective of capitalism surmounting . . . (*Partido dos Trabalhadores* 1999: 20–1). Another indication of a product orientation is that the party refused to consider coalition with any but leftist parties, even though this restricted it to an average of 30 per cent of the total valid votes (see Jacob *et al.* 2003: 305 for analysis of the PT's results in the three former elections).

The party organisation is somewhat complex, encompassing several ideological trends, from those of the extreme Left to those of the Centre-Left. The seven internal pre-candidatures who campaigned to be nominated as the party's presidential candidate in 2001 embodied as many as twenty different trends (Meneghelo 2003: 49). Membership is a very important aspect of the PT. Despite losing three presidential elections and experiencing an inevitable fall in mobilisation from defeats, PT demonstrated an unusual capacity to maintain its internal organisation. 'The Party carried out a membership and renewing subscriptions campaign and started the century with more than 924,000 members, and with directories in 4,016 constituencies out of a total of 5,528 in the country' (*ibid.*: 48).

PT also tried to test new strategies aimed at expanding electoral support, introducing at the local government level an innovative formula for popular participation in the 1990s through public debate on the budget. The 'participatory budget program', as it was known, was particularly successful at the Brazilian industrial port of Porto Alegre (a three-time host of the World Social Global Forum), the capital of Rio Grande do Sul (*ibid.*).[8] Overall, however, the party maintained an internally focused ideological POP approach although it selected Luiz Inácio Lula da Silva as its official candidate for the fourth time even though he had been unsuccessful in the elections of 1989, 1994 and 1998. It was only in 2002 that it changed its approach and began to use political marketing in a market-oriented form.

PT's quest to win the 2002 presidential election campaign

This section explores the extent to which the PT's successful electoral strategy in 2002 was market oriented, demonstrating how the party's behaviour fitted the different aspects and stages of the MOP as proposed by Lees-Marshment (2001a). It also aims to show how political marketing techniques are evolving in Brazil, the third-largest democracy in the world in number of voters (Figueiredo 2003: 57). Methodologically, the empirical sources for this analysis were collected from the media, the PT's website and direct observation of the (30- and 60-second) party's television broadcasts during the electoral period.[9]

After three mayoral electoral defeats, it became clear that the PT's traditional product orientation was not proving successful and the leader, Lula, was beginning to change his attitude. As Almeida (2002: 221) observed, qualitative focus-group research which evaluated the PT's free political advertising on television in the 2002 campaign found that 'Lula's image had improved. He was perceived as more prepared, less radical, less aggressive and therefore able to carry out the position he was asking voters to elect him to.' This was a reflection of the more thorough change in the party's strategy, policies and overall behaviour to be explored in this section.

The motivation for PT to adopt a market orientation came from successive elect-oral defeats and the accumulation of political and administrative experience from one election to another.[10] As Rubim (2003: 10) states, in political and media terms, the image conversion of PT and Lula da Silva was in fact a long time in the making (see also Almeida 2002: 221). The 2002 campaign reflected departure from the party's past product-oriented behaviour and represented a conscious decision on the part of the PT leadership to change its attitude to politics; as Rubim (2003: 10) has observed, the change was not something merely electoral or even a genial mar-keting invention from PT's strategist Duda Mendonça.' Nicolau (2003: 18) has pointed out that other, more pragmatic, Brazilian parties seem to enjoy greater electoral success and that 'Luiz Inácio Lula da Silva and the PT direction members seem to have learned that lesson'.

Market intelligence

As already noted, PT used former electoral results as a form of market intelli-gence and a guide to areas in need of change; it also made use of consultants and utilised quantitative and qualitative research. In terms of professionals, the most notable appointment was that of the political marketing expert Eduardo – 'Duda' – Mendonça. In the first months of 2001 Lula da Silva commissioned him to create a campaign to convey Lula's new approach and to make sure voters knew he was now offering what they wanted. However, as Lees-Marshment (2001b: 32–3) has noted cautioned, there was some internal resistance to the use of professionals. Certain party members were uncomfortable with the commis-sion of Duda Mendonça to design the presidential campaign. As Mendonça (2001: 236) recalled: 'I knew some PT sectors were resistant to the commission of my name to coordinate the campaign.' He was aware that the resistance derived from the fact that earlier he had worked for politicians who were long-time opponents of PT, such as Paulo Maluf, ex-governor and mayor of Sao Paulo (*ibid.*).

Duda Mendonça developed the strategy for the campaign from the results of survey analysis.[11] Indeed Mendonça is known for his obsession with surveys and himself admitted:

> I never devise a campaign without carrying out an analysis or diagnostic. This diagnostic takes into consideration data from quantitative and qualitative research, exhaustive interviews, analysis of the political situation, and comparative work with the main opponents. (quoted in Figueiredo and Coutinho 2003: 34)

PT utilised market segmentation, focusing on voters who had never supported the party but who might do so. Mendonça (2001) noted that in May 2001 (seventeen months before the election's first-turn vote) it commissioned a number of qualitative and quantitative research projects in order to understand the views of people who had never voted for the candidate Lula da Silva but who might in 2002. Mendonça (2001) commented at the time that 'those surveys uncovered a huge amount of information. Unfortunately, I cannot talk about it here because I would finish by giving too much information to the opponents'.

Qualitative research on the electorate's perception of Lula also generated positive results, indicating that voters perceived the candidate as someone who would attend to social problems and would administrate with vigour and emotion (Figueiredo and Coutinho 2003: 19). Lula did, however, change his behaviour in response to awareness that his background as a radical union leader, his lack both of formal education and of administrative experience had lost him the support of significant segments of the electorate, leading him to become less radical and more centrist.

The adoption of a market orientation need not result in drastic change: it all depends on what the electorate wants (Lees-Marshment 2001b: 33). The electorate had demonstrated a desire for change, but not of a radical kind. Once PT's product was designed it became evident that moderation was the style adopted to please the electorate. 'People were looking forward for change but not for a revolution' (Figueiredo 2003: 79). The PT made a number of changes to aspects of its product in response to market intelligence.

Product design

Leader   PT's leader Lula da Silva changed his approach considerably from what it was when he had been a radical union leader who wanted to break the national economical model. In 2002, Lula changed to suit public opinion in several ways: his speeches became more moderate, moving away from his previous radical discourse; and communication strategies were designed to convey this new approach to avoid radicalism and confrontation, accompanied by subtle but significant changes in his personal appearance.

Lula was not university educated, and this was emphasised by his opponents during the campaign. Lula sought to counteract the perceived weakness of this lack of formal education by surrounding himself with a team of academics and experts (Figueiredo and Coutinho 2003: 19), and by projecting an undeniable charisma and an effective verbal delivery (despite grammatical flaws). Furthermore, his impoverished background – Lula da Silva is a migrant from the Brazilian north-east, one of the country's poorest regions, who had started his political career as a union official – was used to electoral benefit. While his humble origins and class were highlighted by his opponents, who insisted that he was incapable of being president, PT strategists neutralised that argument by emphasising Lula da Silva's ability to identify with people who were socially excluded (see Barreira 2002: 173).

Policy, strategy and the coalition   In terms of policy, PT moved to the ideological centre in its communication style and its approach to coalition-making. In March 2002, a meeting of PT's National Directory approved the proposed co-operation with conservative parties (PMDB and PL) opposed to the Cardoso Government. PT formed a coalition with the conservative PL, a medium-sized party whose leader, José Alencar, is a wealthy textile-mill owner. This move improved the PT's electoral prospects, while consolidating Latin America's biggest left-wing party's shift towards the center.

As Meneghelo (2003) noted, in 2001 PT began to forge an alliance with entre-preneurs at the national level in order to reform the economy, reinforce the national market and fight unemployment. The coalition also produced policies which 'benefited from a pragmatic expansion of the various forces of opposition to the government' (Meneghelo 2003: 46). Lula made clear his readiness to con-tinue present economic policies,[12] to deal prudently with foreign investors and to be flexible in negotiations. Responding to the electorate's desire to avoid substan-tial change, the PT produced a relatively ideology-free manifesto.

Product adjustment

PT manifesto and the final policies the party and its coalition partner, PL produced were more pragmatic than ideological. As Aldé (2003: 108) writes, the manifesto that PT released in Brasilia prior to the campaign was perceived as 'non ideological' although it was criticized as vague or incoherent; 'more significantly,' however, the manifesto attracted 'approval for its political maturity and flexibility'.

Achievability characterised also Lula da Silva's stance on the crucial issue of the international debt. In the 1980s he had argued that debt to foreign nations should never be paid; but in 2002 radical speeches against foreign banks were replaced by pledges to pursue the rules of the latest Brazil–IMF agreement fixed by Cardoso's Government. This was in response to the apprehension expressed by some sectors of the economy that an eventual Lula's victory could result in reduced foreign investments in the country.

As for the media's analysis of that episode, Aldé (2003) notes how impressive it was that the newspapers changed their treatment of Lula da Silva after he had agreed in front of President Cardoso to abide by the IMF agreement's rules. The receptive stance that the candidate assumed towards the agreement was treated ambivalently by the media – as on the one hand a proof of maturity yet on the other as an inconsistency. Either way, the survey of the last poll undertaken before free electoral propaganda time was launched indicated 'the candidate's improvement and a gain of 10 points ahead of the second placed candidate' (*ibid.*: 108).

In terms of internal analysis, there was some opposition to the move to a market-orientation, though the shift was born of the PT leadership's experience of losing so many elections. While PT's more leftist groups and the MST (Movement of Landless People) raised doubts about the new praxis of moderation but according to Aldé (2003) opposition to Lula da Silva's 'centrism' remained minor. The focus moved externally and away from ideological concerns.

Support analysis, segmentation and targeting were carried out effectively, developed from market intelligence. First, analysis of electoral sectors which had not voted for Lula before but might be convinced to do so in 2002 was undertaken with the aim of surpassing the 30 per cent share of the vote that the Left had managed in previous elections. Support analysis also indicated that Lula had previously alienated female voters. The PT's 2002 campaign strategy therefore targeted the female vote as Luiz Inácio Lula da Silva pursued an integrated political marketing strategy, following Mendonça's suggestion that the candidate's wife Marisa da Silva accompany him at campaign rallies. Marisa da Silva, who had kept away from politics and the public eye in previous elections, became a constant presence at public meetings and canvassing events, her apparel carefully designed. Lula da Silva also brought into the spotlight Marta Suplicy, a female PT mayor: as Aldé (*ibid.*: 109) commented, 'in order to reverse his bad performance among the female voters, the campaign starts to focus on Marisa da Silva, his wife, who began to show up in the papers, and on Marta Suplicy, the PT mayor of São Paulo'.

The PT also exercised careful competition analysis. The flow of public opinion in 2002 with regard to the Government was somewhat paradoxical: while surveys found that the public perception of Fernando Henrique Cardoso's administration had become mainly negative, the personal image of the president remained positive (Figueiredo and Coutinho 2003: 3), suggesting that despite the prestige lost by Cardoso's Government the situation candidate José Serra was not certain to lose the election. Political and economic experts, as well as the public, acknowledged the positive achievements of Cardoso's Government, economic stability in particular. The surveys confirmed that President Cardoso had maintained a positive personal image throughout the term (table 9.1).

Table 9.1   *Voter evaluation of the president, 1990, 1994, 1998 and 2002*

President	Date	Excellent–good (%)	Average (%)	Poor–very poor (%)
Sarney	March 1990	9	34	56
Itamar Franco	December 1994	41	48	8
Fernando Henrique Cardoso	September 1998	43	37	17
Fernando Henrique Cardoso	October 2002	23	42	32

Source: Instituto Datafolha (in Figueiredo 2003: 66).

PT understood that, even though the Brazilian electorate was dissatisfied with the Government and was looking for a change, to attempt to discredit everything Cardoso had achieved would be unwise: 'Lula and his team understood the message and during the campaign they managed to tell the electorate what [it] wanted to hear' (Figueiredo 2003: 4). In this way Lula da Silva exercised careful, mature, competition analysis in formulating the PT's strategy with regard to the incumbent Government and Cardoso's party's candidate to government, José Serra.

Implementation

Any proposed change in a party's political stance is likely to generate conflict, especially in a party that like PT, encompasses such diverse political beliefs. The adoption of a strategy to develop alliances with conservative political forces, while making victory and, arguably, deliverable policy more achievable, generated internal opposition. The formation of the PT–PL coalition initially triggered intense internal debate. At the beginning of 2002 media coverage focused on this internal disagreement 'pointing at and reporting the PT's members' criticisms of the incoherence that the alliance with PL represented'. This episode generated unwanted negative media coverage for the party for some weeks and the impasse was resolved only in June, when after a difficult process of negotiation with the PL's José Alencar, Lula da Silva succeeded in reversing pessimistic forecasts and consolidating the coalition (Aldé 2003: 101).

The loss of party cohesiveness was never completely overcome and certain party members in Parliament continued to blame the party's changed attitude and guiding principles (this group became well known as 'hard-line PT'), although divergent opinions had been commonplace in PT since its inception. However, the divergences and eventual hard exchanges were well-absorbed and managed, and were taken as reflecting the diversity of belief typical of the PT. Overall, implementation was successful: a large majority within the party supported the changes and it remained relatively unified during the campaign (*ibid.*).

Communication and campaign

Communication about the leader was obviously extremely important for the PT. Mendonça's strategy to launch 'the new Lula' and 'the new PT' was very effective, the latter being called a 'light PT' by the media, while Lula, in a humorous attempt to show how he would avoid confrontation and radicalism, called himself 'peace-and-love-Lula'. Rubim (2003) considered such emblematical images as 'peace-and-love-Lula' and 'negotiator Lula' to have been very significant electorally. There were also changes in Lula's appearance, such as a tidy head of hair, well-groomed beard, good quality suits to replace his former image as an angry, T-shirted metal-worker. The candidate was portrayed as 'a conciliator, elegantly dressed and supported by high standard team of academics and technical experts' (Figueiredo and Coutinho 2003: 19). Appearances by Lula's wife at public events promoted his solid twenty-nine year-marriage, fostering his image as a trustworthy man and also humanising him.

PT's communication structures were re-organised and made more professional, and benefited from greater investment (Rubim 2003: 10). This was evident from the party's high quality use of radio and television and its advertising campaigns. The party's communication team made more effective use of the non-electoral communication (*ibid.*): for example, it ran a very direct publicity campaign with the simple message 'Deep, deep you are a bit PT' (*No fundo, no fundo, você é um pouco PT*).

As noted by Rubim (*ibid.*) in an analysis of Porto's research database on the free electoral propaganda time on radio and television, the PT communications approach to television communication was very effective. Lula da Silva dedicated 28.2 per cent of the party's total free time to conjuncture analysis. 'PT's television campaign prioritised diagnostic solutions to the country's problems. It was the political party that dedicate most time to this subject. Attention to future policies came in second place with 18.4 per cent of the total time' (Rubim 2003: 5). Rubim also argued that PT had a 'soft' campaign style, citing Porto's research which found that 'Lula da Silva was the candidate who dedicated more time to music and jingles (10.6%) and who made less use of negative advertisement resources' (p. 6).

Election and delivery

Lula and the PT won the election. Together with the PL's leader, José Alencar, as vice-president, they almost won outright on the first election stage (46.44%) in October 2002. In the second stage, in November, they achieved a spectacular victory with 61.27 per cent of the total valid votes (Jabob *et al.* 2003: 292).

Other indications of success were the polls conducted throughout the campaign: '"marketing" worked well and the candidate maintained a leadership throughout the campaign' (Figueiredo 2003: 77). The only real doubt was over which of the other main presidential candidates (José Serra, Ciro Gomes and Anthony Garotinho) would get second place. Surveys also revealed that Lula's affiliation with professionals was highly evaluated by the public who thought that their education and qualifications could to some extent compensate for the candidate's lack of both academic background and practical experience in government (Figueiredo and Coutinho 2003: 19). Measures to target the female vote were also effective: surveys demonstrated that the rejection level among the female electorate fell from 47 per cent to 31 per cent in six months (*Veja Magazine*, 'A presença de Marisa', May 2003: 42).

Once in office President Luiz Inácio Lula da Silva put together a Cabinet that was received with some surprise by political commentators. In Maxwell's opinion (2003), Lula da Silva 'put together an eclectic cabinet', reflective of Brazilian diversity. It included, on the one hand, the popular singer and composer Gilberto Gil as culture minister; Marina Silva, a PT senator from the Amazon rubber-tapping region, as minister of the environment; and Benedita da Silva, the first black person and *favela* dweller to be elected a senator and governor in Brazil, as minister of social development and aid. On the other hand, Henrique Meirelles, the former president of global banking at FleetBoston Financial and well known in US financial circles, was appointed the Central Bank's president. 'Brazil's "chicken king", the successful businessman and exporter Luiz Fernando Furlan' (web@nybooks.com) became minister of development, industry and commerce.

The media criticised this Cabinet as well as the new administration's initial policy implementation. Maxwell (2003) observed how 'even Lula's most dramatic early initiative, his Fome Zero program, which pledged that by the end of his four-year term in office no Brazilian would go hungry, has been dismissed by critics as window dressing, a regression to failed "welfare policies"', an unfair criticism 'since Fome Zero, despite the ineptitude of its bureaucratic beginnings, is slowly taking hold'. The PT Government has also been attacked for developing policies it had previously condemned, and the Government has continued macro-economic practices very similar to those of its predecessor, led by Cardoso.

Nevertheless, despite criticism, public opinion has at least so far (i.e. the end of 2003) supported Lula da Silva. Maxwell, an expert on Brazilian history and politics, concluded in June 2002, six months after Lula obtained power, that 'he remains immensely popular, with 75 per cent approval ratings in the opinion polls, and with only 13 per cent thinking he is doing a "bad job," a substantial improvement on his negative rating of 25 to 30 per cent during the campaign. The latest polls show that 80 per cent of Brazilians "trust" him' (Maxwell 2003). It is too early to offer a complete assessment of delivery: the campaign promises included a handful of reforms not yet achieved – social security and tax systems, for example – so the debate will continue beyond this chapter.

The effectiveness of PT's political marketing, the efficacy of the Lees-Marshment model, and its application to Brazil

The application of the Lees-Marshment political marketing model – developed in the UK for its particular political context – to the Brazilian electoral reality, is by no means an easy task considering the differences between the party system of the UK and that of Brazil. The differences between Brazilian and UK democracies are varied. For instance, in the UK, the dynamics of national political life are dictated by party activities, rather than by the dynamics of personal leadership. Brazilian parties are less ideological or bound by tradition, and there is a more direct focus on the leaders who have more room to change party behaviour. Another difference is that while UK and other European countries face an increasing problem of low voter turnout during elections, compulsory voting and a genuine desire to participate produces a much higher turnout in Brazilian elections.

However, from a political marketing perspective, those differences seem to diminish in importance. The steps to be followed by an MOP do not vary according to the nature of that party or the party system in which it operates, and the electoral effects of adopting a market orientation in Brazil appear similar to those in the UK. The Lees-Marshment's model therefore remains valid even when applied to a political environment and reality that are as distinctive as Brazil's. Moreover, the adoption of political marketing by Brazilian politicians appears to be as successful as it has been for British politicians such as Tony Blair – political marketing has utility in practice as well as in academic theory.

Democratic implications of political marketing

The idea that 'market oriented parties aim to discover voter demands in order to respond to them when they design their behaviour' (Lees-Marshment 2001a: 698) does not fit the traditional views of politics of the mid-twentieth century, which gives rise to questions as to whether the MOP is good for democracy. In twenty-first century Brazil, the idea that political parties should design their product to suit the voters' preferences may be seen as signifying a degree of democratic maturity. Signates (quoted in Jury 2003) argues that 'PT has changed because the country and the Brazilian people have changed'. PT adopted a democratic stance by analysing the changes in the political environment and updating and adopting new policies in order to match those changes. However, only a comprehensive assessment of the Government after a full four years of office which takes account of its success in delivery and analyses the maintenance of internal party unity will permit a conclusive evaluation of its contribution to democracy.

It was by adopting a marketing-oriented stance, as this chapter shows, that the PT–Workers' Party candidate Lula da Silva won the presidential election in Brazil. His victory was undoubtedly a triumph for Brazilian democracy. His election was viewed with great interest in the international context and was celebrated all over Brazil. Lula da Silva's campaign has since become an object for study and observation not only in Latin American democracies but in more distant European countries and North American States. International scrutiny and observation will now move to his performance in government and only time will demonstrate whether political marketing provides real democratic benefit: by improving the lives of its citizens and giving satisfaction to his supporters.

Notes

I wish to acknowledge the assistance of Flávio Vicente of Centre de Ensino Superior de Maringá, Brazil, who contributed historical data and references to this chapter.

1 Major elections, for positions at different administrative and legislative levels, are held every 2 years; presidential elections are held every 4 years.
2 This and subsequent quotations are translated from the Portuguese by the author.
3 The 'Real Plan', or *Plano Real.*
4 Cardoso was a member of PSDB, a party that aimed to offer an alternative to the 'Left – Right' divide, positioning itself in theory as Centre-Left.
5 This so-called *horário de propaganda eleitoral gratuita* (free electoral propaganda time). The amount of time to be used by each party is determined according to its representation in the federal deputy's chamber. In the case of the presidential election the formation of a coalition guarantees to the coalition's candidate the use, both on the radio and on television, of the daily time of the parties entering the coalition. In 2002, the free electoral propaganda time was developed in two periods: 'From August 20 to October 3,

before the first turn, it was shown in two blocks of 50 minutes presented daily – a total of 65 hours. The second period went on from 14–25 October, before the second turn. It was divided in two daily blocks of 10 minutes for each candidate' (Figueiredo 2003: 73).

6 The 2002 HPEG was aired in two periods: from 20 August to 3 October, before the election's first-round vote and from 14 to 25 October, before the second-round vote (Figueiredo and Coutinho 2003: 10).

7 Four of the main public opinion polling institutes in Brazil.

8 However, despite national and international recognition of the participatory budget as a democratic practice of public administration and its successful use by the Porto Alegre administration, PT did not yield electoral dividends. After twelve years of control of Porto Alegre's government machine the party lost the local elections and failed to remain in power at the state level. There was little difference in the support gained by Lula da Silva in Rio Grande do Sul at the presidential level and other areas.

9 The images were obtained from the Doxa database, IUPERJ.

10 This motivate for moving to the MOP model is one noted also by Curis Rudd in discussing the political marketing history of New Zealand parties (see chapter 5 of this book).

11 Those surveys have been a major source of journalistic attention. According to Figueiredo and Coutinho (2003: 18) the strategies adopted by the campaign professionals were the subject of several newspaper, magazine and television reports and analysis: 'even the qualitative research, which is normally overshadowed by the impressive figures from quantitative analysis, won space in the media'.

12 In 1994 PT had considered the economic plan called *Real* as an electoral fraud.

Bibliography

Aldé, A. (2003), 'As eleições presidenciais de 2002 nos jornais', *ALCEU – Revista de Comunicação, Cultura e Política*, 3(6): 93–121.

Almeida, J. (2002), *Marketing Político – Hegemonia e Contra-Hegemonia*, Perseu São Paulo: Abramo, Xamã.

Barreira, I. A. F. (2002), 'Um operário presidente? Ideologia e condição de classe no universo da representação política', in B. Heredia, C. E. Teixeira and I. Barreira (eds), *Como se Fazem Eleições no Brasil*, Rio de Janeiro: Relume Dumará: 157–216.

Figueiredo, R. (2000), 'O marketing político: entre a ciência e a falta de razão', in *Marketing Político e Persuasão Eleitoral: Pesquisas*, Loyola, São Paulo: Fundação Konrad Adenauer: 11–41.

Figueiredo, R. (2003), '2002: uma eleição fenomenal', *Cadernos Adenauer*, special issue, 'Eleições e Partidos', 4(1): 57–81.

Figueiredo, R. and Coutinho, C. (2003), 'A eleição de 2002', unpublished paper.

Jacob, C. R., Hees, D. R., Waniez, P. and Brustlein, V. (2003), 'Eleições presidenciais de 2002 no Brasil: uma nova geografia eleitoral?' *ALCEU – Revista de Comunicação, Cultura e Política*, 3(6): 287–304.

Jury, L. (2003), 'Quem gauhou as eleiçoes: Duda ou Lula? Online: www.facomb.ufg.br/farofino/sociedad.

Lees-Marshment, J. (2001a), 'The marriage of politics and marketing', *Political Studies*, 49: 692–713.

Lees-Marshment, J. (2001b), 'The product-, sales- and market-oriented party and how Labour learnt to market the product, not just the presentation', *European Journal of Marketing*, special issue, 35(9–10): 1074–84.

Lees-Marshment, J. (2001c), *Political Marketing and British Political Parties*. Manchester and New York: Manchester University Press.

Lees-Marshment, J. and Lilleker, D. (2001c), 'Political marketing and traditional values: "Old Labour" for "new times"?' *Contemporary Politics*, 7(3): 205–16.

Mainwaring, S. (1991), 'Políticos, partidos e sistemas eleitorais: o Brasil numa perspectiva comparativa', *Novos Estudos do Cebrap*, 23 (March).

Maxwell, K. (2003), 'Lula's surprise', *New York Review*, 50(11), available: www.nybooks.com/ article.

Mendonça, D. (2001), *Casos e Coisas*, São Paulo: Editora Globo.

Meneghelo, R. (2003), 'A face dominante da esquerda brasileira: avanços, mudanças e dilemas do Partido dos Trabalhadores', *Cadernos Adenauer*, special issue, 'Eleiços e Partidas 4(1): 39–54.

Miguel, L. F. (2004), 'Discursos cruzados: telenoticiários, HPEG e construção da agenda eleitoral', paper presented at the 12th conference of the National Association of Post-Graduate Programmes, Recife, Brazil.

Nicolau, J. M. (2001), *Sistemas Eleitorais: Uma Introdução*, 3rd edn, Rio de Janeiro: Editora Fundação Getúlio Vargas.

Nicolau, J. M. (2003), 'Notas sobre as eleiçoes de 2002 e o sistema partidário brasileiro', *Cadernos Adenauer*, special issue, Eleigos e Partidos', 4(1): 11–36.

Passador, Cláudia S. (1998), 'A forma da política contemporânea enquanto sistema de estrelato e o surgimento do marketing político neste processo', dissertation, EAESP/ Fundaçao Getulio Vargas, São Paulo.

Rubim, A. A. C. (2003), 'Cultura e política na eleição de 2002: as estratégias de Lula Presidente', paper presented at the 12th conference of the National Association of Post-Graduate Programmes Recife, Brazil.

Sallum Jr, B., Graeff, E. and Gomes de Lima, E. (1990), 'Eleições presidenciais e crise do sistema partidário', *Lua Nova*: Revista de Cultura e Política, 20: 69–87.

Partido dos Trabalhadores (1999), *Cadernos de formação* 'O que é o PT?' 3, June.

Internet resources

Electoral Supreme Court of Brazil (Tribunal Superior Eleitoral, Governo do Brasil): www.tse.gov.br (accessed June 2003).

Official website of the Workers' Party – Partido dos Trabalhadores (2002): www.pt.org.br (accessed September–October 2003).

University of Goiás, Brazil, Faculty of Communication and Library Science, Farofino Newsletter (2003) (Universidade de Goiás, Faculdade de Comunicação e Biblioteconomia, *Jornal Farofino*): www.facomb.ufg.br/farofino/sociedade (accessed May 2003).

10

The re-launch of the Popular Revolutionary American Alliance: the use of political marketing in Peru's new political era

Pedro Patron Galindo

Theory can only be applied where it satisfies the needs of the people.[1]

This chapter explores the way in which the Peruvian central-leftist party Popular Revolutionary American Alliance (APRA) has utilised political marketing to re-organise and re-launch itself for the next election. Peru has a very different political context from those of most of the other nations studied in this book. It lacks a solid political system and Peruvian democracy is weak due to recent changes introduced by former president Alberto Fujimori's regime in the 1990s. APRA lost popularity at the end of the 1980s not only because of economic and political crises during its term of office (1985–1990) but because of restrictions on political parties as representives of the people. Nevertheless, the APRA has successfully utilised all stages of the MOP model, albeit in a manner adapted to suit the Peruvian political and social reality. Indeed, as Tanaka and Zárate (1998: 141) noted, we can see 'most of the dilemmas in the [Peruvian] democracy and partisan system, the rationale of the partisan actors in the different arenas, and its representative performance' by examining the APRA case.

In the 1980s the political market was dominated by four parties: Acción Popular (AP: Popular Action, Centre-Right), Partido Popular Cristiano (PPC: Popular Christian Party, liberal), Partido Aprista Peruano (APRA: Peruvian Aprist Party, Centre-Left) and Izquierda Unida (IU: United Leftist Parties, socialists and communists). According to Tanaka (1998), behind these four organisations was concentrated almost 90 per cent of the votes between 1978 and 1989; in 1989 this percentage fell to 71.5 per cent and in 1995 it was an extremely low 6.3 per cent in the presidential elections (Tanaka and Zárate 1998: 53). These more established political parties lost their capacity to represent Peruvian voters, who were increasingly voting for independent candidates. As Tanaka and Zárate argue, this was due to the polarisation of the system between uncompromising conservatism (i.e. IU–PPC) and 'anti-system' parties such as the Shining Path and the MRTA,[2] while society was divided along ideological lines; furthermore governance was also a problem (Tanaka and Zárate 1998: 54).

APRA responded positively to the changed conditions that emerged after the collapse of the Fujimori regime (1990–2000). That regime had restricted political freedom, but the nature of the market that subsequently emerged was one not dictated by partisanship, enabling a degree of openness in electoral competition. APRA rejuvenated itself by forming an organisation of successful entrepreneurs, charismatic celebrities and popular radio broadcasters, albeit with little or no political experience (Meléndez Guerrero 2003).

This chapter therefore analyses why APRA was successful in the 1980s and then collapsed in the 1990s, and considers its latest efforts to re-launch itself. First I discuss the problems of using political marketing in an underdeveloped country, where political participation is limited by economic and political instability. Second, I outline recent events that have profoundly affected Peruvian politics – the fall of the (so called) 'traditional parties' and the rise of the independents and the 'anti-politics' decade – which are crucial for understanding how political marketing may assist the democratisation of Peruvian society. Third, the evolution of the oldest Peruvian party, APRA, is analysed. Discussion in this main section centres on how the party's early reliance on political propaganda has been replaced by sophisticated techniques associated with market-oriented strategies, and in doing so APRA has become the leading opposition force in the country, as well as re-organising and re-launching itself for the next election. Finally, I consider the applicability of the Lees-Marshment (2001) model to the behaviour of APRA, and offer some conclusions about the use of political marketing both in winning elections and re-invigorating democracy in Peru and other underdeveloped countries.

Political participation and political marketing: the Peruvian case

The Republic of Peru was founded in 1821, when the country's independence from Spain was declared. Though conflict characterised the nineteenth century, the constitutional division of powers is as entrenched in Peru as it is in most established democracies. Public acceptance of the system appeared to break down in the 1990s, especially after the collapse of President Alberto Fujimori's Government. As Martín Tanaka and Patricia Zárate's study (2002) of citizens' participation and democratic culture in Peru showed, Peruvians' appreciation of democracy was dependent on governmental performance and the 'consumerist' inclination of citizens:

> The support for the political system and the State institutions appeared relatively greater in rural areas, among the least educated and among those who showed less interest in public affairs. [In contrast] the most critical towards the way the political system and the democratic institutions were working were the ones showing greater interest in public affairs, with greater educational levels, who lived in urban areas and were more attached to democratic values. (Tanaka and Zárate 2002: 4)

Tanaka and Zárate's research suggested that changes in the political and governmental arena were not matched by changes in participation and culture between

1998 and 2001. Democracy in Peru still has weak foundations and is thus quite vulnerable to fluctuations in its economic conditions.

Peru presents a distinctive and less than stable context. Political marketing, however, is a discipline and an activity created in a context of solid institutions. Nevertheless, it can be argued that its methodology can be applied not only to promote democratic values but to propose a systematic action plan that involves all agents through organisational change, assuming that the state in question is focused on providing for the needs of the population. People in Peru do, after all, pay taxes, even if they are low (the Peruvian tax burden is approximately 12 per cent of the GDP), and to that extent have a stake in societal organisation.

Another important feature of developing countries like Peru is the unofficial black economy, which is, according to many scholars, a key influence on political participation. In 1990 sub-employment had increased in Peru to 86.6 per cent and according to Barnechea (1995: 61) this led to a collapse in Peru's social institutions. It also had political consequences: Tanaka and Zárate's analysis of the same period showed that the parties had difficulties developing representation in a context characterised by unemployment, an expanding informal economy and a general weakening of the institutions in Peruvian society (Tanaka and Zárate 1998: 174).

The fall of Alberto Fujimori in 1990, however, became a milestone for Peruvian politics, as it provided an opportunity for the so called 'traditional parties' to return to the political arena. Their weakened structure, however, encouraged the development of 'anti-politics' in Peru (Degregori 2000: 35), and their collapse ensured its success and longevity. In response, parties such as APRA, AP and the PPC have re-launched their organisations. They had worked together to oppose Fujimori's regime, and since its collapse have sought to rebuild their capacities, ideologies, infrastructure and, most importantly, their recruitment procedures.

Political marketing in Peru

The current political panorama in Peru offers a unique context in which to test the universality of Lees-Marshment's model. After ten years of 'anti-politics' (Degregori 2000), the circumstances in which Haya de la Torre's APRA emerged as a political alternative for the new social and economic groups that appeared with the incipient industrialisation in the 1930s are politically similar to the circumstances in which Alberto Fujimori emerged as a political figure and to the circumstances in which Alan García, APRA's leader, has returned to the political arena.

Although there are several distinctive features that make the three historical moments unique, it is interesting to note that all three figures appeared after periods devoid of political representation. Haya de la Torre founded the APRA while living abroad, and launched the party when he returned to Peru; Alan García has worked on the re-organisation of the party from Bogotá (Colombia) and his home in Paris (France); and Fujimori, now in Tokyo, has announced on his official website that he is restructuring 'Fujimorism' and will return to Peru in 2006. The political and economic instability of the region seems to provide fertile ground for political leaders with redemptory discourses. As Fernando Tuesta Soldevilla (2002: 144) argues, 'leaders [who] emerge beyond the margins of the political system must assume a discourse of redemption and a mandate for social change. Their arrival to power expresses the discredit of the representational institutions and the [non]existence of stable political identities.'

In attempts to analyse the fall of the Peruvian parties 1989 has become a milestone. Television broadcaster Ricardo Belmont won the municipal election in Lima at the end of that year, and that was the first signal of the citizenry's dissatisfaction, showing that the 'screening' capacity of the parties was starting to fail (Tanaka and Zárate 1998: 169). This is one of the reasons why Fujimori, an independent without a solid party or even a political programme, was so successful in 1990 and throughout the decade that followed.

In the 1990 presidential elections, APRA obtained 20.4 per cent of the vote, a very high percentage given the crisis faced by the party and its leader. According to Tanaka and Zárate (1998: 185), this is one reason why we should not assume, as many people do in Peru, that the failure of APRA to perform in government was solely responsible for the collapse of the political system in the 1990s: tables 10.1 and 10.2 shows that it was not until 1995 that the traditional parties started to collapse.

Despite Peru's distinctiveness, we can observe at work in Peru a process similar to that found in developed countries: from POPs to SOPs, and on to MOPs; in fact, up until the 1990s all the Peruvian parties have been either in a product- or a sales-oriented phase. The Lees-Marshment model applies in Peru, although aspects such as organisation and citizens' participation are now being taken into account by Alan García and adapted to the country's social institutions.

Table 10.1   *Votes in Peru by party, 1978–95 (%)*

Year	AP	PPC	FREDEMO	PAP	IU	CAMBIO 90	Independents
1978 (A)	NP	23.8	–	35.3	29.4	–	11.5
1980	45.4	9.6	–	27.4	14.4	–	3.2
1980 (M)	35.8	11.1	–	22.5	23.3	–	7.4
1983 (M)	17.5	13.9	–	33.1	29.0	–	6.7
1985	7.3	11.9	–	53.1	24.7	–	3.0
1986 (M)	NP	14.8	–	47.6	30.8	–	7.8
1989 (M)	–	–	31.2	20.4	20.2	–	28.2
1990 (V)	–	–	32.6	22.6	13.0	29.1	2.7
1990 (V)	–	–	37.5	NP	NP	62.5	–
1992 (A)	NP	9.7	–	NP	5.5	49.2	35.6
1993 (M)	11.6	5.7	–	10.8	3.9	NP	64.7
1995	1.7	–	–	4.1	0.6	64.4	29.2

Source: Tuesta Soldevilla (1995).
Notes: NP = did not run; (M) = municipal elections; (A) = constitutional elections; (V) = first and second electoral round.

Table 10.2 *Evolution of the votes (%) in the party-political system and the independent vote, 1978–95*

	1978 (C)	1980 (P)	1980 (M)	1983 (M)	1985 (P)	1986 (M)	1989 (M)	1990 (P)	1992 (C)	1993 (M)	1995 (P)
Principal political parties of the system[a]	88.5	96.5	92.7	93.5	97.0	93.2	71.5	68.0	15.3	33.3	6.3
Vote for independent candidates[b]	11.5	3.2	7.4	6.7	3.0	7.8	28.2	31.7	84.8	64.7	93.7
Empty votes	3.2	7.7	4.9	5.4	6.5	3.7	6.2	8.0	4.0	5.5	9.16
Invalid votes	12.6	14.5	9.7	12.3	7.3	11.1	15.4	7.2	19.7	19.7	8.72
Absenteeism	16.0	21.0	31.0	36.0	9.0	22.0	31.0	22.0	29.0	34.4	26.15

Source: Tuesta Soldevilla 1994.

Notes: (C) = Constitutional Assembly, though in 1992, the elections were to seats in the Congreso Constituyente Democratico; (M) = Municipal elections;
(P) = Presidential elections.
[a] Includes AP, PPC, APRA and IU.
[b] Includes all the percentages of the valid votes obtained by the independent lists and small parties.

The oldest Peruvian party: APRA

APRA was founded as a movement in 1924, in Mexico, by Victor Raul Haya de la Torre. Since its foundation it has been one of the most important and influential parties in Latin America. As Haya de la Torre stated in *El anti-imperialismo y el APRA* (1936) (*Anti-imperialism and APRA*), in 1927 the party had branches in Mexico, Argentina, Central America, and Europe; France was the main branch in Europe, with a great number of students and workers in different sub-sections in Germany, Spain and England. According to Barnechea, it became the prototype of the populist party, a mass-organisation model. It was registered as a party in Peru in 1931 under the name of Partido Aprista Peruano (Peruvian Aprist Party).

> The party had, however, two unusual characteristics. First, unlike other populist movements – like Peronism in Argentina or Gertulio Vargas' movement in Brazil – it had been organised 'from the bottom'; from the opposition, not from the government. Perhaps that is the reason why it resisted very harsh situations. Second, between 1963 and 1968 it had a majority in Congress, but it was not until 1985 that the APRA won the presidential elections (Barnechea 1995: 46).

According to Quiroz (1990: 272), Haya de la Torre's initial speeches were directed towards workers, professionals and the youth of Peru in general; their attraction derived from neither historical documents nor ideological traditions, but from his individual 'power of redemption'. The influence of individual leaders is central to the Peruvian political context; as Tuesta Soldevilla explains, there is a belief that 'strong and straightforward men can implement relevant changes in the state within in a society characterised by its rigidity and by exclusion' (Tuesta Soldevilla 2002: 147). Alan García offered this style of strong leadership. His biography by the Catalan research institute CIDOB described García as a brilliant and talented orator, capable also of delivering a traditional populist discourse. His image is, in part, that of a 'Latin-lover', standing 1.93m tall, which is quite uncommon in South America (Fundació CIDOB 2001a).

Most political movements in Latin America are founded around strong leaders, a consequent according to most scholars, of the rural background of the working class in the region's incipient cities in the middle of the twentieth century. The lack of political institutions and representation for such 'new citizens' created the need for new political movements, especially those with leftist discourses (Barnechea 1995: 46). A leader's charisma helped to provide a symbolical bridge between the old and the new order and to appeal to the workers. In the case of APRA, there was a movement away from the more radical ideological phase in the 1920s and 1930s to a more political and leader-focused period, once Haya de la Torre returned to Peru, after several years' living in exile, to stand in the presidential elections. Any ideological basis was continually modified, depending less and less on a Marxist conceptual framework (Planas and Vallenas 1990: 218).

Thereafter, Haya de la Torre led the party's development. He argued for the re-distribution of wealth but became severely anti-communist (*ibid.*). He adapted Marxism, arguing that there were certain privileged groups (the local bourgeoisie) that were temporarily threatened by imperialism, but that political strategy should forge short-term alliances with them. It was a very different approach from that of other Leninist groups at the beginning of the twentieth century. It is important to take these foundational elements into account when analysing the party's adaptability and its capacity to work on partnerships with different interest groups, as is now the case. In 1980 APRA had obtained a majority in the Constitutional Assembly, formed by the military government (1968–1980), to draft a new constitution. However, Haya de la Torre died in 1979, and because the party had been so focused around him its performance in the presidential elections in 1980 was significantly impaired.

Nevertheless, in 1982 APRA became the first opposition party, mainly because of the efforts of its young leader Alan García Pérez, aged 33 at the time. García created a new image for the party in just a few years: it became a modern political party with a social democratic ideology, replacing the elite with a new generation of *Aprists* (Tanaka and Zárate 1998: 142). In 1985, APRA won the presidential elections and García began his presidency with 96.1 per cent support.

This positive start gave García the power to implement the policies outlined during the campaign. However, economic, social and political problems brought García's Government into a deep crisis. According to Tanaka and Zárate, between September 1988 and the beginning of 1989, many people demanded García's resignation, and there were some hints that the military would take over through a coup (*ibid.*: 163). In 1989 the National Congress elected Luis Alva Castro, another important figure, as secretary general of the party in García's place. García's loss of popularity – and along with it that of APRA – led the electorate to think that the system was not working out. Mario Vargas Llosa and other independent candidates started to jump into the political arena, which, up until then, had been reserved for candidates from the traditional political parties (AP, PPC, IU and APRA).

As Lees-Marshment argues, political marketing is an adaptation of commercial marketing to the public sphere; therefore, because it is adaptable, it can be applied in different contexts regardless of their stage of economic and political development, which will in the end shape the way it is applied (think globally, act locally). Based on this assumption, we can use the model to identify three phases in APRA's history:

1931–82

Here APRA was in a product-oriented phase, when it created an ideology to meet most of the people's demands. A *product*-oriented business is focused on producing the best product possible, in the most efficient and inexpensive way, and assumes that it will 'sell'. This is what happened during the so-called Aristocratic Republic,[3] when upper-class intellectuals designed political programmes for the country and thought of Peru as if it was a European country, with a high level of industrialisation. Haya de la Torre made an effort to apply existing ideological currents to the Peruvian situation in a pragmatic way. We should also consider a previous phase, though, between 1924 (when the APRA was founded as a movement) and 1931 – what Planas and Vallenas (1990: 218) call the 'literary' phase of APRA – which coincides with the period prior to Haya de la Torre's return to Peru to run in the 1931 election. This was essentially a phase when ideology was used to design the core product.

1980–95

As mentioned above, Haya de la Torre died in 1979, which caused a deep crisis within the party. According to the Lees-Marshment model, this period in APRA's history corresponds to the sales-oriented phase. Following the 1980 presidential elections, Alan García took over the secretariat general of APRA and transformed it, through a process of restructuring, into the leading opposition party. At this point, the party became a *sales*-oriented organisation, continuing its attitude towards the design of the product but now with an emphasis on selling the discourse, making use of advances in information and communication technology.

This continued throughout the 1980s and the beginning of the 1990s, during which time the most powerful advertising campaigns were run in Peru. The Mario Vargas Llosa campaign in 1990, for instance, is an interesting example of advertising expenditure in a developing country that failed because, among other reasons, it seemed a waste of money to the majority of poor voters (Daeschner 1993; Vargas Llosa 1991 and 1993).

Tanaka and Zárate (1998) argue that the fall of the traditional parties (including APRA), and consequent success of Fujimori in the 1990s, was due in part to the rise in importance, politically speaking, of the arena of public opinion over that of social movements. As they point out, these new times presupposed the end of the era of the public plaza and the *direct* relationship between the politician and the voters. That dynamic was replaced by the 'mediated language' of the mass media.[4] In this new political arena, the diverse political discourses correspond to the various interest groups gathered around a certain issue, struggling symbolically to obtain a *discursive hegemony*.[5] For Tanaka and Zárate, the main reason for the fall of Peru's traditional political parties in the 1990s was the fact that they had not familiarised themselves with this new relationship between politicians and the electorate.

Fujimori on the other hand, did seem to be ready to face this new situation and, in fact, used it to gain political support. He realised early on that, lacking a solid partisan organisation, he would need a strong political communication apparatus. Fujimori's government produced a film called *Tres Años que Cambiaron la Historia* (*Three Years that Changed History*) as part of the campaign for the 1993 elections, the referendum for the new constitution drafted by the CCD, in which there was a sophisticated use of political communication elements that was in fact quite effective – the constitution was approved by the voters- and summarised Fujimori's discourse in terms which contrasted with those of the 'traditional' parties.

1995–

As a consequence of the 'anti-politics' decade, the fall of the traditional party system in the 1990s and the experience gained by the traditional parties during

Fujimori's regime, there was clear potential for a *market*-oriented approach. APRA has started to form new responses to issues such as globalisation, privatisation, external debt and the development of Third World countries (see, e.g., García 2003), challenging the neo-liberal proposals at the heart of the current political agenda. APRA has always been the party with the most solid base, because of its effective partisan machinery and its political experience. In spite of the crisis, there remained consistent support for 'Aprist' candidates (Tuesta Soldevilla 1995: 106).

Another factor to consider when analysing the current situation of APRA is the relationship between the Government and the party while it was in office. Tuesta Soldevilla (1995) stresses the fact that the party filled most of the public administration's positions with party members. However, there was a conflict since some *Aprists* thought that *real* members were not in key positions in the Government, believing rather that it was President García's friends who were benefiting. Tuesta Soldevilla argues that this is key, as APRA is a party that emphasises the collective spirit of the group as vital for cohesion (*ibid.*: 119).

APRA appears to agree with Lees-Marshment (2001: 23) that 'a market orientation is much more likely to satisfy its customers and will stand a better chance of securing their long-term custom', and has set about the task of rebuilding democratic and political participation. Alan García and the current Secretary General Jorge del Castillo are working towards that end, as the remainder of this chapter shows. I have made use of party documents, such as the four letters published on APRA's website (www.apra.org.pe) explaining the re-launch and reorganisation of the party and summarising the foundation of the new political marketing strategy.

The new APRA: an MOP?

Stage 1   Market intelligence

The APRA documents demonstrate that the party used various means of data collection among the different voter segments, classified according to geographical location, gender, age, etc. In fact, Alan García refers in the letters to clear distinctions among voter segments and their interests, for each of which there are different strategies, with a special emphasis on the youth of Peru. García mentions that, according to the polls, out of 5 million people (approximately) who voted for the APRA, almost 3 million were under 30 years of age. As García (2001) puts it: 'we are not the owners of those votes ... most of them are not *Aprists* ... And according to the new times and culture [of the youth], most of them do not want to become members or even accept one single ideology.'

García is pleased with APRA's use of marketing research methods, considering it a positive development that the party is gathering data on people's expectations. For him, 'the human being is much more related to the facts, to the news, and that is why he or she refrains from being associated with complex organisations or accepting hermetic ideologies' – a clear indication of the market-oriented approach. APRA's politics is not controlled by the membership and is no longer territorial; programme development is far more objective, being founded on public opinion.

This is highlighted when García (2001) states that 'the polls are as important as the elections in determining political behaviour, and that is also why [other] associations are so important to us'.

Stage 2   Product design

'The right to work, reconstruction of agriculture, free access to education, controlling the monopolies and their abuse, decentralisation with a baseline' are the basic tenets of the discourse of the new APRA, an instrument of social justice that contrasts with the autocratic administration of Fujimori. It is a New Minimum Programme that embraces the recent economic and technological changes, the hegemony and decadence of neo-liberalism. It takes account of the utility of information technology and its impact on international trade and world finance, the social role of the State in these new circumstances, the greater importance of the market and world trade, the challenges of continental and hemispheric integration, and it combines a set of anti-imperialist imperatives with updated ideologically led commitments. The product, then, is an adaptation of Haya de la Torre's 1936 doctrine, one which has had a favourable impact on the 'conservatives' in the party, who recognise that little of the core discourse is changed, and on the 'liberals' who wanted to see a more up-to-date programme.

The other element in the product design is Alan García himself, at present one of the most important politicians in Peru. Peruvian analyst Javier Barreda has noted that Pervian voters have shown a 'memory lapse' with regard to García, dismissing his previous performance in government in 1989–90 when voting in the 2001 presidential elections. First of all, because it is mandatory to vote in Peru,[6] voters have only two options: either they vote for a candidate or they leave the ballot empty. Barreda was reported in the press as saying:

> in the last elections, Alan García kept his promises of welfare from the past while including new elements of the future: From political re-foundation to the proposal for the Peruvian youth and their access to the information society, technology and informatics. That's the reason why he connected so well with the young voters'. (Barreda 2001)

Stage 3   Product adjustment

Product adjustment has been achieved through adapting the party's discourse to Peruvian society. APRA has challenged (current) President Toledo to live up to the great expectations he has created among the people, for whom *achievability* has been a key issue. APRA has offered a set of proposals on areas where Toledo is weak, but where the party believes it can succeed.

Internal reaction has also been important, especially because the more conservative factions have been reluctant to accept the re-positioning of the party. García appealed to them, saying that 'if for some *Aprists* of good faith this term is excessive, since they think it might bring the party to change its name or Haya de la Torre's principles, I would like to tell them they are wrong. Nobody and nothing can change the name, the ideals or the inspiring presence of Haya de la Torre.'

Regarding competition analysis, APRA's relationship with the other left-wing parties is significant. Their failure in general to represent the poorest in Peruvian society (see Ames 2001) left a gap in the marketplace that APRA has filled, ideologically positioning itself at the Centre-Left as a reflection of the specific circumstances of the Peruvian political situation. APRA is managing to represent the poorer Peruvians without appearing too radical or extremist because it is taking care also to develop other key sectors, such as the private sector and international organisations and corporations. There are similarities here with what, for instance, is being done by Luiz Inácio Lula da Silva's PT in Brazil, the first leftist party in government in that country (see chapter 9 of this book).

Substantial effort is being expended to engender and sustain support from APRA's members, loyalists and the broader electorate. Barreda (2001) claims that in the website's letters addressed to party members García has made a call for modernising and re-launching APRA before the eyes of Peru's public, with the objective of maintaining the relationship with those voters who gave him almost 5 million votes in the 2001 presidential elections (Barreda 2001). There are some groups, especially the more conservative enclaves in APRA, that do not agree with this way of conducting politics, of using political marketing, of being an MOP. Nevertheless, García is, as noted, attempting to assuage their fears and has targeted the electorate with messages explaining the new direction and how this will change politics in Peru for the better.

Stage 4   Implementation

The organisation of the party has been changed to adapt it to the new State structure. There is a new School of Training in Municipal Issues and the *Comité Ejecutivo Nacional* (CEN – national executive committee) of the party has been divided into several national secretariats, specialising in key areas such as education, public health, labour, the agrarian sector, international relations, etc. These branches are charged with producing updated documentation for policy-making and preparing party members for lobbying, negotiation and governing.

The unions' presence, now diminished in the country by unemployment, has been replaced by associations linked to APRA. As García underlines, 'this is the way we can get more party members, as these people will not have to leave their main activities'. APRA also intends to work with different levels of the Peruvian community through meetings with professional associations, educative institutions, industries, informal vendors, etc. In November 2003 APRA called independents and liberal professionals who might be interested in forming a 'popular' front around the party with García to stand as leader in the 2006 elections.

Stage 5   Communication

APRA's reconstruction of its political image is being communicated using a sophisticated marketing strategy to promote García's new stance to voters and to party members. This is in response to public concerns about the party – there is a degree of anti-APRA sentiment among a significant proportion of the population combined with negative perceptions of García when he was president.

When García's Government tried to expropriate the banks from the private sector in 1988, inflation rose to 1,722 per cent, production fell 7.3 per cent and both private and public incomes decreased – by 30.8 per cent and 9.6 per cent respectively. In 1989 inflation was at 2,775 per cent and the GDP fell 13.8 per cent. Unemployment rose to 8.3 per cent in 1990 and sub-employment to 86.4 per cent. As Barnechea observes, 'the result of all this was the increase of critical poverty in Peru. In July 1990 the critical poverty index was 49 per cent, greater than in 1985 [when García entered government]' (1995: 62). All this inevitably raises questions about Garcia's ability to change public perception and gain support. According to *Cuestión de Estado* (2001), there is a section of the electorate that says it would never vote for him and APRA is regarded as a party that acts in its own interest rather than that of the country. APRA has therefore tried to offset these weaknesses in designing its communication strategy.

Stages 6–8   Campaign, election and delivery
These stages cannot be applied properly because there are three more years before the presidential election campaign in 2006. Some initial speculations may, however, be offered. As the Peruvian magazine *Cuestión de Estado* (2001) has highlighted, APRA has a real opportunity to do well. Over the last few years no political party has been able to offer a political programme that appears relevant or is supported by the majority of Peruvians. *Cuestión de Estado* (2001) believes that García could win support through his discourse, underpinned as it is by public opinion, and because the campaign is designed to build on the support gained in the 2001 elections, when he took second place (with 32.92 per cent of the vote) – Toledo won with 37.24 per cent. More recently, in a poll on political preferences carried out by the University of Lima in September 2003, APRA is the most popular party, with 27.4 per cent. This is a key indicator that the party is successfully applying its strategy.

Conclusion: towards market-oriented practices, how does it work?

APRA is clearly applying the techniques of political marketing, making it the first of Peru's *traditional* political parties with a systematic market-oriented strategy. This demonstrates that it is possible to apply a market-oriented approach in an underdeveloped country, though in the process one must take into consideration distinctive local characteristics, as APRA has done.

Among the biggest problems facing all political parties in Peru are the lack of participation and a weak democratic political culture, which not only constitute barriers to voter engagement, but actually threaten Peruvian democracy itself. As Grompone (2001: 10) points out, when the Fujimori regime collapsed the opposition parties, leaders and social movements that had fought against it (including Toledo's party, Peru Posible) were not properly prepared to take over, as its collapse took them by surprise (Grompone 2001: 10). Parties behaved differently in other countries, such as Brazil, Chile, Uruguay, Argentina, Portugal and Greece, in their transitions to democracy. In Chile, for instance, the political parties analysed their own mistakes instead of simply blaming Pinochet's regime. They renewed their ideological proposals and understood the importance of reaching strategic agreements among themselves (*ibid.*: 2001: 11), a strategy which presupposes a market-oriented approach.

In Peru, however, this did not happen;[7] its political and social leaders had to go through a fast learning process. Grompone contends that in other transitions to democracy the parties retained their communication structures, which could be re-activated when democracy was achieved, widening their support bases and adapting their discourses to the new times. This did not happen in most Peruvian political organisations, and in that respect APRA was an exception.

A market-oriented organisation has as its goal the satisfaction of the user, and so it tries to understand those whom it intends to serve, delivering a product that reflects their needs and wants. It is willing to change its behaviour in order to increase its support: APRA follows this model. It will depend on its behaviour during the next campaign, and the extent to which the other parties roll out a consistent campaign, whether the APRA is able to capitalise on what is has achieved thus far and turn its market orientation into an election victory and, afterwards, political delivery.

APRA's tradition of adaptability is one of its core strengths. The interpretation of Marxism is based on Hegelian dialectics that allows constant adaptation to different realities. This is key to understanding the way in which the APRA has evolved ideologically and strategically in order to achieve power, for instance, participating in the movement against the Fujimori's regime with other parties, even those which were historically political enemies.

APRA has led the opposition against the privatisation of some public companies, precipitating the first crisis to be faced by President Alejandro Toledo. The demonstrations against the privatisation of two of the most important electricity companies in Arequipa, the second largest city in Peru, appear market oriented. However this strategy also raises questions: is it because of their ideological belief that state capitalism would redistribute wealth – and, therefore, that privatisation is not a good option for public companies – or because it responds to the demands of those people who fear privatisation will result in the loss of jobs? APRA is leading the leftist movement in the Peruvian political spectrum, basically against neo-liberalism, indicating that García has applied Haya de la Torre's anti-imperialism to current times. Issues such as privatisation, external debt and the prescriptions of other international organisations (International Monetary Fund, World Trade Organisation, World Bank, etc.) profoundly affect the development of countries like Peru, and García appears to be attempting to develop ideological solutions that link to the desires of the electorate. Hence, key words such as 'anti-imperialism' have been replaced by, for instance, 'anti-neo-liberalism', which is the new buzzword that political leaders argue dominates the current Peruvian political agenda.

The transition from *state*-centric politics to *market*-centric politics, through the changes introduced in the 1990s, has also reconfigured the organisations of labour, the unions and social movements, and has transformed political participation. We are witnessing a debate between the different segments of society, in which the role of the mass media is crucial. This opens up new forms of participation and inter-action with power that need to be accounted for (Tanaka and Zárate 1998: 245). García is taking advantage of this by linking APRA with new and current organi-sations in Peruvian society of the twenty-first century.

There is an interesting point in Knuckey and Lees-Marshment's essay on the US Republican Party that I would like to highlight: 'the political marketing of parties is now truly international: Indeed there may be a globalisation of political market-ing with links forged and ideas shared between similar parties across countries' (Knuckey and Lees-Marshment 2002: 1). This is indeed true, and in particular it is time to have a debate on the way in which South American countries like Brazil, Argentina or Peru relate to international organisations and address issues such as the external debt. Social democratic parties such as the Partido dos Trabalhadores, the Partido Justicialista, and APRA (not in government), respectively, are becom-ing increasingly market-led on these issues.

Democratic communication is another aspect for further research within the political marketing field. Building democracy in contexts such as developing coun-tries is a key issue when discussing how these techniques can be used to increase political participation and disseminate democratic values. We have to take into account that there are epistemic and political implications: implications for the way we learn and think and implications for the ways we exercise power and authority (Karlberg 2002: 11). Another key issue is voters' expectations and needs. Customers do not always know what their real needs are, and when they do they cannot always verbalise them; often they are able to articulate their needs only in terms of the familiar, and cannot predict how their needs will be changed by social interaction (Johansen 2002: 19). Communication is here a key role of the political parties – and is what APRA is doing when re-connecting with social, political and economic institutions in Peru – while informing their solutions with longstanding ideological constraints, such as those on the legitimacy of leftist parties in Peru.

The use of political marketing might enhance democracy in Peru, through polit-ical participation. However, economically speaking, in a country where people's attitudes to democracy depend on their standards of living, the use of political marketing might easily become a further source of division and exclusion, as not all parties and political movements would be able to use its techniques. In the end, the utility of such a models will depend on the practicability of applying them to the specific characteristics of the country.

Alan García reorganised and re-launched the party between 1982 and 1985. He won the presidential election in 1985, but after five years of severe crisis the APRA lost most of its credibility and popular support. Now that García is giving it another try, we might witness the cyclical tendency of Latin American history to repeat itself. Alternatively, we might see Peruvian political parties take advantage of the new means of political participation and economic development. It is a great challenge, at the heart of which is political marketing.

Notes

1 Karl Marx *Hegelian Philosophy of Right*: *Selected Essays*, quoted in Haya de la Torre (1936: 187).
2 For more information about political violence in Peru, see Gorriti (1990) and Pareja and Gatti (1990).
3 This is what Jorge Basadre, a leading Peruvian historian, called the period 1895–1930, in *Peru: Problema y Posibilidad* (1994).
4 We should, however, take into account that interpersonal communication is a very important element when defining a communication plan for a candidate, especially in rural and less developed areas where access to technology is limited.
5 For this approach I am taking into consideration also elements of Kenneth Burke's 'Dramatisation' theory; concepts such as *selection, reflection and deflection, identification, terministic screens* or *motives* (1945: x), are valuable components of discourses and have a role in the configuration of political spectacle (Edelman 1998: 90).
6 For failing to turn out, there is a fine of approximately 30 Euros, which is 10 per cent of the average income of a public-school teacher.
7 In the paper I presented at the Political Marketing Conference in the University of Aberdeen in 2002, I spoke about politicians treating Fujimori's regime as a 'scapegoat', at tactic which does not seem to be working any longer for Toledo or other politicians (see Patron Galindo 2002).

Bibliography

Ames, Rolando (2001), 'Un tiempo para el sinceramiento social y cambio de rumbos', *Revista Cuestión de Estado* (Lima: Instituto de Diálogo y Propuestas), 27–8.
Barnechea, Alfredo (1995), *La República Embrujada*, Lima: Editorial Nuevo Siglo.
Barnechea, Alfredo (2001), *Para Salir del Laberinto. Del Neoliberalismo a la Nueva Socialdemocracia*, Lima: Editorial Santillana.
Barreda, Javier (2001), 'Relanzamiento y refundación', *Diario Correo* (Lima), 9 August.
Basadre, Jorge (1994), *Perú: Problema y Posibilidad*, Lima: Fundación M. Bustamante.
Burke, Kenneth (1945), *A Rhetoric of Motives*, New York: University of California Press.
Cuestión de Estado (2001), 'Elecciones otra vez. Entre las opciones y los deseos', 27–8.
Daeschner, Jeff (1993), *The War of the End of Democracy*: *Mario Vargas Llosa versus Alberto Fujimori*, Lima: Peru Reporting.
De Soto, Hernando (1987), *El otro Sendero*, Lima: Instituto Libertad y Democracia.
Degregori, Carlos Iván (2000), *La Década de la Antipolítica. Auge y Huida de Alberto Fujimori y Vladimiro Montesinos*, Lima: Instituto de Estudios Peruanos.
Edelman, Murray (1998), *Constructing the Political Spectacle*, Chicago, IL: University of Chicago Press.
Fundació CIDOB (2001a), Biografías de Líderes Políticos: Alan García Pérez, Barcelona, available at: www.cidob.org/bios/castellano/lideres/g-014.htm (accessed November 2003).
Fundació CIDOB (2001b), Biografías de Líderes Políticos: Alejandro Toledo Manrique, Barcelona, available at: www.cidob.org/bios/castellano/lideres/t-021.htm (accessed November 2003).
García Pérez, A. (2000), *La Década Infame, Deuda Externa 1990–1999*, Cali: Fundación para la Investigación y la Cultura.

García Pérez, A. (2001), 'Sobre la modernización y el relanzamiento del aprismo', available at: www.apra.org.pe/modernización.asp (accessed November 2003).

García Pérez, A. (2003), *Modernidad y Política en el Siglo XXI: Globalización con Justicia Social*, Lima: Editorial Matices.

Gorriti Ellenbogen, G. (1990), *Sendero: Historia de la Guerra Milenaria en el Peru*, Lima: Apoyo.

Grompone, R. (2001), 'La obligación de una transición audaz', *Revista Cuestión de Estado* (Lima: Instituto de Diálogo y Propuestas), 27–8.

Haya de la Torre, V. R. (1936), *El Anti-imperialismo y el APRA*, Santiago de Chile: Ediciones Ercilla.

Johansen, H. P. M. (2002) 'Political marketing: more than persuasive techniques. An organisational perspective', paper presented at the 2002 Political Marketing Conference, University of Aberdeen, 19–21 September.

Karlberg, M. (2002), 'Partisan branding and media spectacle: implications for democratic communication' *Democratic Communiqué*, 18 (summer).

Knuckey, J. and Lees-Marshment, J. (2002), 'American political marketing: George W. Bush and the Republican Party', paper presented at the 2002 Political Marketing Conference, University of Aberdeen, 19–21 September.

Lees-Marshment, J. (2001), *Political Marketing and British Political Parties*, Manchester: Manchester University Press.

Lees-Marshment, J. and Bartle, J. (2002), 'Marketing British political parties in 2001: an impossible challenge?', paper presented at the 2002 Political Marketing Conference, University of Aberdeen, 19–21 September.

Meléndez Guerrero, Carlos (2003), 'Adiós a los outsiders?' *Revista Quehacer* (Lima: Fundación Desco), 140 (March–April), available at: www.desco.org.pe/qh/qh140cm.htm (accessed November 2003).

Pareja Pflucker, Piedad and Gatti, Aldo (1990), *Evaluacion de las Elecciones Municipales de 1989 (Impacto de la Violencia Terrorista)*, Lima: INC.

Patrón Galindo, Pedro (2002), 'Symbolism and the construction of political products: analysis of the political marketing strategies of Peruvian President Alejandro Toledo', paper presented at the 2002 Political Marketing Conference, University of Aberdeen, 19–21 September.

Planas Silva, Pedro and Vallenas Málaga, Hugo (1990), 'Haya de la Torre en su espacio y en su tiempo', in *Vida y Obra de Víctor Raúl Haya de la Torre*, Lima: Instituto Cambio y Desarrollo.

Quiroz, María Teresa (1990), 'El partido: obra principal de Víctor Raúl Haya de la Torre (1930–1934)', in *Vida y Obra de Víctor Raúl Haya de la Torre*, Lima: Instituto Cambio y Desarrollo.

Tanaka, Martín and Zárate, Patricia (1998), *Los Espejismos de la Democracia: El Colapso del Sistema de Partidos en el Perú*, Lima: Instituto de Estudios Peruanos.

Tanaka Gondo, Martín and Zárate Ardela, Patricia (2002), *Valores Democráticos y Participación Ciudadana en el Perú 1998–2001*, Lima: Instituto de Estudios Peruanos.

Tuesta Soldevilla, Fernando (1994), *Perú Político en Cifras: Elite Política y Elecciones*, Lima: Fundación Friedrich Ebert.

Tuesta Soldevilla, Fernando (1995), *Sistema de Partidos Políticos en el Perú, 1978–1995*, Lima: Fundación Friedrich Ebert.

Tuesta Soldevilla, Fernando (2002), 'El liderazgo político en el Perú', in W. Hofmeister (ed.), *Liderazgo Político en América Latina*, Rio de Janeiro: Fundación Konrad Adenauer.

Vargas Llosa, Álvaro (1991), *El Diablo en Campaña*, Madrid: Ediciones El País.

Vargas Llosa, Mario (1993), *El Pez en el Agua*, Barcelona: Seix Barral.

11

Political marketing in Scotland's devolved system

Declan P. Bannon and Robert Mochrie

Scotland – a unique political arena in Britain

The Scottish political market has been shaped by the country's history. Although part of the UK, Scotland has always been a distinct entity with its own political, legal, religious, educational and cultural framework. The second largest political party in Scotland, the Scottish National Party (SNP), has no effective presence in the rest of the UK. While the distinctive elements of Scottish politics are often attributed to the influence of the SNP, we argue that Scottish and English politics have always differed. For example, the alignment of social groups with political parties has differed between Scotland and England for many years, with religious affiliation and attitudes to national identity shaping political participation much more in Scotland than in England.

From the Treaty of Union in 1707 to the establishment of the Scottish Parliament in 1999, the country had no national parliament. Yet, throughout that period Scotland has enjoyed greater autonomy than any other part of the United Kingdom (Paterson 1994). For many years, Scottish political affairs were managed within the UK through the Scottish Office (established in 1885), with the secretary of state for Scotland sitting in the UK's Cabinet. Scotland's distinctive political position within the UK is reflected by various considerations:

- Scotland is not a region within the UK, but rather a country of the UK (Brown *et al.* 1999).
- Scotland has traditionally had a disproportionately high number of MPs.
- Bodies such as the Scottish Grand Committee (comprising all MPs representing Scottish constituencies) and the Scottish Affairs Select Committee at Westminster have no regional counterparts.

The presence of the SNP simply emphasises the role of the national question in Scottish politics. All Scottish political parties have recognised that they need to be able to represent Scotland's political and economic interests, and they have succeeded when they defend and extend Scottish interests. We interpret the Liberals' domination of Scottish politics in the nineteenth century, their replacement by the Tories in the early twentieth century and, finally, the rise of the Labour Party in the latter half of the twentieth century as indicative of changes in the public's perception of the national interest. When the Liberal and Conservative Parties weakened thirty years ago, primarily due to a sense of injustice over the ownership of North Sea oil, a market space opened that the SNP, until then a minor party, was able to fill.

In the UK general election of 1997, the 72 Scottish constituencies returned MPs from 3 parties, 56 representing the Labour Party. Exactly six years later, in the Scottish general election using the additional member system (AMS) of election, which is analysed below, 129 members of the Scottish Parliament (MSPs) were elected, representing 6 parties, as well as 4 independents. While the fifty-six representatives of the Labour Party formed the largest group in the Scottish Parliament, they had to enter into a coalition agreement with the Scottish Liberal Democratic (SLD) Party to form the Scottish Executive (government). In this chapter, we describe how the structure of the Scottish political market, the behaviour of political parties and the voting behaviour of the electorate have changed during 1997–2003. We argue that the electoral system used in Scottish general elections has given minor parties much greater influence than they had previously. While we use the comprehensive political marketing (CPM) model (Lees-Marshment 2001a) to explain differences in the parties' electoral success, our case study is of the Scottish Socialist Party (SSP).

This minor party has achieved only modest electoral success in the Scottish Parliament, securing the election of one MSP in the 1999 election and six in 2003. The case study demonstrates how the party has developed from having a product orientation in 1999, with elements, at least, of a sales orientation emerging by 2003. We contend that the party's ideological commitment prevents it from adopting a market orientation, and we use the case study to suggest how the CPM model might be developed to take account of ideologically distinct niche parties that can survive by attracting substantial support from well-defined segments of the electorate.

Scotland's political market

The Labour Government, elected in 1997, had a clear manifesto commitment to the devolution of power to Scottish and Welsh institutions. This took effect through the Scotland Act (1998), which created a devolved Scottish Parliament with legislative powers across a wide range of policy issues, including education and health services, criminal justice, and environment and transport policy. Policy is implemented by the Scottish Executive, composed of ministers who are members of the Scottish Parliament. These new institutions are subsidiary to the Parliament sitting at Westminster and the UK Government, which retain powers to deal with fiscal policy (including social security benefits) and foreign policy, incorporating relations with the European Union. We consider it unlikely, given the process leading to the establishment of the Scottish institutions, that their UK counterparts could exert their implicit authority over devolved matters without creating a constitutional crisis, leading to the (threatened) withdrawal of Scotland from the UK. The substantial powers vested in the Scottish institutions should ensure an active market for representation in Parliament and strong competition between parties wishing to form the Scottish Executive.

We are interested in explaining here the ways in which the extensive changes to the nature, composition and structure of the political market affect political marketing activity. The Scotland Act prescribes a method of election of members of the Scottish Parliament, the AMS, which is designed to increase the extent to which representation in Parliament is proportional to the support of political parties. In this system of election, there are two separate ballots. In the first ballot, to elect MSPs for seventy-three territorially distinct constituencies, each elector casts a single vote, the winner being the candidate first past the post (FPTP), i.e. receiving the greatest number of votes. In the second ballot, to elect 56 additional members from 8 regional lists, electors again cast a single vote, this time for a political party. For each political party, in each regional ballot, the number of votes cast is divided by the number of seats already won (in constituency elections) or allocated to them (from the regional list). The party for which this ratio has the highest value is allocated a further MSP and its ratio is recalculated, increasing the divisor by one. This process is repeated until all of the available seats have been allocated.

Since voters in most regions elect 16 MSPs, any political party that obtains at least 6.25 per cent of the regional list vote is certain to obtain one seat. In constituency elections contested by 4 parties, no party can win a seat without obtaining 25 per cent of the votes cast. The introduction of the regional list therefore increases opportunities for minor parties to be represented. In the first Scottish Parliamentary elections, in May 1999, the Scottish Conservative Party failed to win a single constituency ballot in spite of attracting 15 per cent of the votes cast. However, by securing eighteen regional list seats, it was able to form the third largest group within the Parliament.

The introduction of the AMS had, therefore, greatly increased the opportunities for tactical voting. However, because this is a novel voting system, it might be expected that some voters will be uncertain how to use it effectively.[1] Assuming that all voters will participate in both ballots, they can vote for the same party twice, or split support between two parties. Polling data indicate that up to 40 per cent of Scottish voters might consider splitting their votes, either by conscious choice or as a result of misunderstanding the purpose of the regional list ballot, supposing it to represent their second preference.[2]

Intentionally splitting support between two parties might result from voters understanding how votes cast will benefit parties. For example, voting SSP in the FPTP and Labour on the regional list vote is pointless: the SSP is unlikely to win any FPTP seats because it lacks sufficient concentrations of support, and so relies on the lower threshold for support to return members in the regional list ballot. The Labour Party has very highly concentrated support, and so is more likely to be a contender for FPTP rather than the regional list allocation. Confusion and misunderstanding over the regional list ballot will occur if voters treat it as a second preference ballot. While the two ballots remain separate – and there are issues of public education for the Electoral Commission and political parties to consider here – the problem is exacerbated because the terminology of 'first' and 'second vote' has already established itself.

As well as the SSP, which we study in detail here, the Scottish Green Party (SGP) has also achieved a degree of electoral success under AMS. However, where the SSP has adopted the traditional approach of fielding candidates in all constituencies, the SGP has run candidates only in the regional list. Tactically, this is problematical, for it suggests the message: 'Vote for me; our's is the best party, but only vote for me second.' For a niche party, this is credible because of the relatively weak affiliation of voters to specific parties observed in polling data.

We expect political parties' and voters' understanding of the system to improve over successive elections. Parties will direct their marketing efforts to maximise returns in terms of seats held, while voters will become increasingly adept at ticket-splitting. We also consider that the many innovations in the Scottish political market have created opportunities for the entry of new parties, though it is not clear that the proliferation of parties (and policy stances) will be sustainable in the long run.

A brief history of political marketing in Scotland

Factors peculiar to Scotland have long affected voting preferences. Since the work of Lipset and Rokkan (1967) political scientists have recognised that partisan divisions within Western democratic societies may be based on religion, social class and core issues such as national identity. We believe that Scottish voting patterns in the 1950s and 1960s were based on an alignment of interests in which working-class Protestants tended to identify themselves as unionists, a feature of Scottish politics that goes back to the 1920s and the rise of the Protestant Action Party in Edinburgh. As recently as 1968 in Dundee, nearly 40 per cent of Protestant manual workers voted for the Conservative Party, compared with 6 per cent of Catholic manual workers. Hence Seawright and Curtice (1992) argue that the Labour Party was able to establish itself as the representative of the whole of the working class only as the importance of such religious affiliations declined.

The emergence of national identity
Matching the diminishing importance of religious affiliation as a determinant of voters' preferences, attitudes towards national identity have become more prominent in Scottish politics since the 1960s. The two major parties, Labour and Conservative, had adopted unionist policies, according to which Scotland was to be treated very similarly to the rest of the UK. As voters' opinions began to alter, the SNP, previously a fringe group, was able to emerge as an important political party; by the 1997 general election, it was the second largest party in terms of votes cast, although only the third measured by constituencies held.

Table 11.1 *National identity in Scotland (%)*

	Scottish, not British	Scottish more than British	Scottish equal to British	British more than Scottish	British, not Scottish	Sample size
1992	19	40	33	3	3	$n = 957$
1997	23	38	27	4	4	$n = 882$
1999	32	35	22	3	4	$n = 1,482$
2000	37	31	21	3	4	$n = 1,663$
2003	30	32	30	3	9	$n = 1,100$

Source: Curtice and Seyd 2001.

Brown *et al.* (1999) argue that attitudes towards national identity affected voting decisions strongly in the Westminster elections of 1992 and 1997. They also argue that all of the political parties operating in Scotland have changed their policies and behaviour in response to shifting voter attitudes.

Certainly, during the last twenty five years, there has been a persistent increase in the proportion of people who identify themselves in some sense as Scottish rather than British. In table 11.1, we show the proportions of respondents in successive ICM opinion studies by perception of their national identity. The number of those who regard themselves as more British than Scottish has remained very low throughout the period 1992–2003, while the majority, generally between 60–70 per cent, consider themselves to be primarily Scottish. The survey conducted in 2000 found that, within this group, the majority believed themselves to be purely Scottish.[3]

Similar results can be obtained from Scottish Election surveys for 1979, 1992, 1997 and 2000, in which one question invited respondents to classify themselves as either Scottish or British. On this cruder measure, the number of those who regard themselves as Scottish has increased from 57 per cent in 1979 to 80 per cent in 2001, while the proportion responding 'British' has fallen from 39 per cent to 13 per cent. These data suggest that, were the respondents in the ICM survey who consider themselves equally Scottish and British compelled to choose between those alternatives, an increasing majority would favour Scottish.

The policy stance of Scottish political parties

The importance of addressing the national question has created degrees of complexity in the Scottish political market not found in the wider British market. Political activity prior to the emergence of the SNP can be modelled by treating the country as an integral part of the unitary UK State, although one with institutions (including judiciary, Church and higher education) constituted by distinctively Scottish legislation and operating quite differently from their English counterparts. Choice between the Labour and Conservative Parties could then be reduced to a single dimension in which voters' preferences for collective over market-based solutions to problems of policy determine the party that they will support.[4] The emergence of the 'Scottish question' indicates a second dimension, in which voters' preferences for creating and strengthening autonomous Scottish institutions might be indexed.

By the general election of 1979, the three parties had established distinctive characters that have largely endured for the last quarter century. The Labour Party, the market leader, was to the Left of Centre on economic issues, and supportive of limited Scottish autonomy (figure 11.1). The Conservative Party, although the UK's market leader, was never more than the challenger party in Scotland. Its position has been to the Right of Centre on economic issues, while generally opposed to increased autonomy in Scottish affairs. The SNP, although defined primarily in terms of support for full Scottish autonomy (possibly outwith the UK), gradually adopted a position to the Left of Centre on economic issues. Lastly, the Liberal Party, while the smallest of the major parties, experienced some resurgence of support following the formation of the Social Democratic Party in 1981. It is centrist on economic issues, and moderately supportive of increased Scottish autonomy.

The effects of devolution

Accepting the importance of the Scottish question in defining the political market during the 1990s, one reason for the leadership of the Labour Party agreeing to support the establishment of devolved institutions was to confront the appeal of the SNP. In the same way that the Labour Party in the 1992–1997 political marketing

Figure 11.1   *Positioning of political parties in Scotland*

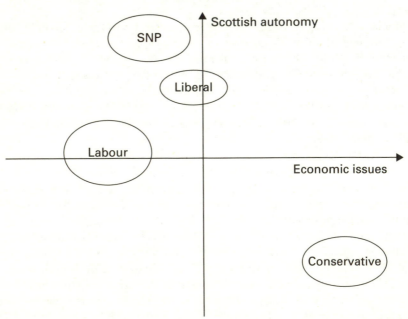

cycle used the development of a policy that would be 'tough on crime, tough on the causes of crime', to counter Conservative Party leadership on issues of law and order, the creation of devolved institutions granted the degree of autonomy sought by most Scots, reinforcing the Labour Party's claim to be the best representative of the interests of the Scottish people. For Labour Party strategists, the SNP exists to promote a single policy, and once that policy has been realised, it will be unable to sustain a significant challenge to the Labour Party. To the extent that the new institutions meet the needs of the Scottish electorate, the importance of this dimension to the political marketplace should diminish, and this might be expected to benefit the Conservative Party, which has traditionally offered distinctive policies on other issues.

In addition, while all of the Scottish organisations of the UK's political parties have traditionally had some degree of autonomy in determining policy, they have concentrated their efforts on participating and winning UK general elections.

Conjecture 1   Market-oriented British parties will permit their Scottish organisations to develop distinctive policies that enable them to address the needs of the Scottish electorate more effectively, especially in areas of social policy such as health and education provision.

Differences between Scotland and the rest of the UK in support for political parties are quite complex. Between 1979 and 1997, the Conservative Party was in government, while the Labour Party was the main opposition.

Conjecture 2   For the SNP to become an effective challenger party (or the market leader) within the Scottish political market, it will have to become more market oriented, developing and promoting policies that positively attract a broad segment of Scottish voters.

The SNP's central ideology is self-governance for Scotland. At its spring 2004 conference, this position was strengthened by enshrining *independence* in the constitution for the first time, replacing the ill-defined goal of self-governance (Swinney 2004). While the majority of the Scottish electorate are against independence (although 80 per cent believe it to be inevitable), the SNP must, and does, adopt a sales orientation, pushing the benefits of independence. It would be contrary to its stated aims to be simply pro-devolution; so the SNP has adopted a pro-devolution stance as a stepping stone to independence. However, the SNP adopts policies and a presentation style that attempt to appeal to the political marketplace, which is left of centre. In so doing (with the exception of its independence stance) it is in a position to develop a more market-oriented approach on other policy issues. This positions the SNP in a hybrid orientation. To some extent, this is inevitable, for we suggest in our analysis of the most recent political marketing cycle that the party's behaviour was that of a follower, rather than of a leader (either nationally or in a specific market niche). The structure of the Labour Party and of the SLD mean that they displayed a strong element of a market orientation during that political cycle, and so they have converged in terms of policy. This has enabled them to work in partnership, forming a majority in Parliament and controlling the Scottish Executive since 1999. However, there are still some notable differences in their policy orientations and structures, with the Liberal Democrats being the more flexible and decentralised.

> **Conjecture 3** Labour and the SLD will continue to dominate the devolved institutions. Over time, the SLD's strength within the partnership will increase.

The political marketing stance of the major parties

With the adoption of new standing orders in 1998, the SLP replicated the decision-making structures of the UK's Labour Party, which we consider to be the most thoroughgoing attempt by any UK political party to institutionalise a marketing orientation. Within a scheme called 'Partnership in Power', the national party drafts consultation documents covering the main responsibilities of government, in which market research is used to identify the unmet needs of individual voters and party members are invited to suggest appropriate responses. The process by which policy is developed involves extensive dialogue within the party and the adaptation of initial proposals following further public consultation. The time from initial public consultations to the launch of the pre-manifesto document is nearly two-and-a-half years. This is possible for the UK's Labour Party because it has sufficient resources, including salaried staff, to pay for market research, assimilate findings and disseminate them within the party, and then collate the responses, and draft further policy proposals, working by iterations to definite conclusions. We do not believe that the SLP has such extensive resources, having been treated for many years as a regional party office by the UK party, and so the marketing process is perhaps not so well defined. Nonetheless, the number of steps in the process, especially open consultation with outside organisations, should ensure that party policy will continue to address the felt needs of voters. This degree of market orientation entrenches the party's market leadership.

The SNP's internal debate between 'fundamentalists', who believe that the party exists principally to secure the establishment of a sovereign Scottish state, and 'gradualists', who wish first to obtain control of the devolved institutions, and then make the case for independence, came to public notice in the leadership election in 2000. The ease with which the winner, John Swinney, who is seen as a leading gradualist, defeated the challenge of Alex Neil, seen as the leading fundamentalist, suggests that this debate is largely settled. This in turn suggests that the SNP does not wish to be characterised simply as the party of independence, but wishes to work within the devolved institutions, making the case for the transfer of reserved powers over time within the context of specifically Scottish needs. While this demonstrates that the party has moved well beyond product orientation, the internal debate suggests that the SNP is not yet market oriented.

We consider that the SNP does not have either the resources or the structures in place to become market oriented. Its constitution continues to offer party members the opportunity to participate in policy development, and it is the responsibility of party committees such as its national council to formulate policy. Although outside bodies are invited to contribute to such discussions, these party organisations retain a higher degree of control over process than their equivalents in the Labour Party. We believe that there is therefore less opportunity for external comment on policy through formal mechanisms. In addition, the SNP does not have the financial resources of the Labour Party. It has to rely heavily on the opinions of members in developing policy, and we expect members of any political party to be committed to the achievement of specific objectives, so that their attitudes on certain matters may be quite different from those of the majority of the electorate. We therefore conclude that during the last political cycle, the SNP was largely a follower and that it will become a challenger to the Labour Party only when it is able to match it in developing a *market*, rather than a sales orientation.

For example, the party has recently put considerable effort into the establishment of Business for Scotland, a non-affiliated organisation that seeks to build up links between the SNP and the Scottish business community, among whose members there are many doubts about the value of the devolved institutions. We think that this can be likened to the Labour Party's 'prawn-cocktail offensive' under the leadership of Neil Kinnock, when the party, in sales-oriented mode, sought to persuade business that its policies would not have an adverse effect on them. Under the direction of economics spokesmen Andrew Wilson and Jim Mather it has advocated a reduction in business taxation, arguing that the stimulus to entrepreneurial activity would lead to higher rates of business formation, exports to England and the rest of the EU, and tax revenues. We consider that these proposals do not fit in well with promises to increase spending on public services. While the party has correctly identified the needs of this market segment, it has not been able to develop a policy that addresses its needs well.

We have already hinted that the SLD might have the capacity to develop a market orientation because of the party's decentralised decision-making structure, which is designed to compensate for its limited resources by responding very precisely to local issues. The SLD tends to concentrate activity in those wards in local authority elections where it considers itself to have a reasonable chance of success. Its strategy is to obtain market intelligence based on local contacts, and to respond to matters of concern through such means as regular newsletters. Thus, the party concentrates much more on serving the needs of local communities than its opponents. While this strategy has its problems, not least the possibility that SLD councillors will support strongly opposing policies once elected, it is consistent with a party developing the sort of relationship marketing techniques that we expect to see in an MOP. This policy of working within very restricted areas enables the party to achieve a degree of credibility that its national representation, reduced to very low levels for many years, would not otherwise permit.

It is therefore interesting to note that the constitution of the Scottish Liberal Democrats specifies that policy formation is the responsibility of the party conference, but that policy will normally be developed by a policy committee, which may consult with outside bodies. Again, the policy-making process is largely under the control of the party membership. While this has the same disadvantages as with the SNP, we consider that the process adopted in which policy is revised bi-annually at party conferences ensures regular scrutiny and review of all policies, increasing the effectiveness of external scrutiny. (How effective the SLD policy of requiring constituency parties to elect conference representatives who attend a number of meetings is in ensuring that external voices are given a fuller hearing by the party's decision-making procedures is less certain.)

The SLD have also had the advantage of being a partner in the Scottish Executive during the political cycle. Its leader was the Scottish deputy first minister, and 4 of its 17 MSPs were members of the Executive. These were the first SLD ministers in UK since the wartime coalition. The party skilfully used these representatives to claim that all of the popular achievements of the entire Executive were the result of party policies being implemented. For example, under the direction of Henry McLeish, the first minister, the Scottish Parliament agreed to provide for the cost of personal care for residents of nursing homes, a policy recommended by the Royal Commission on Personal Care (the Sutherland Committee), but rejected by the British Government. Although agreement on the policy was the result of a commitment by Labour ministers, their partners were very quick to claim the credit (Mitchell 2003; see the party manifestos for 2003).

This is simply extending to a national scale the policy adopted at the local level, where local councillors from other parties find the effects of their actions being reported in SLD *Focus* newsletters as resulting from prospective (SLD) candidates' interventions. We conclude that this party has developed the sorts of procedures necessary to become a challenger to the Labour Party. It is also possible, however, that the two parties will reach an accommodation in which the SLD would accept the role of the junior partner, being more effective in rural areas than the Labour Party, seeking together to retain control of the Executive.

Communication and campaigning

Burnside, Herbert and Curtis (2003) note that all four major parties appeared to have converged on policies that were very similar in both character and presentation. All were concerned to address the priorities of the electorate, as expressed in market research conducted for BBC Scotland, addressing issues of crime and disorder, health, education and the economy. This suggests that all of the parties have understood the importance of positioning their products in order to appeal to key voters, and that they now rely on attack and defence lines in communications to achieve product differentiation. Thus the Labour Party and the SNP wanted to argue that only they could lead the Executive, so that a vote for the other parties would be wasted.

The SNP appeared to follow a sales management approach. The party developed its policies and its campaign for the Scottish parliamentary election early in 2002. The release carried positive messages on school class size, nursing pay and police numbers (matching many of the themes of Labour's 1997 UK election victory), set against attacks on Labour management of health care (especially increased waiting times for critically ill patients) and the slow pace of economic growth in Scotland compared with that of the UK as a whole. This took attention away from discussion of the constitutional settlement, and was therefore consistent with the gradualist policy of the leadership. This approach was designed to consolidate SNP support by avoiding the mistakes of the poorly managed campaign of 1999, where the party's economics spokesman was forced to admit at a press conference that a key policy on taxation could not be sustained, with the party changing policy abruptly in mid-campaign.

The Labour Party, having refined its policy carefully to emphasise the need for continuity, argued that after 4 years in office (and with a first minister who had served less than 18 months) improvements in key areas such as health and education could already be perceived. The title of its manifesto, 'Just the Beginning', was intended to echo a theme used successfully by the national party in the UK election of 2001, 'A lot done, a lot to do'. Its main line of attack was that an SNP-led Executive would provoke 'divorce' as Scotland separated from the UK. However, given its previous use and the gradualist approach of the SNP, this did not seem to have any great effect. Overall, the party seems to have continued to rely on market-oriented activity based on centralised campaigning. This was perhaps making a virtue out of necessity. Political debate in the three months preceding the election was dominated by the decision of the UK Government to support the US-led coalition's intervention in Iraq. The Scottish Labour Party conference was unable to proceed until time was given to delegates to express their often strongly negative opinions about this, and many activists appear to have taken little part in the election. Local activity to support candidates was therefore in many places quite minimal.

The SLD had used the pre-election campaign to develop its key claim that it had 'made a difference' in the Scottish Executive, pushing forward its key themes, in particular the abolition of university tuition fees (achieved through the deferral of payments), the implementation of free personal care for the elderly and the introduction of freedom of information legislation. As the smaller coalition party, the SLD faced difficulties in achieving credibility, especially since it had indicated that it would be unwilling to enter into a partnership with the SNP. While reasonable in many ways, it meant that the party could expect to achieve influence within the Executive only by continuing the existing partnership, and this was seen to limit its post-election freedom to negotiate with the Labour Party. Its message was further confused by the party's refusal to specify policies on which it would not be willing to negotiate changes in the partnership agreement. We consider that this reflects concerns within the party about conceding too much to the Labour Party in negotiating the partnership agreement in 1999 in order to achieve the SLD's very public commitment to reforming student tuition fees. Thus important themes for the SLD, including a rehabilitative approach to anti-social behaviour, reform of the electoral system for local government and the transfer of power from central institutions to local ones, were never developed fully in the campaign. The good groundwork of policy development did not translate into effective communication in this electoral cycle because the party has yet to define a sufficiently strong identity, differentiated from the Labour Party's.

While the other three parties were seen to be contesting very similar ground, the Conservatives were able to develop their unionism into a critical commentary on the working of the devolved institutions. The Conservative leader David McLetchie led the attacks on First Minister Henry McLeish that led to his resignation over the management of his constituency party's accounts. The Conservative Party has also made much out of the difficulties in the construction of the Scottish Parliament building, where costs have quadrupled in the past four years. While these are very strong attack lines, they have the drawback of suggesting that politicians are not to be trusted, and a party has to be careful not to suggest that its own representatives could not be trusted with positions of power. The difficulty for the Conservative Party is that it has not yet developed strong themes that might enable it to build on its relatively low current levels of support.

Polling and party representation

During the electoral cycle, the only regular published polling information comes from the survey undertaken every month by NFO System 3 on behalf of the *Herald* newspaper. While all the major parties are actively involved in episodic canvassing, the need to commission polls is diminished by regular large-scale polls commissioned by the newspapers. In addition, other government-funded research projects, such as the British Electoral Surveys, CREST and various academic research, provide ample *marketing data* on which to base sales and marketing decisions. This, of course, is in addition to the most accurate marketing information system of the majority of industries, kindly providing regular, if not frequent, state of the market surveys (i.e. election results). The Scottish parliamentary election takes place every 4 years, and this in conjunction with Westminster election allows a more regular market report and aids the marketing segmentation process.

Polling data suggest that for long periods within this electoral cycle, support for the major parties remained more or less constant. Support for the Labour Party and the SLD increased immediately after the election – but this is quite normal for parties in power – and then fell away, the SLD reaching a low of 12 per cent on the regional list ballot in the months before the UK general election in June 2001. Towards the end of that year, there was consolidation of Labour Party support, while SLD support increased steadily from then until the start of the Scottish general election campaign. Polling suggested that support for the SNP fell immediately after the election, but then rose in late 2000 to a level achieved prior to the 1999 election campaign. A relatively poor performance in the UK general election does seem to have affected support in the Scottish polls, but this was reversed in part as the SNP benefited from the Labour Party's loss of support in the months leading up to the election as the Government prepared for military intervention in Iraq.

During the election campaign, the Labour Party was able to regain support that it had apparently lost, benefiting from the 'Baghdad bounce' following the successful invasion of Iraq. The effects of the modest loss of support in the constituency and regional list ballots were mitigated as SNP support fell away considerably. Whereas in 1999, 62 per cent of the votes cast in the regional list ballot were for the two leading parties, their combined share in 2003 fell to 50 per cent (see table 11.2).

While the Conservative Party improved its position slightly, the main beneficiaries were the minor parties, such as the SGP and the SSP, but also independent candidates. However, the geographical pattern of support for the major parties did not change substantially during the political cycle. As in the previous Parliament, the Labour Party and the SLD are over-represented relative to their support, while the minor parties remain extremely under-represented.

We have also shown the relative efficiency of each of the parties. This is defined as the average number of votes per seat gained for the party of interest divided by the number of votes per seat gained for the Labour Party. Consequently, for the Labour Party, the measure takes the value one(1). The higher the value, the greater the disparity between the party's success in attracting votes and winning seats: thus the Labour Party, the market leader, is most efficient in this respect. It is interesting to note that the minor parties (SGP and SSP) reduced their efficiency measure considerably between the two elections. In 1999, these parties won only one seat each. In 2003, both obtained enough votes in regional list ballots across Scotland to win at least one seat in the majority of these contests. The improvement is especially marked for the SGP. Its share of the regional list vote increased from 3.6 per cent in 1999 to 6.9 per cent in 2003, but the party managed to increase the number of seats won from one to seven. Thus, while the SSP can claim to have grown more rapidly in terms of votes cast, increasing its share from 2.0 per cent to 6.7 per cent, the

Table 11.2 *Party representation in Parliament, 2003*

Party support	Labour	SNP	Cons	SLD	Greens	SSP	Other
Constituency ballot (%)	34.6	23.8	16.6	15.4	a	6.2	3.4
Regional list ballot (%)	29.3	20.9	15.5	11.8	6.9	6.9	9.0
Constituency seats	46	9	3	13	0	0	2
Regional list seats	4	18	15	4	6	7	2
Seats allocated in proportion to regional list support	37.8	26.9	20.0	15.2	8.9	8.6	11.6
Over-representation relative to share of vote (%)	32.3	0.3	−10.0	11.9	−21.4	−30.4	−65.5
Relative efficiency	1.00	1.32	1.47	1.18	1.68	1.90	3.83
Efficiency relative to 1999	0.95	0.99	1.01	0.95	0.27	0.56	0.40
Relative efficiency in constituency ballot.	1.00	3.51	7.36	1.57	a	a	2.28

Note: [a] Not applicable.

number of seats increased only from one to six. This outcome suggests a profound change to the political market. In constituency elections, the larger parties have always made the claim that a vote for a minor party would be wasted since it could not affect the outcome. But these data show that the smaller parties are now nearly as capable of turning votes into parliamentary representation as the larger parties. It is interesting, however, to note that the improved position of the minor parties does not appear to be at the expense of the Executive partners, the Labour Party and the SLD, for whom the share of votes per seat held fell only slightly. Improved efficiency for all parties is consistent with better targeting of marketing effort and more complete market segmentation.

Case study: the SSP

We now turn to our case study of the SSP, in which we analyse its political marketing stance. Established in 1998, it achieved its first electoral success during the 1999–2003 political marketing cycle. By securing the election of a group of six MSPs – enough to form a parliamentary group with the associated privileges, such as membership of the parliamentary business group, the right to nominate the convenor of one parliamentary committee and the right to initiate business – it has established itself as a minor party within the Scottish political market. We argue that in this process the SSP has already developed from having a very pure product orientation at the time of its formation, introducing (elements of) a sales orientation in the course of the political cycle. However, we consider that the party's ideological commitment prevents it from attaining a market orientation.

A study of the SSP is especially interesting since we are not aware of any previous work in which the CPM model has been applied to organisations at such an early stage of development. Following Lees-Marshment (2001b), the CPM model identifies eight distinct stages in a political marketing process:

1 market intelligence;
2 product design;
3 product development;
4 internal marketing;
5 external communication;
6 campaigning;
7 election; and
8 delivery.

We believe that previous work has examined how organisations which have already contested elections respond to changes in market conditions by adapting elements of their product – structures, policies and leadership – to changes in market conditions. The SSP, created to exploit a perceived gap in the Scottish political market created by the devolution settlement and the emerging socio-economic policy consensus among its rivals, is not bound by its history. It may therefore have greater freedom than its rivals to design and develop its product.

It is difficult to incorporate the final stage of the CPM process within the analysis. The SSP was established to represent the opinions of a relatively small group of the Scottish electorate, and its founders had not expected to be in a position to challenge the major political parties during the initial political cycle. In addition, the party's policy is not to support the Scottish Executive, even where a minority administration requires the party's support in a vote of confidence. Such ideologically based decisions limit its opportunities for engaging in delivery, but are consistent with its potentency as a vehicle for protest against current trends in political activity.

The strongly ideological SSP has tended to make documents publicly available in electronic form that other parties do not. As well as documents published in other forms, such as election manifestos, it has been possible to obtain detailed policy documents, internal discussion papers, agendas and minutes of the party conferences and a complete archive of the *Scottish Socialist Voice*, the SSP's weekly newspaper. Our method has been to use these documents to assess the ways in which the party's interactions with the electorate changed during the period 1999–2003. Restricting our attention to the differences between a product and a sales orientation, we looked for evidence both of the collection of market intelligence prior to the communication stage, and of external communication other than campaigning, these being indicators of a sales orientation.

Goals, market and product

The origins of the SSP can be traced back to the national campaign against the council tax in the late 1980s and early 1990s. Campaigners associated with the Militant Tendency were expelled from the Labour Party, but were able to use the experience of large-scale mobilisation to establish Scottish Militant Labour (SML). Sheridan and McAlpine (1994) relate the emergence of SML to the Anti-Poll Tax Union's provision of services to 'constituents', a role in political marketing identified in Butler and Collins (2001).[5] By 1996, realising the need to expand support beyond Glasgow, SML joined with groups that had previously been affiliated to the SNP and the Labour Party to found the Scottish Socialist Alliance. The SSP also allowed the Socialist Workers' Party's Scottish Aggregate to become an affiliate early in 2001, creating a 'broad front' of left-wing groups. As might be expected given the foundation process, the party has retained a strong ideological bent.

As a niche party, the SSP has directed its efforts towards securing support among two segments of the electorate: the poorer voters who stand to benefit from the SSP's strongly redistributive policies; and middle class voters who feel alienated by the other political parties' convergence on the Centre.[6] In the SSP's manifestos for the elections between 1999 and 2003, there is a strong appeal to class identity. In 1999, the SSP proclaimed that it was the 'only party that stands unequivocally [sic] on the side of the working class and the poor against big business and the rich'.[7] It also sought the support of 'others who may not personally suffer poverty and insecurity but who are dismayed by a government that can spend billions on nuclear weapons and military planes, yet can scarcely find pennies to wage war against poverty at home'.[8] In the 2003 manifesto, this appeal has been softened to read:

> If you're against the war on Iraq; if you're in favour of a fair deal for our low paid workers; if you're dismayed by the growing gulf between rich and poor; if you want quality public services; if you want to move towards an independent socialist Scotland based on the principles of equality, solidarity, social justice and generosity, this is your party.

Given its origins and political ideology, the SSP might be expected to be unsympathetic to the development of marketing tools, believing that their use would lead to the abandonment of socialist principles. The SSP's internal organisation probably prevents it from becoming an MOP in the near future. It has vested considerable power in its members in order to create conditions in which members can trust the party's leadership to remain committed to the SSP's programme. Thus the ultimate authority of the party is its national conference. In February 2003, the conference agreed that the SSP group in the Scottish Parliament should not join the Scottish Executive's administration, and that the group should not offer a minority administration support in votes of confidence. The conference also confirmed that elected representatives are expected to take part in 'non-violent direct action', and to meet with the party's executive committee to discuss their work.[9] Such efforts to bring the parliamentary party under the control of the wider party are mechanisms to ensure that the product offered to the electorate retains its strong ideological identity, and are indicative of the SSP's public eschewal of conventional marketing techniques.

These comments suggest that the SSP is likely to develop policy simply by reference to its internal structures. Furthermore, given the limited resources available to the party, external communication tends to be minimal outside of the campaign period. This suggests that the SSP is a POP, using only the minimum set of elements from the CPM approach – firstly, product design (a purely internal process) and campaigning immediately prior to the election.

Sales orientation in the SSP

Further analysis suggests that there is evidence of the SSP using political communications in the more sophisticated manner of a SOP. The SSP has developed two quite distinct channels of external communication and promotion. First, given its roots in protest, it remains involved in very localised campaigning based on strong networks, especially within peripheral housing schemes in Glasgow. As noted in the case of the SLD, lack of resources precludes the formal use of market intelligence. And so this community-based activity provides both a means of communicating with voters away from elections (stage 3 of the CPM process for an SOP) and informal methods of acquiring market intelligence (stage 2 of the CPM process for a SOP). This activity shifts the party away from a product orientation towards a sales orientation. However, there is little evidence of the party attempting to use such consultations to develop ideas for policy, as an MOP would.

The second channel of external communication is its newspaper *Scottish Socialist Voice*, which offers a mixture of internal and external communication. The paper is written from the viewpoint that capitalism is destructive of communities, public services and nations in its remorseless pursuit of profit, an objective that is permissible, according to *Scottish Socialist Voice* because of the capitulation of other political parties to business interests. Thus the party's attack lines are expressed with vitriol and are frequently directed at individuals in other political parties, large businesses and media organisations that are critical of the SSP. This recalls the definition of political communications as propaganda (O'Shaughnessy 1990).

We consider that there is considerable evidence of the SSP engaging in product development and communication (stages 3 and 5 of the CPM process for an MOP) throughout the political marketing cycle. For example, the SSP is increasingly concerned to cost proposals and to demonstrate their feasibility. At its formation, shortly before the 1999 general election, the party listed '100 steps towards a socialist Scotland'. No clear suggestions were provided about funding, apart from noting that 'Scotland possesses large oil reserves' and that funds under management in Edinburgh were 'more than ten times the entire budget for the Scottish Parliament'.

By 2003, the SSP had identified key pledges that its members considered to be priority objectives. Of these, the best developed was the proposed introduction of a Scottish service tax, based on income, to finance local authority expenditure. To justify its proposals, the SSP commissioned research (Danson and Whittam 2002) showing that such a tax could raise the same revenue as the current system of finance, yet, unlike the present system, be strongly redistributive. In commissioning this research, the SSP indicated that it required proposals for a 'progressive tax, with all the poorest in society, those with incomes under £10,000, exempt from the tax, and others contributing according to their ability to pay'.[10] The data in Danson and Whittam (2002) suggest that were the tax to be set so that local authorities would face no loss of revenue, people with an income of over £30,000 (11 per cent of the total) would tend to lose in the redistributive process. In addition, for those people with incomes in excess of £50,000 (approximately 2.5 per cent of the total), combined council tax and water charges would average £13,500, or slightly over 15 per cent of their mean income. The highest marginal tax rate of 23 per cent would be levied on all income in excess of £90,000 per annum.[11] In making these proposals, the SSP is addressing a problem that is widely recognised. However, its solution, in which an individual's tax burden increases sharply with income, is strongly differentiated. Again, the party has undertaken activities consistent with being an SOP.

Difficulties translating UK practice to another country

While marketing practice may indeed be translatable from England to Scotland the political environment in each case will differ in terms of voter behaviour, demographics, socio-economics, culture, religion, legal framework, media coverage, elections and parliaments, all of which contribute to the diversity. While London-based central political offices may wish to ignore the distinctiveness of the Scottish political situation purely for simplicity, they do so at their peril. The whole underlying rationale of devolution was to recognise this diversity and encourage political decision-making north and south of the border: a policy might be supported in England and have no support in Scotland. For example, Jack McConnell, Scottish Labour leader and first minister, announced that there would be no tuition fees introduced in Scottish higher education. Frank Roy, MP for the same constituency represented by the first minister, is in favour of tuition fees in English higher education establishments.

David McLethie and Michael Howard, the leaders of the Conservatives in Scotland and England; have similar problems. In a visit to Fife shortly after becoming Tory leader, Howard stated that the party in Scotland would fight campaigns as it would in England, thereby simplifying the marketing and the message. Nevertheless, the Scottish Conservative Party is an independent organisation, only *affiliated* to the UK Conservative Party, and can run a different campaign from that of the UK party if it so chooses.

Issues arising from the use of political marketing

The Scottish political market has recently experienced many changes. Our case study of the SSP has shown how a small party has been able to exploit some of the opportunities created by such changes. As noted above, the introduction of AMS lowers the threshold for minor parties to obtain seats in the Scottish Parliament. But differences between the Scottish and UK political markets might also have made it easier for small left-wing groups to emerge in the former than in the latter political context. In addition, the willingness of the SSP leadership to develop a broad front in which there is tolerance of competing opinions in internal debates has enabled previously disparate groups to work together. Lastly, the apparent shift towards a market orientation among the larger parties has apparently created a market segment whose interests were not being addressed in the political process. The SSP has been able to exploit the lack of representation of that niche.

The emergence of minor parties, especially the SSP and the SGP, during this political marketing cycle suggests that there is scope for refinements to the CPM model. As argued by Butler and Collins (1996), niche parties seek to become the market leader in a very specific context. A niche is defined as a political market segment that can be easily identified, but which is not a key target for other political parties. The SSP's target niche includes people who have been disappointed by the Labour Party's delivery phase, but who are not attracted to the other political parties.

Assuming either that members of the niche have relatively uniform needs, distinct from those of other and larger groups of voters, or that members of the group have an identity sufficiently defined as to have no wish to be represented by parties seeking to obtain office and represent a large part of the wider community, a niche party may have no need to market itself using the same channels as a larger party, and be able to work satisfactorily with rather more limited market intelligence. For example, where the niche is defined by ethnic origin or ideological commitment, Butler and Collins (1996) suggest that a niche party might form long-term relationships with supporters and informal links with the communities that it seeks to serve. This suggests a customer services marketing orientation, in which policy is developed on the basis of the known needs of the groups that the party seeks to represent.

A further consideration is the reliance of political parties on the support of volunteers. Because it is consistent with the CPM to treat members overtly as a special class of customers, to whom the party has to provide services, we have redefined the fourth stage of the CPM process as that of *internal marketing*. In a fuller discussion, an analysis of internal orientation would complement the analysis of external orientation and relationships with the wider electorate.[12] These two orientations are distinct, and so it would be possible for a POP on the basis of external orientation to be an MOP internally, providing services to members such as the opportunity to campaign on matters that they consider important.[13] It is then possible that a party's membership will have such strong needs that they prevent the development of the party's external market orientation and its capacity to achieve electoral success.[14]

We consider that successful political parties will tend to develop internal and external market orientations so that they have a well-motivated membership, committed to promoting policies that address the needs of key voters. Internal orientation, expressed in the degree to which a party attends to the needs of its members, will affect electoral success, if only because of the role of public trust and political unity in the electoral process. We believe that the SSP has demonstrated an internal market orientation. As a niche party, it has been able to establish itself within the political market. Being compelled to remain a POP with SOP tendencies can be explained both by its internal orientation and by the lack of resources currently available to it.

A further argument is that the SSP's marketing can be consistent with its service concept only if it avoids the processes of the CPM and concentrates instead on building relationships with members of its target niche, providing services through direct action. Again, a comparison with Sinn Féin, which McGough (2002) identifies as serving groups that are alienated from the wider political process, is instructive. Both parties appear to have consciously differentiated themselves from their competitors, using an amorphous and vaguely defined claim to be socialist, and have thus achieved success among younger voters. On this interpretation, the populist nature of the product means that its authenticity would be threatened by the (overt) use of conventional marketing techniques.

Conclusion

We began by suggesting how political parties would respond to the introduction of the devolved institutions. We have noted that all parties were able to maintain their efficiency (measured as the share of votes required to win a seat in Parliament) during this electoral cycle, with the minor parties increasing efficiency very considerably. The outstanding example of an intelligent response to the system is the SGP's decision to contest only the regional list ballot, allowing it to direct resources towards the election of a much larger groups of MSPs. On a smaller scale, the three constituency ballots won by the Conservative Party reflect a greater degree of targeting. Although we have chosen to study the SSP in detail (a decision based on polling evidence prior to the general election), the party failed to convert support during the political cycle into electoral success as effectively as some of its rivals.

While we have not yet seen the entry of new parties, our case study of the SSP, formed just before the devolved institutions were established, shows how minor parties have been able to increase their influence within the new electoral system. We have emphasised the extent to which marketing activity undertaken by other political parties created the niche which the SSP has exploited, and also the willingness of the party to abandon a product orientation in order to increase its electoral success.

We have also seen that during the political marketing cycle, the position of the Conservative Party seems to have stabilised. This is interesting because the party's support in opinion surveys had remained much lower than was achieved in the elections in both 1999 and 2003. We consider that the party has begun to address the changed environment of Scottish politics, but that it does not yet have a positive identity. The problems facing the SNP turnout to be similar in nature, for with devolution many of its supporters might consider that it has achieved its principal goals. Among the major parties, the SLD, as members of a federation of national parties, has the greatest autonomy to develop a distinctively Scottish policy, and this helps to explain the relatively strong support that this party achieved in opinion polls during the cycle. However, it does not yet have a strong presence in many of the areas where the Labour Party dominates political activity.

Throughout April 2003 commentators repeatedly stated that the election campaign was uninteresting, with the major parties offering policies that were almost identical. The result was much more interesting. It demonstrated that the minor parties were sufficiently well organised to achieve their objectives, while all the larger parties suffered reverses. The outcome has been the emergence of a multi-party system, in which there are clear threats to the positions of all of the parties. We believe that parties will be under increasing pressure to enter into market-oriented activity through the coming political marketing cycle because of the increased competition in the market. The minor parties have managed to win a number of seats by very small margins, and so are unlikely to be able increase their representation substantially without large increases in their support. They now have to use their representatives to demonstrate that they are able to influence the Executive, and also to find ways of expanding beyond their niche, identifying needs and addressing them fully. The challenge for the follower parties is similar, or else they will risk losing support, but it is possibly the partnership parties (Labour and the SLD) that face the most complex challenge. Having fought the election on the basis that more time is required to complete their programme of government, they must now deliver on their pledges, communicate success with the electorate and identify challenges for the future.

It is the contention of this chapter that a true and complete market orientation is inappropriate for political parties: applying a commercial marketing approach does not take cognisance of ideology, belief structures, historical development, the voluntary nature of politics and the lack of resources to implement a true marketing orientation. This is not to say that marketing has no relevance in politics. On the contrary, the application of marketing is immensely important and relevant to the creation, maintenance and understanding of political exchanges.

Notes

1 In contrast, the Scottish electorate and opposition parties showed themselves to be very capable of using the electoral system to eliminate the Conservative Party's representation in Westminster in 1997. In every Conservative-held seat, there was a swing of at least 11 per cent against the incumbents, but the beneficiary of that swing was always the party that was the runner-up in the 1992 election.

2 It would also be possible for voters to believe that they must vote for the same party in both ballots, though there is no evidence of this occurring.

3 The results of the 2003 survey suggest some changes that are not consistent with previous trends. However, the proportion of respondents who regard themselves as more Scottish than British is still five times the proportion of those who consider themselves more British than Scottish.

4 This does not take account of the element of religious affiliation in determining choice at that time.

5 A comparison might be made with the strategy of Sinn Féin. McGough (2002: 16, 18) argues that 'Sinn Féin appeals to all the working classes by emphasising its role as the representative of the oppressed, excluded and deprived'. In addition: 'Relief from the effects of sectarianism . . . or normal criminal activity are sought from the efforts of Sinn Féin and not from the Security Services in the North of Ireland'. While there are many differences in the situation that the SSP and Sinn Féin face, both are overtly socialist parties embedded in the communities that they seek to represent.

6 We consider that it is quite difficult to explain such behaviour within the CPM model since it is not clear whether the market for the party is then the entire electorate (as we have assumed in analysing the behaviour of larger parties) or only the target segments. There is also the difficulty of trying to explain the goals of such a party, for it does not enter an election campaign with the intention of attaining office. The limited objectives of such a party must include securing the election of a sufficiently large number of representatives that it is able to exert some degree of influence on policy implementation. We argue below that this is easier to achieve in a system where elections use some form of proportional representation.

7 Defined as the poor, lone parents, pensioners, students, low-paid workers, the disabled, council tenants, trade unionists, slave-labour trainees on government schemes, the unemployed, the homeless, and asylum seekers: Manifesto for the 1999 Scottish Parliamentary Elections.

8 2001 Manifesto.

9 SSP Conference 2003, motions B and C.
10 Danson and Whittam (2002; 24)
11 However, note that in order to finance the higher levels of public expenditure now current, the SSP's 2003 Manifesto proposes higher tax rates. Retaining the exemption of the first £10,000 of income, marginal rates would be 4.5 per cent on the first £20,000 of taxable income, and 15 per cent on the next £20,000. Water charges would be abolished and replaced with a tax of 1 per cent of turnover, levied on all VAT registered businesses.
12 While Lees-Marshment (2001b: 37–8) includes a number of suggestions about ways in which the 'implementation' stage of the CPM model might be effected to ensure widespread acceptance of the policies developed by a political party, Johansen (2002) argues that such internal marketing is an integral part of the service management orientation of a business, developed in the 'Nordic School' and summarised in Grönroos (2000). In addition, Granik (2003) analyses the services provided by parties to members in the context of the decision to continue in membership.
13 For example, the democratic decision-making structures of the SSP might be interpreted as a set of communication procedures designed to ensure that the leadership of the party is attentive to the desires of members.
14 This is not simply a feature of politically active members of left-wing parties. Lees-Marshment and Rudd (2003) suggest that the Conservative Party under the leadership of William Hague failed to resolve problems of internal marketing, so that it was unable to reorganise the party sufficiently to develop a strong external orientation.

Bibliography

Ansolabehere, S. and Iyengar, S. (1995), *Going Negative*, New York: Free Press.
Baker, M. (2000), *Marketing Strategy and Management*, 3rd edn, London: Macmillan.
Bannon, D. (2000), 'Political marketing: plotting the development of political activity into an evolutionary framework', in *Proceedings of the UK Political Studies Association Media and Political Group in conjunction with the UK Academy of Marketing Special Interest Group on Political Marketing*, Loughborough: Loughborough University: 461–2.
Brassington, F. and Pettitt, S. (1997), *Principles of Marketing*, London: Pitman Publishing.
Brown, A., McCrone, D., Paterson, L. and Surridge, P. (1999), *The Scottish Electorate: The 1997 General Election and Beyond*, Basingstoke: Macmillan.
Butler, P. and Collins, N. (1996), 'Strategic analysis in political markets', *European Journal of Marketing*, 30(10–11): 32–44.
Butler, P. and Collins, N. (1999), 'A conceptual framework for political marketing', in B. I. Newman (ed.), *The Handbook of Political Marketing*, London: Sage.
Butler, P. and Collins, N. (2001), 'Payment on delivery: recognising constituency service as political marketing', *European Journal of Marketing*, 35(9–10): 1026–37.
Campbell, A. (1957), *The Voter Decides*, Evanston, IL: Row, Peterson & Co.
Crewe, I. (1985) 'Great Britain', in I. Crewe and D. Denver (eds), *Electoral Change in Western Democracies*, London: Croom Helm.
Curtice, J. and Seyd, B. (2001), 'Is devolution strengthening or weakening the UK?', in A. Park, J. Curtice, K. Thomson, L. Jarvis, C. Bromley and N. Stafford (eds), *British Social Attitudes: Public Policy, Social Ties, 18th Report*, London: Sage.
Danson, M. and Whittam, G. (2002), *Paying for Local Government, Water and Sewerage Services Fairly: The Case for a Scottish Service Tax and Scottish Water Charge*, mimeo, University of Paisley.

Doyle, P. (2000), *Value-Based Marketing*, Chichester: Wiley.

Gould, P. (1999), *The Unfinished Revolution: How the Modernisers Saved the Labour Party*, London: Abacus.

Granik, S. (2003), 'Part of the party: continuity and discontinuity amongst political party membership', paper presented at the PSA Annual Conference, Leicester.

Grönroos, C. (1994), 'From the marketing mix to relationship marketing', *Management Decision*, 32(2): 4–20.

Heffernan, R. and Marqusee, R. (1992), *Defeat from the Jaws of Victory: Inside Kinnock's Labour Party*, London: Verso.

Johansen, H. (2002), 'Political marketing – more than persuasive techniques: an organisation perspective', paper presented at the 2002 Political Marketing Conference, University of Aberdeen, 19–21 September.

Kirchheimer, O. (1966), 'The transformation of the Western European party systems', in M. Weiner and J. LaPalombara (eds), *Political Parties and Political Development*, Princeton, NJ: Princeton University Press.

Kotler, P. (1997), *Marketing Management*, 9th edn, Englewood Cliffs, NJ: Prentice-Hall.

Lambin, J.-J. (2000), *Marketing Driven Management*, London: Macmillan Business.

Lees-Marshment, J. (2001a), 'The marriage of politics and marketing', *Political Studies*, 49(4): 692–713.

Lees-Marshment, J. (2001b), *Political Marketing and British Political Parties: The Party's Just Begun*, Manchester: Manchester University Press.

Lees-Marshment, J. (2001c), 'The product-, sales- and market-oriented party: how Labour learnt to market the product, not just the presentation', *European Journal of Marketing*, 35(9–10): 1074–84.

Less-Marshment, J. and Ruid, C. (2003), 'Political Marketing and party leadership', paper presented at the 2003 PSA Conference, Political Marketing Group Panels, 15–17. April.

Lipset, S. and Rokkan, S. (1967), 'Cleavage systems, party systems and voter alignments: an introduction', in S. Lipset and S. Rokkan (eds), *Party Systems and Alignments*, New York: Free Press.

Marsden, C. (1998), 'Scottish Socialist Party fosters nationalist divisions', available at www.wsws.org/polemics/1998/oct1998/ssp-o24.shtml

Mitchell, J. (2003), 'Politics in Scotland', in P. Dunleavy, A. Gamble and G. Peele (eds), *Developments in British Politics*, London: Palgrave.

McGough, S. (2002), 'Selling Sinn Féin: the political marketing of a party in conflict resolution', paper presented at the 2002 Political Marketing Conference, University of Aberdeen, 19–21 September.

McKay, E. (1972), *The Marketing Mystique*, New York: American Management Association.

O'Shaughnessy, N. (1990), *The Phenomenon of Political Marketing*, Basingstoke: Macmillan.

Palmer, A. (2000), *Principles of Marketing*, Oxford: Oxford University Press.

Paterson, L. (1994), *The Autonomy of Modern Scotland*, Edinburgh: Edinburgh University Press.

Seawright, D. and Curtice, J. (1992), 'The decline of the Scottish Conservative and Unionist Party: religion, ideology or economics?' *Contemporary Record*, 9(2): 319–42.

Seyd, P. and Whiteley, P. (1992), *Labour's Grass Roots: The Politics of Party Membership*, Oxford: Clarendon Press.

Shama, A. (1976), 'Marketing the political candidate', *Journal of the Academy of Marketing Science*, 4(4): 771.

Sheridan, T. and MacAlpine, A. (1994), *A Time to Rage*, Edinburgh: Polygon.

Sheridan, T. and McCoombes, T. (2000), *Imagine: A Socialist Vision for the 21st Century*, Edinburgh: Rebel, Inc.

Smith, G. and Saunders, J. (1990), 'The application of marketing to British politics', *Journal of Marketing Management*, 5(3): 295–306.

Surridge, P., Paterson, L., Brown, A. and McCrone, D. (1998), 'The Scottish electorate and the Scottish Parliament', special edition: 'Understanding constitutional change', *Scottish Affairs*.

Swaddle, K. (1990), 'Coping with a mass electorate', unpublished PhD, University of Oxford.

Wring, D. (1999), 'The marketing colonisation of political campaigning', in B. I. Newman (ed.), *The Handbook of Political Marketing*, London: Sage: 41–55.

12

Conclusion: towards a comparative model of party marketing

Darren G. Lilleker and Jennifer Lees-Marshment

There can be no doubt that marketing is being employed, in a variety of ways, by political parties across the world. Its effectiveness, however, varies; Moreover, a number of democratic and pragmatic issues have been raised by comparative analysis. The Lees-Marshment (2001) model has provided a useful framework within which to explain and analyse party behaviour for all of the contributors to this book, but it requires development and refinement before it can be considered generally applicable. There are therefore a number of aspects which will be discussed here: systemic differences that have an effect on the application of marketing tools and concepts; specific weaknesses with the model; and broader practical and normative issues with political marketing. Firstly, however, the chapter will consider the extent of the evidence for the increase in political marketing activities globally and the phenomenon of the political consumer.

The global rise of political marketing and the political consumer

This book developed out of research by individual political scientists, scholars of communication, marketing analysts and sociologists who all suggested that political marketing has global reach and actually applied the Lees-Marshment model as a route by which to explain the shifts in party behaviour. This was somewhat surprising, given that the model was developed purely for UK politics, so we approached these works with a degree of scepticism. The empirical data outlined in each chapter has nevertheless shown that the model is an efficient explanatory tool, though in need of slight modification, and that political marketing has indeed gone global. Critics of this book may argue that this finding is the result of our authors searching for evidence to fit the model, but that claim would be a disservice to them all. A more refined contention would be that political parties are just cynically manipulating their electorate in order to gain power, rather than adopting a new and full form of market-oriented behaviour. This and diverging forms of political marketing approaches will be discussed later, but it is important to look first at a force that allegedly drives political marketing. This is claimed to be the new breed of voter that defies the politician to attempt manipulation: the political consumer (Lees-Marshment 2004).

Is there evidence that such a creature exists? It is possible to argue that de-alignment is not as serious as some claim, as Knuckey and Lees-Marshment (Chapter 3) note in their study of the Bush campaign, and there is also evidence to suggest that there realignment is taking place in the UK. However these are duopolistic systems where it is always tempting to view politics as black or white, Left or Right. In the majority of the polities our authors have studied the voter has far more choice; not only this, but the voters demand a greater say over the way politicians run their nations, and in whose interests. John Street (1997) discusses these themes in terms of the globalisation of popular culture, a factor that is reshaping political culture. Regardless of the current debates about the causes and extent of globalisation, it appears to be enabling political power to pass to the voter, and for the voter to take on the role of the political consumer.

This is highlighted in the arguments of the political leaders that have featured in the chapters. Marland (Chapter 4) quotes a leading author who argues 'no government is prepared to risk major policy initiatives without gauging public opinion' (Whitehorn 1997: 91). Such observations come across clearly in the studies of Brazil, Austria and Peru. Cotrim-Maciera notes (Chapter 9) that the public were demanding change, which led PT leader Lula da Silva to design the product they wanted, and similar themes recur in the studies of Peru's APRA and Austria's Freedom Party. Lederer *et al.* (Chapter 8) argue that increased voter volatility, combined with voters' search for independently produced political information, led all parties to raise their game as the parameters of competition were fundamentally altered. Even Sinn Féin may well be forced towards a market orientation as, McGough notes (Chapter 6), 'policies that address individualism have more credibility for the [Irish] voter than the collective patriotism of Irish republicanism'. This electoral volatility, and the demands placed on parties to be responsive as well as credible in government, forces changes in behaviour. This is often a shock to the party system which, as Patron Galindo notes in his study of APRA (Chapter 10), become destabilised as the electorate form a new relationship with its representatives.

The fact that all our authors note that it is the voters, not the parties themselves, who are commanding the behavioural shift leads us to argue that it is the political consumer who is now sovereign. In this new-found political terrian it is vital for politicians to adapt to this new consumerism as the indications are that the more market-oriented the party is the more likely it is to have electoral success. Thus the Lees-Marshment model is found to be a tool of high utility in explaining behaviour and offering pointers for future developments, though this was less true of its original (2001) form, and the model needs further discussion and development, both for comparative practice as well as theoretical use. To that end; we now outline the respects in which systemic differences and specific weaknesses hinder the model, and comment on problems with political marketing.

Systemic differences

The following systemic differences have been shown to be obstacles to implementing the MOP approach and to using the Lees-Marshment model for explanatory
or predictive analysis.

Electoral and party systems

Both the UK and US electoral systems encourage a strong duopolistic party system,
though that is not the global norm. Forms of proportional representation pre-
dominate, encouraging a broader range of parties with different goals, ideologies
and approaches to political behaviour, some of which may well combine to form
coalition governments. This affects the application of political marketing in a
number of ways. First, and perhaps most importantly, it has been theorised that
the effectiveness of the MOP approach can be diluted, once parties are elected to
government, because the delivery of a political design becomes compromised by
coalition governance. This point has, however, been somewhat muted by the
empirical work in this book, because it is largely absent from our case studies. In
fact, it seems that coalitions tend to move towards the centre ground and seek to
be led by majoritarian opinion, thus reinforcing the MOP strategy.

There is an internal issue, though, because compromise positions lead to
disaffection among party members. As Rudd notes (Chapter 5), coalitions 'may
lead to a party sacrificing, or at least de-emphasising, policies that it knows are
attractive to its own supporters but are anathema to a potential coalition partner's
voters'. This means that parties within proportional representation systems may
have to market themselves also to their opponents' supporters, making the product
adjustment stage even more complex.

The possibility of coalitions also encourages smaller parties to adopt a POP or
SOP approach. Coalitions often allow marginal parties, even those with below 10
per cent of the overall votes, to have a role in government. Such parties derive electoral votes from committed supporters who tend to hold strong ideological attach-
ments to them, as with the Greens in Germany. Therefore, within these systems it
may be more appropriate to remain a POP. These parties are able to gain influence
within the electoral system (their dominant goal) and may well broaden their
appeal, but it would be a mistake for them to move towards the sales- or market-
oriented models, as to do so would lose them their core support while pitting them
against the major parties without the benefit of an established electoral base.
Therefore Canadian parties can successfully adopt niche-marketing strategies
because of the country's voting system and strong regionalism. This means that we
cannot justifiably claim the MOP to be the superior form for all parties, and we
accept that the POP does have a role.

In other systems, with particular histories, it is perhaps also appropriate to have
a combination of approaches. Though we discuss this in more detail later, it is possible that among certain voter segments a party can act like a POP, while being a
SOP among others and developing some policy strategies as would a MOP. This

may indicate that the divisions between each approach are not as clear as we first imagined; political reality can be highly complex, refusing the constraints imposed by models.

Differing importance of the leader within the party organisation

A further area where the stage of product adjustment is complicated is where a party leader has differing levels of power over particular aspects of political marketing and governing. In the US George W. Bush found that the contrasting demands of the wider electorate and of party politicians made delivery a complex task, particularly when faced with issues such as tax reform and Clinton's environmentalist policies which party supporters wanted him to reverse. This put him at odds with Democrat voters and Congress. His lack of power was, perhaps, reversed by the events of 9/11, but he continued to face the task of balancing competing sources of influence. Adjustment was also a problem for the Canadian parties, where strong organisations continually attempt to pull parties back towards a more traditional political pro-gramme – as was true of William Hague when he led the UK Conservatives.

Such problems were not faced by the leadership of PT in Brazil and of APRA in Peru; both were able to use market intelligence to create a series of policies that their parties were then forced to adopt. In Brazil this was aided by a tradition of personal leadership, while in Peru de la Torre became as much the product as the party became an organisation designed to facilitate his rise to power. This, however, can be dangerous. In Austria the leader developed a personalised policy designed to win an election that later collapsed in government, along with the leader's control of the party. A similar example can be found in the UK: since 2001 Tony Blair was moved towards a personal conviction-based, product-oriented approach in which he became 'the product' and seemed to sideline the party. Such leadership-driven product design can be a tenable approach when the public is behind the party, as in the case of the New Zealand Labour Party. If public support for the leader drops, however, as occurred with the FPO in Austria, the loss of a market-orientation is likely either to result in a party's loss of power or an individual's removal from office.

The power of the leader and the importance of the rest of the party in the pur-suance and success of an MOP strategy therefore depend partly on the system. In the UK the party remains an important part of the product and can block change, as the Tories did with Hague; yet leaders have the potential to drive and implement a market-oriented strategy in the party and in the government if they can generate internal support and win a strong majority in Parliament. In the USA, the separa-tion of powers gives the president greater independence from the party organisa-tion, yet less control over what it does. Coalition systems may require leaders to listen to their parties much more attentively, thereby offering greater incentive to them to maintain a market orientation and a successful electoral strategy. The importance of product adjustment may therefore be also nation-specific, being a necessity for a leader with a strong party organisation, but of less importance where there is a tradition of personal politics. These issues will be revisited as we review the product adjustment stage in the model.

Differing political cultures and participation

A political culture and its level of participation shape the way an electorate behaves, and the extent to which a party can adopt a market orientation. We posit that the rise of the political consumer is a feature associated with de-alignment, though de-alignment is not as widespread or as sharp as many academics suggest. In the USA, for example, we see that there are still clear social schisms affecting party loyalty and affiliation, meaning that the MOP approach is limited. Traditional supporters are as important as are the undecided, or floating, voters, highlighting the importance of balancing competing interests and moving to a more centrist position in a number of policy areas, while maintaining a clear link to the party ideology.

Weak political culture is also an obstacle to adopting a market orientation. If the electorate does not believe in democracy then it is unlikely to be sufficiently informed to provide input to the product design. Education and information availability are also influential on the ability of electors to act as political consumers. However, as Patron Galindo points out, Peruvian voters are exercising their power, and APRA's market orientation is actually building and enhancing Peru's democratic culture, so political marketing there has the potential to respond to and change such conditions.

Available resources for marketing activities

The extent of a party's resources for marketing activities will clearly influence their effectiveness, and will differ between parties and from one nation to another. With two main parties, both of which are highly skilled at attracting funding, the USA is able to hold elections that see MOP pitted against MOP. This is less likely to be the case in most of the nations studied in this book: being an MOP *costs*. In Canada the incumbent has the (unfair) advantage of having the resources to adopt a market orientation while the opposition parties do not. New Zealand parties' use of political marketing is limited by the funds they have available to conduct wide and objective market intelligence. Parties in Brazil and Peru do not confront this obstacle, however, while the Austrian FPO circumnavigated its lack of funds through informal intelligence gathering, though intelligence of an informal kind may be subject to bias and can result in a product-oriented attitude by over-reliance on a party's electoral base.

Specific model weaknesses

A number of weaknesses in the model have been exposed by this comparative study. We presented them here in question format, then debate the issues prior to making suggestions for revision.

Are the POP–SOP–MOP approaches distinct and discrete?

At a conceptual level, there seems to be a clear distinction between the three approaches. One indication is the role of market intelligence: the POP will not use market intelligence; the SOP will use it only to inform communication; and the

MOP will use it to inform product design and so have to balance all competing claims when adjusting the product prior to launch. Rudd points out, however, that it could be the aim of the marketing that differs: is it to sell or to build a relationship? Several of our case studies highlight that there is a blurring in terms of the orientation adopted. Lederer *et al.* argue that the orientation could be specific to particular areas of party behaviour: for example the leader could be the product of market intelligence, while the policy is ideological. Does this require us to weigh each aspect of behaviour and then find the orientation that fits most closely (as citizens themselves have to do so when they assess a party prior to deciding for whom to vote), or is there evidence that parties are in fact adopting hybrid orientations and that the POP–SOP–MOP distinctions are artificial?

The FPO offers evidence that there were clear elements of a market orientation in designing its product: the leader's image, party image and the policies. The communication strategy, though, was one of persuasion, the territory of the SOP. Marland finds the same with the Canadian Liberal Party, while Rudd suggested that the New Zealand Labour Party offered leadership on some issues while listening to the market for information on others. The clearest example of the latter behaviour is that of Sinn Féin's amalgamation of socialist and nationalist principles, together with its offer of market-led solutions to the concerns of key segments of the electorate, which have allowed the party to stake claim to a growing electoral base. McGough notes how 'the voters are left in no doubt as to what it is they are voting for, while simultaneously believing that their own issues are being listened to and dealt with'. This leads us to suggest that parties can be, for example, market-oriented on health policy while disavowing nuclear weapons on ideological grounds. They could interweave free-market economics and state provision of services in the form the public demands, thus borrowing from a range of approaches without allowing themselves to be classified under a single heading.

Marketing, as a philosophy, therefore offers a range of tools, any of which can be chosen and rejected based according to principles relating to the use of marketing and it appropriateness within a given democracy and the specific political context. Therefore, some parties may well adhere to the stages of Lees-Marshment's MOP, while others will appear to take a pick-and-mix approach. Had the model been developed to address the Canadian system, for example, it might look very different, and that would indicate that we are in danger of forcing a fit to the model when using each approach as separate and having declared which of them has the greatest utility.

There are, however, alternative ways of reading the hybrid variants. First, we can see SOP-style communications as a necessary tool for persuading the electorate of the party's credibility. Second, we can view some of the deviation from the MOP model as necessary to the adjustment, so adapting to internal reaction, differentiating the party from the competition, as well as appealing to the voter segments required to win. These hypotheses will be explored further in relation to the case studies.

Rudd notes that the challenge facing Helen Clark's Labour Party was to show the voters that it was not only 'saying what they wanted to hear' but, more importantly, was convincing voters 'that [we] had credibility and were trustworthy'. This was also noted by Marland in arguing the Liberals used sales-oriented communication, while Lederer *et al.* talked of Haider 'actively creating demand for his policy'. Policies may be based on market intelligence but, as this is a new departure for many political parties, why should the public believe that the party is not just using those policies for cynical ends and that, even if it is true to its word, is it a party able to govern? Therefore, while market intelligence is important in terms of an MOP's policy design, it is important also for its communication – something that needs stressing within the model. This does not on its own suggest a hybrid variant, though it might seem to do so; rather, it is using marketing at every stage of design, including the design of appropriate communications. This is something any profit-motivated organisation would also engage in within a competitive market.

There is, however, a more complex issue – are we seeing a hybrid version of the POP–SOP–MOP that operates with differing behaviour within different contexts. Marland writes about the Canadian Alliance redesigning the party product in line with voter opinion, but also ensuring that changes were harmonious with the party's ideological traditions. Bush found a similar requirement, though only when fighting John McCain in the primaries, as did Sinn Féin in the contrasting contexts of Eire and Northern Ireland's devolved system. Clearly Bush had to adjust his product in order to defeat McCain, but he had then to reassert the market orientation when fighting for the presidency. Sinn Féin have found a real market for their blend of ideology and core issues, so adjusted their policies to fit the ideological constraints and the voter concerns. The question is: is this part of product adjustment or evidence that an MOP is highly inconsistent?

To judge by the arguments of our authors, it seems that there is some element of inconsistency between the model and the practice, but we would argue that this is not indicative of a hybrid variant. Actually the MOP must take into account ideology, because ideology is what allows the party to be distinctive – in terms of the proposed solution, if not of the political issue – as well as appealing to its loyal support base. This was included and noted in the Lees-Marshment (2001) model, but it was not shown empirically because up until 2001 no UK party has actually followed the MOP model comprehensively, not even New Labour. As Lees-Marshment (2001: 200) noted at the time, 'Blair did not follow the model completely. He neglected the more subtle aspects of marketing, such as the internal analysis part of Stage 3. In many ways Blair failed to carry his party with him.' Indeed, subsequent conflict within the UK Labour Party has been derived from internal concerns about the party's ideological principles, giving rise to the feeling that a 'Labour Party wouldn't do that'. Therefore, we must note that in practice, as in theory, adjustment is crucial and must take into account not just member opinion but the identity, ethos, traditions and ideology of the party to a much greater extent than Blair did. Parties such as Sinn Féin, the Republicans under George W. Bush and the Canadian Alliance could be said to be more highly developed than those parties which attempt to enact a complete *volte-face*. Non-UK practice currently appears to be more developed than the very British party behaviour that led to the original theory. Parties such as the FPO could be described as using marketing cynically, but the others have the greater wisdom and inclination to be true to all sections of their electorate. While this may seem problematical and complex, both to conceptualise and practise, it is perhaps a crucial task of the true MOP that aims to achieve both long-term electoral success and more democratic governance.

Is a market-orientation possible for a party of government?

Chapter 2, which covered UK politics, raised the question of whether a market orientation is practicable for a party in government. While the core objective would be to deliver on promises, designed in response to pre-election market intelligence, once in government a number of circumstances can bring that party to make pragmatic changes that are not always led by public opinion. Therefore the war on Iraq, which was communicated as a necessity, but was an issue on which not all the facts could be made public, became a product that had to be 'sold' by both Blair and Bush. This questions the utility of the MOP approach for a party in government.

There is also the question of whether parties will wish to maintain an MOP approach if they feel secure. The chapters on Canada, New Zealand, Austria and the UK suggest that while in opposition a party may develop an MOP, and win an election: once in government, it either consciously or subconsciously reverts to a more leadership-driven sales orientation. For example the Canadian Liberal Party found its market intelligence continuing to indicate that its leadership, symbols, policies, and candidates were known commodities that many electors generally preferred over the alternatives. The party's secure position reduced its inclination to retain a market orientation. Marland rightly argued that this 'illustrates the trend that the longer that a government is not challenged by another MOP, the further it can descend into a SOP or even a POP, and the less democratic accountability exists for its decision-making'.

This is true also of individual leaders, such as Tony Blair in the UK. It is difficult for leaders to maintain a responsive, mature, market-oriented attitude once in power. Staying in touch with the public is more difficult the more successful a leader becomes: power appears to encourage a feeling of invincibility and superiority – something noticeable in the most successful business managers, let alone prime ministers. Lees-Marshment (2001: 94) argued that market intelligence must be conducted continually and that leaders cannot maintain a market orientation by themselves. A popular leader who moves against his or her party allows colleagues little power to bring the leader back in line with the public. However, as Lees notes, it is far easier for an opposition party to be market oriented. For instance, Lees reminds us that 'the SPD's marketing strategists were working from the *tabula rasa* of a party unencumbered by the compromises and disappointments of government'. This became more difficult as the party came under fire for failure to deliver.

The original model gave insufficient attention to the difficulties of maintaining a market orientation in government and to the importance of leadership in this. In theory, leaders could set up full-scale market intelligence information systems that collect and disseminate feedback both internally and externally, ensuring the leader will always be aware of criticism. In the UK the Tory leaders Margaret Thatcher and John Major stopped commissioning and listening to market intelligence during their decline into a product orientation – and in each case subsequently lost power. Persuading a prime minister to commission a *compulsory* market intelligence programme over a parliamentary term, when the results may well be negative, would be no easy task. The psychology of leadership and the handling of market intelligence results are crucial factors, therefore, in maintaining a market orientation in government and is an area that needs further research.

Maintaining a market orientation in government is not simply about following the polls. Governing means making tough decisions. While leaders may need to focus on the issues that the public sees to be important, they can combine a blend of data from marketing research with internal party discussions and advice gleaned from consultations with experts – as was the potential with the UK government's 'Forethought' project – to create solutions. Thus what the public wants – high quality services for the minimum expense – may be unrealistic, and a party in government must focus on delivering on its promises in the most equitable way possible. There are also serious doubts as to whether following public opinion, however that may be derived, is the right course. For example, Lees argues that, given the voters' 'increasing volatility and inchoate, contradictory and often illiberal preferences', it could be said that governments should not listen to them at all. Political consumers may not always know what they want, and short-term wants may conflict with long-term needs.

Clearly this aspect of the model needs to be developed in order to be factored into the delivery stage, as well as the product design – adjustment stages in terms of achievability. Marketing in government is clearly difficult, and the business of governing may reduce the space as well as the incentive to continue to develop fully fledged market oriented policy in all its complexity. We do not wish to suggest that maintaining a market orientation in government is easy, but equally, it would be futile to do anything other than advise parties in government of the importance of continuing market intelligence and policy discussion if they wish to stay there.

Does the market-oriented strategy guarantee election?

Perhaps one of the most contested statements in Lees-Marshment's elucidation of the models of political party marketing is that 'if the party is the most market-oriented of its main competitors, it then wins the election' (2001: 211), and some of the case studies have further questioned this argument and 'equally' the appropriateness of the MOP within certain contexts.

One key question is what happens when two MOPs face one another at an election? The US case study (Chapter 3) tells us that here credibility is key, thus underlining the importance of persuasive communications targeted at key voter segments. However, we have not found a case study that sees MOPs competing with POPs or SOPs and losing. Perhaps, then, the statement is true. Nevertheless, the key question concerns motivation.

The niche-marketing strategy is clearly effective in regional political systems or those with proportional representation systems of voting. Parties such as the SSP and the SLD (see Chapter 11), the SPD in Germany (Chapter 7) and the BQ in Canada (Chapter 4) effectively used the sales-oriented approach to gain major electoral advances. This is also seen as the best approach under the proportional representation voting system, where many examples demonstrate the inappropriateness of appearing too similar to other parties rather than identifying core voters and marketing the party to them alone. In contrast, Sinn Féin is employing a MOP approach effectively, one predicated on a strong ideological foundation, to gain influence within the Irish political system. Therefore we have to ensure that the approach is appropriate to the political context and to the motivations of the party, thus enabling the Lees-Marshment model to have greater predictive ability.

A further point to be raised here, however, is that MOPs can suffer from media criticism, as has been seen in the UK, Brazil and the USA. This can lead to marketing itself becoming unpopular as parties are condemned for their lack of principles, ideology, for being followers of fashion or for cynically manipulating the electorate. This even led Howard Dean, one of the candidates for the US Democratic Party nomination in 2003–4 to stand as the 'anti-marketing candidate'. Similar trends can be seen in Austrian politics following the collapse of the FPO. Most of the parties studied in these chapters have not been in office for a significant length of time, so this factor did not emerge in all the case studies, but it could present MOPs with problems in the future. This could well be a result in the failure of continuing a market orientation in government and resorting to communication by spin, though it could also be the result of many dissenting politicians acting solely out of conviction and so seeing marketing as anathema to democracy, which is a problem for the use of marketing irrespective of the approach they choose.

Are there dangers when appealing to conflicting market segments?

A further difficulty emerging from our case studies is that of segmentation. In the UK the Labour Party's concentration on 'middle England' lost them support among the heartland electorate, a particular problem when core voters perceives the Government to be ignoring them after election. This conflict was also seen within the Republican Party in the USA and could well be faced by PT in Brazil and the New Zealand Labour Party.

The alternative is to ensure that policies, and in particular the delivery aspect of the programme, satisfies all aspects of the market, but this can be extremely difficult. Appealing to different voter segments can lead to the criticism that the party is trying to be all things to all voters – as with the Austrian FPO – and makes delivery impossible because the promises are unachievable. Given the range of competing segments targeted by Sinn Féin, this could be a particular problem should that party ever be elected to government, while also highlighting key problems with the implementation stage, which are dealt with below.

Is implementation achievable?

Implementation is one area that was under-explored previously and raises the most complex issues for the would-be MOP. Implementation, and in particular the adjustment to suit competing voter segments and internal opinion, seem to be the aspects of the MOP model that are the least practised. While George W. Bush is said to have completed this stage, there are those critics who argue that this was a cynical manoeuvre. He designed his product on the basis of market intelligence, but found himself under threat from John McCain, his rival for the Republican nomination. In an attempt to ensure he was not seen as 'the Republican Clinton', or as too centrist, he re-invoked more traditional Republican policies and imagery, and, after defeating McCain, he then moved back towards the centre ground. Since his election he has followed a similar course, combining traditional, ideologically driven republicanism with a more centrist and consensual programme. Is this a fully implemented MOP or is it evidence of Bush's skill at the game of politics?

The New Zealand Labour Party generated a 'pragmatic acceptance' of the new MOP approach because it promised victory. Helen Clark managed to build a consensus, but this appears to have been built by her as *leader*, and was not reliant on extensive adjustment. It did not win new members or even win back lapsed members. A similar attitude is apparent in most of the other case studies. Some, such as the Brazilian PT, witnessed conflict resulting in media criticism, a situation averted by Jorge Haider because of the extraordinary level of personal power he enjoyed. Personal power was equally pivotal for García in Peru, though not without dissent among the conservative wing of APRA. This indicates that the role of the leader, and the level of power vested in the position, is key to implementation. However, a strong leader, able to force a market-oriented programme on a party with the promise of victory, is not guaranteed to have long-term success; this is evident from the experience of Haider and to a lesser extent of both Tony Blair in the UK and German Chancellor Schröder. Lack of implementation was also key to the failure of the UK Conservatives under Hague to adopt an MOP.

We contend, however, that this is a flawed version of implementation practice rather than a problem with its theory. While balancing competing elements is a difficult task, it is impossible to hold together an MOP without completing it: effective adjustment and implementation are crucial to the success of political marketing. Yet this stage does need further theoretical consideration by academics, particularly in the light of the effects of systemic differences. It may well be the case that an MOP must have a weaker organisation than other traditionalist parties to enable greater flexibility in its behaviour. For example, the membership of the UK's Conservative Party have traditionally played a very strong and influential role in the selection of candidates to stand for election and in policy-making; but if that membership is non-reflective of UK society, it is unlikely to aid – and, indeed, may impede – the development of a market-oriented product. This is not the case for a party seeking only to gain influence; to achieve a long-term electoral victory, however, a party must have a clear link to the broader electorate and a programme that is achievable, and it must appear credible as a government. Some of these aspects are predicated on effective implementation, so this aspect of the model needs further research both theoretically and empirically.

Philosophical and democratic issues with global political marketing

Many of the above issues have ramifications for the use of political marketing. While we accept that it is a worthwhile and interesting area of study, we welcome debate on its potentially negative impact on democracy and party politics. We briefly consider the problems with implementing a market orientation, as well as the disadvantages and advantages of political party marketing in terms of democracy, prior to considering the Lees-Marshment model.

Some difficulties in adopting a market orientation

First, we focus on difficulties that emerge for the practicalities of a market orientation. These fit into five areas: the uniqueness of politics; the role of the media; the nature of the party; the nature of the public; and the question of delivery. These have been raised to differing extents by each of our case studies and are therefore in need of discussion.

There are a variety of concerns raised regarding the differences between profit-motivated corporate organisations and organisations which seek political power. Politics is very different from business, and though we can apply corporate marketing terminology in political contexts, there is always some lack of fit (Moloney 2004). This has led some to claim that marketing does not fit within the political sphere and so we should council against its use and not grant it status through academic study. While to ignore marketing would be wrong, to question it is absolutely correct. Marland raises the point that marketing is often predicated on co-operation. A market will be segmented and lines drawn by competing players: companies will not use negative advertising or may not target the market of a rival. Politics would adopt a reverse view. Politics is about seeking the support of the majority, in most political systems, and so the opposition has to be attacked. This, Marland argues, is unattractive and not what the market wants; however, if we are to retain a competitive political system, this is necessary.

Political marketing could perhaps encourage greater co-operation. However, political marketing involves analysing the competition and seeking weaknesses in their products, suggesting that negative communication will increase in line with the growing adoption of marketing. Yet, Bush refused in 2000 to take this line because the results of market intelligence indicated that voters disliked overly-negative advertising. A mature market-oriented-approach could lead to a more dignified, reflective and detailed debate about proposed policy than has hitherto been the case.

Political marketing has, however, sometimes encouraged negative criticism, and cynicism is heightened by media attacks on SOPs or MOPs. The Brazilian PT found itself under attack for weakening its ideology and seeking compromise over issues; this has occurred also in Peru and the USA where parties have been criticised for 'swinging like a pendulum' as public opinion changes. Such criticisms were also made of Blair's Labour Government, perhaps encouraging him to move away from a market orientation.

Party unity is key to political marketing, yet sales-oriented media (see Lees-Marshment 2004: chapter 4) enjoy the spectacle of division and dissent because it enables them to attract a higher audience. This makes it more difficult for a party to adopt a full market orientation. A party that is out of favour, the Labour Party in the UK or New Zealand for example, may have unity if victory is promised, but maintaining unity is difficult. Rudd in particular notes this, highlighting the difficulties in implementing a market orientation from the top down.

Media criticisms and party disunity all fuel public cynicism about the party, the political process and democracy as it is conducted. Many of the parties studied found it difficult to convince the electorate that their new programmes were genuine and that all aspects of their products were credible as a basis for government. Often this means performing a balancing act, appearing neither too left- nor too right-wing, but not claiming to be too centrist as this could put off loyal voters, potential voters or both. Therefore being elected as an MOP is not as straightforward as simply communicating the product and leaving it to be 'bought'. As one marketer argued: 'Selling in politics is like selling something that looks like soot when calling it gold dust. No one believes you, no one wants it, not even when it is real gold dust that has just been made to look dirty' (Mauritian political advisor with the authors in interview, December 2003). This statement highlights the problem that exists when political products are generally perceived with cynicism, or are seen as sleazy, inconsistent or incoherent. The quality of the product can often be obscured by the noise of opposing voices.

This is particularly the case with delivery, when expectations commonly far exceed reality, and presents clear problems for an MOP. This can result from the party's failure to ensure that its product design is achievable, as with Austria's FPO which failed to follow all stages of the marketing process. However, an MOP can find that public demands are simply not satisfiable within the given political environment. The Bush administration post 9/11 has had difficulties in delivery, and Brazil's Lula da Silva is now facing the task of balancing social reform with the forces of global economic competition. Delivery in opposition is also difficult: this will be an issue for Sinn Féin as its contrasting target markets compete for different political outcomes. Failure, or the perception of failure, to deliver increases cynicism and can lead to an anti-marketing backlash, as discussed earlier.

All of these practical issues are worthy of consideration by a party intending to adopt a market orientation; such a party should, however, give thought to the effects on democracy and its practice of adopting that orientation.

Concerns with the market-oriented approach

The contributors raise a number of concerns relating to the nature of the product and how it is developed in the MOP approach. While it is important to integrate public opinion into political policy design there can be problems with this strategy. The weak political culture in Peru, for example, can render people less able to articulate their wants and desires than those in established democracies. They may also be seeking a certain style of leadership as opposed to posting a shopping list of desired political outcomes. However this is not isolated to emergent democracies. Politics is a complex business and initiatives like the UK Labour Government's Big Conversation does not allow true interaction when questions are too difficult for the less-than-well-informed ordinary voter. Furthermore, marketing traditionally focuses on the individual while politicians have to deal with conflicting demands and make decisions for the country as a whole. The fact that much intelligence is gathered in either an *ad hoc* and informal way, or in-house and secretly, makes this aspect of party behaviour difficult to track. What we can track is the use by the UK Labour Party of intelligence data for internal sales, as well as exercises such as the Big Conversation, ostensibly the launching of a consultation process but actually more of a public relations initiative (Lilleker and Negrine 2004). This problem in identifying the link between public opinion-gathering and policy development as a long-term exercise can lead us to question whether there is a link at all, although the fundamental issue is the extent to which it is desirable that political parties base their decision-making on market intelligence among both practitioners and the public at large.

Marland claims that, even in well-developed nations, there is a risk of developing an 'undeveloped', or weak, product if there is a complete reliance on public opinion. He argues that Canadian parties need the anchorage of a core of constraints, based on ideology, which will allow the party to develop solutions and make the electorate aware of what the party stands for. This could be said to be the approach adopted by Sinn Féin, the SSP and the German SPD, and the need for it is perhaps exemplified by Austria's FPO: the product was one that focused on the lowest common denominator, base public opinion; it had few achievables and no practical dimension, and therefore its collapse in government was swift. The UK Conservatives developed a similar approach during the 2001 general election campaign, which was unsuccessful. While the FPO and the Conservatives both failed to follow a market-oriented strategy in full, factoring the ideology of the party into the adjustment stage appears a crucial step to achieving effective and successful MOP behaviour.

The role of ideology is also crucial when a government makes decisions into which the public can have no realistic input. If a party has been guided completely by public opinion, there is little sense as to how it will act when asked to make a decision alone. This again raises the question of a party's anchorage and an understanding what is being elected, so that expectations and reality are relatable. There is a need for a balance between exercising political judgement and following public opinion; or at least utilising both leadership and ideology in responding to the demands of the political consumer.

Positive consequences from market-oriented politics

The global development of market-oriented parties moves political marketing beyond the parameters set by the majority of academics working in this field (see Bowler and Farrell 1992; O'Shaughnessy 1990 and 1999). While marketing is often seen as controlling political party communicative outputs, and is criticised as a manipulative function (Neubaur and Wilkens 1997), our contributors indicate that marketing may also be used to enhance democracy and the interface between the public and political spheres (see also O'Cass 1996). The case studies of Peru and Brazil both highlight this aspect, Cotrim-Maciera arguing that it is evidence of democratic maturity, while Patron Galindo sees it as a step towards embedding democracy in Peruvian society and McGough sees marketing as enabling Sinn Féin to reject terrorism.

Such views suggest that politics is changing, and is now more about providing citizens with what they need, first and foremost, and, within reason, what they want. Such decisions are not taken in isolation, however, as per the model espoused by political theorists from Plato to Burke. That politicians must consult the public, using market intelligence to discover what it is that the public wishes a potential or current government to do, seems both logical and necessary, given that the public is able to, and often demand the right to, have its say and for its voice to be heard, listened to and acted on (Lilleker 2005). In its more comprehensive form, the market-oriented approach does not reduce politics to mere populism, but extends the democratic function of government through an externalisation of political debate in the form of informed consultation in which the public is allowed to take responsibility for areas of policy development in tandem with the experts employed by government (O'Cass 1996). This negates the necessity for spin, which is really only a tool used by organisations trying to sell something in a guise that suits the market, not actually providing something which the market wants. Nevertheless, we might have expected our individual authors to report and account for the dominance of a sales orientation, if that was what they found in their nations.

Market-oriented developments in democracies are said by nation state theorists to be necessary. Many observe that, across the majority of liberal democracies, disaffection is characterising the relationship between electorates and their politicians (Katz and Mair 1994 and 1995; Lilleker 2003; Opello and Rosow 1999). Some recognise that politicians are attempting to re-invigorate community politics over an individualist privatisation of political aspirations, however they also see this as a limited strategy that depends more on rhetoric than on fundamental change in political behaviour.

Opello and Rosow (1999: 252–4) note that more and more political consumers are choosing independent, personalised, non-state brands of political activity. They see this as a move towards a de-territorialising of politics that could threaten the existence of the nation state by undermining its legitimacy. We argue that an alternative and workable strategy is to institute the MOP model, to listen to the people, to get them involved in politics and, ultimately, to return democracy to the *demos*. It seems that this is what the political consumer in the UK demands (Dermody and Scullion 2001; Lees-Marshment 2003 and 2004; Lilleker 2005), and it is a development, as we have seen, that is driven by the economic and political freedoms which are now a feature of global society. Certainly, whatever one's opinions about the democratic implications of political marketing, there is a growing value in studying this phenenomon.

The Lees-Marshment model refined

We expect that the discussion as to how to improve the model will extend beyond the publication of this book. Certainly there are aspects raised that will require further and more detailed research, utilising new areas of literature, such as:

- internal party management and cultural barriers to a market-orientation;
- the role of the leader in introducing a market-orientation;
- constraints of government especially with regard to delivery;
- the most effective mechanisms to handle market intelligence;
- mechanisms to prevent the decline of a market-orientation once in government; and
- the psychology of market-oriented leadership.

We can at this stage recommend a number of revisions to the model, clearly, the use of the model in practice depends on the goals, the market and the product of a particular party in a given nation. This does not really go much against the initial predictions of Lees-Marshment (2001: 220–1) and fits with normative assumptions about designing comparative models for party behaviour (Sodaro 2001). It should, however, be noted, and re-confirmed from empirical study as opposed to theoretical speculation, that:

- Any one of the approaches can be successful, whether POP, SOP or MOP, depending on the systemic nature of the political system, the party and its goals, and the circumstances of the time.
- There is no formal hierarchy of utility and the model does not provide an evolutionary explanation; parties do not have to pass through all its stages and examples of regression can be found.
- Implementation requires strong leadership and, perhaps, a weaker party organisation.
- Successful implementation and agreement at all party levels are required for a party to maintain cohesion.
- Implementation must take into account all groups from which the party seeks support, and all factors that could influence the election result in the given political context.
- Ideology is required to anchor the party within an ethical framework and to ensure that the unknown areas of the product, such as potential behaviour, can be predicted by the voter.
- Communication must be persuasive at all times, but must not resort to manipulation.
- Delivery will be more difficult in some systems than others, especially where coalition government is the norm.

We have a number of suggestions to make as to how the MOP model in particular might be revised to take account of identified weaknesses and to make it more
functional for comparative analysis. In doing so, we stress that a party wishing to
use political marketing should first ask what its goal is, consider its market and the
nature of its product, as well as the nature of the political market environment and
system in which it operates. This will determine whether it chooses to adopt a POP
or SOP approach, as well as how it moves through the process should it choose to
become an MOP.

The MOP: a comparative model

All of the following aspects should be considered, but will vary from one party to
another, and across nations.

Stage 1   Market intelligence

Once the party has determined the nature of its product, intelligence is gathered,
both formally and informally, though the former gains the better results, using internal and external data gatherers. Market intelligence is used to inform the product
design in response to electoral demands, as well as implementation, communication
and campaigning. Internal market intelligence is also a means of communicating
between leader and fellow politicians.

Continual intelligence   Market intelligence, once begun, should never stop: it
should be a continual aspect of party activity. Periodic reviews should evaluate its
effectiveness and consider new means and methods of gaining data, but it should
never be banned.

Identification and segmentation of a party's market   The party needs to identify,
understand and segment its market, which may be the general public, the electorate, target segments of the electorate, key professional groups and/or opinion-
influencers (for instance, in the media, health professionals, business leaders),
representative agencies, MPs, potential candidates for office and core members or
supporters.

Topics of consultation   Intelligence is concerned with understanding market
demands on the party and/or potential government, but also participation levels and
voting behaviour, and how people receive communication. Therefore it includes:

- identification of demands for past, present and potential party behaviour;
- aspects of behaviour most relevant to the party's product – such as leadership,
  policy, organisation, membership, the constitution and proposed policies for
  government;
- complex consideration of fundamental needs, both short and long term, not just
  immediate desires;

- mature, reflective discussion integrating consideration of the complexities of government with competing demands;
- allowance for policy development and governing constraints;
- analysis and understanding of voting behaviour and participation levels within the party, in a manner similar to consumer behaviour analysis by businesses;
- understanding of how people receive information, and of the effectiveness of different media and forms of communication

Consultation organisation   Consultation should be organised in a way that responds to and encourages the emergent political consumer, viewing market intelligence as a means of participation in the political process, whether as a member of the public, party or an elected official. Questions should be presented in a manner comprehensible to the political consumer. The party should use different methods, be open to new means of intelligence, continually evaluating their effectiveness. Internally, there needs to be an understanding of the likely passion and ideological commitment of members, as well as the bias which may produce results unrepresentative of the electorate as a whole.

Managing the results   The handling of market intelligence exercises, as well as their results, needs to be carried out with care. Ideally, results should be disseminated widely, both internally and externally. Independent market intelligence experts should be used to ensure professionalism, but they also need to understand the complexities of political organisations. Professionals will find it easier to show negative feedback than will politicians dependent on the leader for promotion; negative feedback should be presented carefully, however, taking account of the likely psychological reaction to criticism, to prevent the leader and party from dismissing personal attacks and encourage a professional response to any issues raised.

Stage 2   Product design

The product, whatever form it takes for that particular party and nation, will be designed with specific reference to the intelligence gathered. This will take into account the political context, the constraints of government and the nation's political system. The party will begin by designing a product according to the demands of the electorate whose support it needs to win in order to achieve its goals. An MOP seeks to develop a product that meets the long-term needs of its electoral market in a way that does not harm other sections of society. It does not seek to produce populist, opportunist policies or behaviour. The product then needs to be carefully adjusted to ensure it can be implemented internally, maintain unity in the long-term and succeed after the election, whether in government or opposition.

Stage 3   Product adjustment

Adjustment will take into account four factors: achievability; internal reaction; competition analysis; and support analysis. Achievability should look to the long term and take into account the political and economic environment and the context(s) under which the party could govern. Internal reaction will look beyond the party members to the core supporters, as well as factoring in aspects of the party's history, traditions, ethos and ideology, ensuring that critics are unable to claim that the party is out of touch with its roots and has no ethical anchor. Adjustment also encourages the leadership to understand why aspects of its organisation may oppose certain policies, in preparation for implementation. Internal analysis may also suggest that changes are needed to the party's organisation and constitution to encourage the development of a market-oriented culture.

Competition analysis will look at all competitors, including those who may be allies in potential coalitions and partnerships. Importantly, this process will identify how the party can develop ideological solutions to the important concerns of the voters, so allowing differentiation from those of opponents. *Support* analysis ensures that the party does not promise everything to everyone – and so have unachievable goals – and can also provide the opportunity for the adoption of less popular policies, such as those that are unpopular in the short term but will meet the electorate's needs in the long term; or a product change that will satisfy internal members even if it is not a high priority for the electorate. Smaller parties may focus on satisfying a slimmer and more coherent segment of the market; larger parties need to segment their market, so the nature of the support analysis depends on the party's electoral goals and its proximity to government.

The party's product need not be 100 per cent market oriented/popular across the electorate; but overall it needs to provide satisfaction to win enough support from the electorate to achieve the party's goals, while maintaining internal cohesion, and be deliverable after the election. This stage will inform the rest of the process.

Stage 4 Implementation

If stages 1–3 have been carried out effectively, implementation should be a smooth procedure, although this will depends also on the nature of the party–leader relationship, and so will vary from one party to another. In nations where party organisation and unity are influential in respect of voting behaviour and governing, implementation is crucial. It may be an easier process for parties with a more – electorally – professional structure but will require a leader(ship) with developed management skills (see Panebiano 1988). Wider dissemination of market intelligence and the use of literature on marketing information systems, as well as empirical research, to identify internal sources of dissent and sensitivities surrounding the use of marketing may allow members to feel more involved. The culture as well as the organisational structure of the party will play a part in the success of implementation. However, an MOP does not require 100 per cent support; indeed, dissent and debate will be in part positive forces for the continuance of a market orientation after the election, particularly if the party forms the government. Debate will require careful handling, however, and the overall product design should be accepted by the majority of the party.

Stage 5   Communication

Communication should be carried out with voters, the public at large, key target groups, the media, and also internally with members and politicians. It will utilise market intelligence results, but also be targeted in response to support analysis, which identified those voter segments whose support is required to achieve the party's goals. Intelligence will inform the style, content, format, method and timing of communications: for example, it will take account of voters' sources of information, the media to be used and how best to communicate with voters.

While an MOP does not sell an unwanted product, it has to let voters know what it has on offer, and it may also have to persuade voters – *not* that they want what the party offers, but that the party really does offer what the voters want, such as an organisation capable of delivering in government, or one committed to low taxation, or amenable to co-operative governance in a coalition or to influencing the agenda even if it does not win the election and gain control of government. This will be particularly important if the party has changed its product recently or dramatically.

Internal communication aids implementation and post-election delivery. Systems – whether formal or informal – should be put in place to enable multidirectional communication between leaders and politicians, potential politicians and members, and the public and the party. Rather than trying to sell a product, political marketing communication is about promoting a dialogue between the public and political elite.

Stage 6   Campaign

This stage involves designing and executing a short pre-election campaign to focus on the key voter segments that will achieve the goals of the party, be that victory or any other measurable objective. Again the campaign should be designed with awareness of internal and external markets.

Stage 7   Election and measurement

If the MOP is successful, it will achieve its election goal. This may be to:

- win the election and gain control of government, either solely or in coalition;
- make advances in its number of seats;
- place a key item on the policy agenda;
- attract an increase in membership/internal supporters; and
- gain a positive evaluation from the public and party members, as measured by focus group or opinion polls, on any aspect of its product – leadership, main policies, unity, economic management.

Stage 8   Delivery

Post-election delivery is the stage at which the real political marketing occurs, and it depends on the goals and the success in completing the previous stages. Smaller parties may deliver greater representation to their members and supporters by entering into coalition, though that can diminish their potential to deliver on their promises and so weaken the public's perception of that party. Other minor parties may deliver purely by continuing to provide effective opposition and representation, or by attempting to influence government through pressure. These parties will keep key policies on the agenda, retain their radical character and focus on creating new participatory structures to represent their niche market. Parties in government must deliver on their promises, and to ensure this is recognised keep open channels of communication with the electorate, in the same way that companies do with their shareholders to inform them of progress and how they are delivering in key areas and how they are approaching unforeseen problems.

Stage 9   *Maintaining a market orientation*

To maintain its market orientation the party must engage in political marketing continually, whether in opposition, as the sole party of government or in a coalition. There are numerous obstacles to doing this, such as:

- If in government, power, resources and the challenges of the job are likely to encourage leaders in particular to move back to a more sales- or product-oriented approach; furthermore the incentive to maintain a market orientation will depend on the nature of the competition.
- If in coalition, the energy and time needed to maintain that coalition and consider the other party's (or parties') markets can reduce the energy and time available to consider and respond to the main market.
- In opposition, if a party has attempted a market orientation and failed, internal debate and dissent can prevent adherence to the market orientation and it may consider the MOP inappropriate and so revert to a POP/SOP.
- In a weak position of influence, smaller parties can lose the desire to battle to influence a system dominated by larger and better-resourced parties, and turn away from the MOP strategy.

Focusing on an MOP in government, if it wishes to achieve long-term success and continue as an MOP, it should repeat the process at the same time as governing – not an easy task. The party would, however, have government resources at its disposal and the potential to increase its credibility if it is successful in office.

The process will be essentially the same, but undertaken from a different perspective as it will be done while in government, and not in the vacuum that opposition affords. The different stages will be carried out in a more simultaneous fashion, rather than sequentially. An MOP in government therefore would:

- Collect market intelligence both internally and externally; disseminate it; and be seen to be discussing and, at least, considering feedback, as well as current and potential party behaviour.
- Ensure space and time to think about product design/development for the next election. Future product design over time may require established policies to be altered in response to new market intelligence or changed circumstances in the economy or government finances.

- Attend to the need to adjust the product – including the pre-electoral design policies and those for the next election, taking into account achievability in government given any changed circumstances, but also the importance of gaining acceptance internally, responding to developments in the competition and possibly targeting new markets of support. Support analysis may lead to new target markets relating to the reality of governing, including product design and communication efforts – for example, targeting campaign effort in a seat where an MP or minister is particularly effective in delivery or has a special skill so that the party/Government would try to ensure that he or she continues in that post.
- Carry out careful party management in the continued implementation of the product, with effective leadership to ensure party unity and smooth governing, but without suffocating internal debate, which would damage internal market intelligence results. Any policy that has to be changed will require particularly careful internal management.
- Communicate the existing and future design, both internally and externally, as well as information on delivery to gain credit for success in this area. Communication is also important if the promised design has to be altered in any way due to changed circumstances.

Clearly the model could be developed and fleshed out with emergent political marketing management theory. What is presented here is an initial step in improving the model in the light of comparative empirical study and further theoretical reflection. While we have retained the initial values of the Lees-Marshment model, we have increased its flexibility to consider the use of a market orientation by smaller parties and parties in different political systems, and expanded/amended aspects to include consideration of weaknesses, in particular offering a more comprehensive framework for an MOP which wins control of government and then has to maintain that power. We acknowledge that this will not be an easy task. While politics is not an easy business, political marketing continues to offer means by which to make it a more satisfying process for the electorate in receipt of the government/political product, if not for the politicians tasked with design and delivery.

Conclusion

Political marketing is being adopted across the world. This comparative study has shown that, in one form or another, parties in nations with contrasting systems are adopting concepts which originated in business to engage with and gain support of the public in elections. The Lees-Marshment (2001) model, while amenable to criticism and requiring development from an academic point of view, has enabled empirical illustration of how politicians globally are attempting to use political marketing, not simply in election campaigns, but in the design of their policies, in their leadership and overall behaviour. Our contributors have shown that persuasive SOPs do succeed in getting their more ideological/party-driven policies on the agenda in countries that have proportionally representational electoral systems, as also do the smaller POPs. Political marketing practice, studied comparatively, has been shown to be more diverse and supportive of differing forms of representation than was previously thought. Systemic differences between nations can condition the scope and utility of political marketing. Nevertheless, the overall trend for major parties wishing to gain control of government is still to become a MOP, in countries as divergent as Peru and Brazil, as well as the UK and the USA. This raises a number of philosophical, as well as practical, issues, some but not all of them affected by systemic considerations. Delivery, internal implementation, retaining a market-orientation in government, developing policies that will satisfy the needs of the country in the long term while maintaining popular support necessary for the party to stay in power in the short-term, are undeniably serious and significant tasks that are faced by leaders around the globe.

The emergence of the political consumer is a challenge for all democratic political systems, and political marketing could help leaders and parties respond to this twenty-first-century development, though as quickly as we learn something new, other problems present themselves. Political marketing is a new phenomenon that yields fresh challenges for both academics and politicians, and none of us has all the answers. Indeed, by taking the comprehensive approach, utilising all three POP–SOP–MOP types, and studying political marketing in comparative perspective, we have raised new questions. All of those questions are related in some way to classical debates about the organisation of democracy – the relationship between elite and masses; representation; delivering on electoral promises; meeting society's needs versus market demands; when to persuade, to lead, or to follow; whether to focus on winning the election or on ideological beliefs. These issues, predominant in all democracies at the turn of the twentieth century, continue to pervade the twenty-first-century political marketing environment. That political marketing, its practice or its study, can ever provide the solutions is yet to be seen.

Bibliography

Bowler, S. and Farrell, D. M. (eds) (1992), *Electoral Strategies and Political Marketing* Basingstoke: Macmillan.

Dermody, J. and Scullion, R. (2001), 'Delusios of grandeur? Marketing's contribution to "meaningful" Western political consumption', *European Journal of Marketing*, special edition on political marketing, 35(9–10): 1085–98.

Katz, R. S. and Mair, P. (eds) (1994), *How Parties Organise: Change and Adaptation in Party Organisations in Western Democracies*, London: Sage.

Katz, R. S. and Mair, P. (1995), 'Changing models of party organisation and party democracy: the emergence of the cartel party', *Party Politics* 1(1): 5–28.

Lees-Marshment, J. (2001) *Political Marketing and British Political Parties* Manchester: Manchester University Press.

Lees-Marshment, J. (2003), 'Political marketing: how to reach that pot of gold', *Journal of Political Marketing*, 2(1): 1–32.

Lees-Marshment, J. (2004), *The Political Marketing Revolution: Transforming the Government of the UK*, Manchester: Manchester University Press.

Lilleker, D. G. (2003), 'Whose Left' Working-class political allegiances in post-industrial Britain', in B. Altena and M. van der Linden (eds), *Deindustrialization: Social, Cultural and Political Aspects*, Cambridge: Cambridge University Press: 65–86.

Lilleker, D. G. (2005) 'Political marketing: the cause of a democratic deficit?' *Journal of Non-Profit and Public Sector Marketing* (forthcoming).

Lilleker, D. G. and Negrine, R. (2004) 'Mapping a market-orientation: can we only detect political marketing through the lens of hindsight?', paper presented at the conference elections on the horizon: marketing politics to the electorate in the USA and UK', British Library, London, 15 March.

Moloney, K. (2004) 'Is political marketing new words or a new practice in UK politics?', paper presented at the Political Studies Annual Conference, Lincoln, 6–8 April.

Neubaur, C. and Wilkens, L. (1997), 'Propaganda as religion in National Socialism', *Psyche-Zeitschrift für Psychoanlyse*, 51(3): 47–65.

O'Cass, A. (1996), 'Political marketing and the marketing concept', *European Journal of Marketing*, 30(10–11): 45–61.

O'Shaughnessy, N. J. (1990), *The Phenomenon of Political Marketing*, Basingstoke: Macmillan.

O'Shaughnessy, N. J. (1999), 'Political marketing and political propaganda', paper presented at the Political Marketing Conference, Bournemouth University' 15–16 September.

Opello, W. C. and Rosow, S. J. (1999) *The Nation-State and Global Order: An Historical Introduction to Contemporary Politics*, London: Lynne Reiner.

Panebianco, A. (1988), *Political Parties: Organisation and Power*, Cambridge: Cambridge University Press.

Sodaro, M. J. (2001), *Comparative Politics: A Global Introduction*, London: McGraw-Hill.

Street, J. (1997) *Politics and Popular Culture*, Cambridge: Polity.

Whitehorn, A. (1997), 'Alexa McDonough and Atlantic breakthrough for the New Democratic Party', in A. Frizzell and J. H. Pammett (eds), *The Canadian General Election of 1997*, Toronto: Dundurn Press: 91–109.

Index